MEXICO

BRITISH HONDURAS

Belize

Stann Creek

Caribbean Sea

Bay Islands

Utila
Roatán
Guanaja

Manabique point
Puerto Cortés

Livingston

GUATEMALA

Puerto Barrios
Omoa
Tela
La Ceiba
Salado
Trujillo
Iriona

Motagua R.

San Pedro Sula

Cuyamel

Chameleción R.

Cangrejal R.

Guatemala City

Comayagua

HONDURAS

Segovia R.

Cabo Gracias a Dios

San Salvador

Tegucigalpa

Mosquito Coast

Puerto Cabezas

EL SALVADOR

Nacaome

Maraita

NICARAGUA

Choluteca

Namasigüe

Siuna

Prinzapolca

Amapala

Fonseca Bay

Matagalpa

Chinandega

Lake Managua

Boaco

Siquia R.

Corinto

León

Tipitapa

Rama

Escondido R.

Managua

Camoapa

Bluefields
The Blufff

Tisma
Granada

Acoyapa
Recreo

Monkey point

L. Nicaragua

Mico R.

Pacific Ocean

Rivas

San Juan del Sur

San Carlo

San Juan del Norte

El Castillo

San Juan R.

COSTA

Puerto Limón

San José

RICA

0   200
Km

Miles

0   200

THE BANANA MEN

THE BANANA MEN

American Mercenaries
and Entrepreneurs in
Central America,
1880-1930

Lester D. Langley
Thomas Schoonover

THE UNIVERSITY PRESS OF KENTUCKY

Copyright © 1995 by The University Press of Kentucky

Scholarly publisher for the Commonwealth,
serving Bellarmine College, Berea College, Centre
College of Kentucky, Eastern Kentucky University,
The Filson Club, Georgetown College, Kentucky
Historical Society, Kentucky State University,
Morehead State University, Murray State University,
Northern Kentucky University, Transylvania University,
University of Kentucky, University of Louisville,
and Western Kentucky University.

Editorial and Sales Offices: Lexington, Kentucky 40508-4008

Library of Congress Cataloging-in-Publication Data

Langley, Lester D.
  The banana men : American mercenaries and entrepreneurs in Central
America, 1880-1930 / Lester D. Langley, Thomas Schoonover.
      p.   cm.
  Includes bibliographical references (p.   ) and index.
  ISBN 0-8131-1891-3 (acid free)
  1. Americans—Central America—History. 2. Central America—
Relations—United States. 3. United States—Relations—Central
America. 4. Central America—Civilization—American influences.
I. Schoonover, Thomas David, 1936-   . II. Title.
F1440.A54L36   1995
972.8—dc20   94-12864

For
Ralph Lee Woodward, Jr.

Contents

Acknowledgments   ix

Introduction   1

1. The World of the Banana Men   6

2. Banana Kingdoms   33

3. The Central American Wars   58

4. The Campaign for Nicaragua   91

5. The Campaign for Honduras   115

6. A Different World   141

Epilogue   167

Notes   176

Bibliographical Note   204

Index   209

Illustrations follow page 126

Acknowledgments

Thomas Schoonover thanks his wife Ebba for research, editorial, and secretarial assistance; and Walter LaFeber and Ralph Lee Woodward, Jr., for friendship and generous professional support.

Lester D. Langley thanks Hermann Deutsch, biographer of Lee Christmas; and Samuel Zemurray, who was not hypocritical and thus never apologized for having subsidized the Honduran revolution. He apologizes to his mother, Lona Clements Langley—a devout Christian who read Bible stories to her son and stayed in an unhappy marriage so that he could get an education—for publishing the expletive Sam Zemurray used when he took over the United Fruit Company in 1932.

Both authors are indebted to Bonnie Cary, typist in the History Department of the University of Georgia, who herewith adds her own words: "Typing *The Banana Men* was a very interesting experience, and I hope readers will enjoy the book."

Introduction

This is a book about North and Central Americans and their role in the transformation of Central America during the U.S. imperial era from the late nineteenth century to the onset of the Great Depression. It is about modernization, its benefits and often frightful costs. It is about a generation of ambitious entrepreneurs, politicians, and mercenaries who dramatically altered Central America's political culture, its economy, and even its traditional social values. Their story did not begin in the 1880s, nor did the lasting effects of their impact end in the 1930s. The U.S. preoccupation with defiant Nicaragua and dogged support of El Salvador in the 1980s—a policy riddled with opportunism, deceit, and intrigue—is in many respects the most recent chapter in what historians label a sordid record in the annals of U.S. foreign policy. Similarly, the social debilities of modern Central America, often attributed to the indirect costs of ten years of internal wars, must be placed in a larger historical context to be understood. The predicament of Central Americans in our times, as isthmian peoples know, is rooted in their past. North Americans have had a great deal to do with the shaping of their history.

We have chosen to concentrate on these fifty years for two reasons. The first, as we point out in Chapter 1, is that the character of the United States economy and especially the modern Central American economies took form in this era. The second has to do with the values and behavior of the North

Americans who helped to define the U.S. presence in Central America during these years, and of those Central Americans who abetted or opposed them. This was an era when U.S. troops paraded through Bluefields or Corinto or Puerto Cortés under the pretext of restoring "order" or making the region "safe for democracy" or "safeguarding the national interest"—ringing phrases that often concealed other motives. Not even the ignominy of a questionable Central American policy in the 1980s has persuaded many Americans that isthmian peoples do not require our guidance. That arrogance, typical of private citizens and public officials in this country in the early twentieth century, may have diminished somewhat but, regrettably, lingers on. Ordinary North Americans are not directly responsible for Central America's current debilities, certainly, and the culpability of the U.S. government is at least debatable. But there can be little doubt of the conjuncture of powerful U.S. economic forces and influential persons in the shaping of isthmian history during this fifty-year period.

Within our broad chronological focus we concentrate on Nicaragua and Honduras. Undeniably, every country in Central America (including Panama) experienced the economic, political, and military repercussions associated with U.S. expansionism in this era. Nicaragua and Honduras, however, occupy a special place in this story, not only because of the numbers of Americans and Europeans doing business there, the monetary value of their investments, and the frequency of U.S. troop landings but also because of the distortions the North American presence bequeathed these two countries. We are still living with that legacy. The collective anger of Nicaraguans and the embittered frustrations of Hondurans in the 1980s have their historical explanations in the parallel experiences of these countries with the U.S. government and North American intruders during the era we are discussing. Understanding how these experiences came about, we believe, may help us to comprehend the depth of pro- and anti-Americanism in modern Central America. History is often nonlinear. Americans trying to fathom the politics of postwar Nicaragua, where ideologues of left and right often take similar positions or occupy posts within the same government, may find an explanation in the political culture of Nicaragua in the first rather than the last third of the twentieth century. Similarly, those who want to know why Ronald Reagan chose a military option in 1981 in preference to Jimmy Carter's course of negotiation in Central America may find an answer in the imperial sloganeering of Theodore Roosevelt and the political culture of his generation. Among other things, the first and ninth decades of this century—one an industrial, the other a postindustrial epoch—reverberated with concerns over immigration, the economy, and the troublesome disparities between this country's professed purpose and the impact of its conduct in world affairs on national identity and purpose. Race, ethnicity, and class figured importantly in questions of political economy after the turn of the century; they still do, albeit in muted form. As chaos theorists remind us, a fundamental principle of why things work out the way they do is sensitive dependence on initial conditions.

Ours has been an unusual collaboration. Lester Langley began writing this book almost a decade ago as the narrative account of a generation of entrepreneurs and mercenaries—gunrunners, banana barons, mine operators, and soldiers of fortune—who ventured to the Central American isthmus to build a small empire or to escape an unlucky past or the law and who got into the occasionally profitable business of "revoluting." The intent was to produce a companion volume to his book on the U.S. military intervention in the Caribbean and Central America from the Spanish-American War until the marines departed Haiti in the early 1930s.[1] The result was a manuscript about the careers of men who varied tremendously in background and who fared very differently in Central America: Samuel Zemurray, a Bessarabian Jewish immigrant known as "Sam the Banana Man," who made a fortune in Honduran bananas and later (after 1932) ran United Fruit Company for two decades; Minor Keith, who linked San José with the Caribbean coast of Costa Rica by railroad and transformed United Fruit into a business as powerful as any isthmian government, with an empire stretching from Puerto Limón, Costa Rica, to

Puerto Barrios, Guatemala; the Vaccaro brothers, Sicilians out of New Orleans who carved out a banana kingdom on the north Honduran coast; Washington Valentine, who made his mark in Honduran mines and railroads; and vagabonds, tough hombres, and soldiers of fortune who often served as mercenaries—on one or both sides—in the wars that plagued the isthmus.

Much of our story deals with Zemurray and a man who helped him to build his banana fortune—Lee Christmas, a bellicose Mississippian who set off for Honduras in 1894 and made a reputation as a man who could use a weapon, command soldiers of uncertain capability, and generally prove "reliable" in a fight. The New Orleans journalist Hermann Deutsch penned a fascinating biography of Christmas in the early 1930s.[2] Deutsch's emphasis, understandably, lay with Christmas rather than Zemurray, who is referred to as "El Amigo" in the book (as he was in the correspondence Deutsch collected in researching Christmas's life). Deutsch doubtless knew of Zemurray's involvement with Christmas and with the Honduran Manuel Bonilla, and their complicity in the Honduran revolution of 1911, but he may have been reluctant to implicate Zemurray at a time when the "Banana Man" was taking over United Fruit and was living in the New Orleans area. In any event, another journalist, Ernest Baker, wrote that story a few years later.[3] Our account explores in far more detail the relationship between Zemurray, his ally Bonilla, and the mercenaries who served them. We also provide an assessment of the role of the banana barons and mercenaries in Nicaragua and the part they played in the U.S. war on that hostile country. Save for occasional comments, neither Deutsch nor Baker assessed the North American presence there.

Thomas Schoonover came late into this collaboration, but his participation has been critical to its success. Drawing on his pathbreaking study of social imperialism in Central America,[4] he has set the narrative of the banana men into the larger record of Central America's incorporation into the North American economy in the late nineteenth and early twentieth centuries. His command of the relevant literature (in English, Spanish, German, and French) on Central American development is unrivaled, as the notes to this study attest. The first chapter, which details the theory informing this book, is the work of Schoonover, who has drawn upon his published and unpublished scholarship to describe competitive imperialism in Central America from the 1880s to the 1930s. In addition, every chapter bears his imprint, through either revision of or additions to the original manuscript material.

We have studied Central America from different historical perspectives and training. Yet despite our differing historical methods, we have reached remarkably similar conclusions about the North American impact on Central America. We have learned from each other. We have enjoyed and profited from this collaboration. Submitting our contributions to the friendly but serious review of a knowledgeable colleague has prompted each of us to rethink some of our earlier assumptions about Central America and work harder in the areas of our weaknesses. We leave this project believing we might work together again, and we recommend to our other colleagues that they give serious consideration to joint projects.

We alert the reader to several matters, two of which may be confusing. Unless otherwise indicated, translations are ours. We have used "American" to refer to a citizen of the United States *unless* it is necessary to distinguish between North and Central Americans. Our use of "Central America" to refer to the five republics of Nicaragua, Costa Rica, Honduras, Guatemala, and El Salvador may provoke understandable queries about the exclusion of Panama and Belize. In modern usage, certainly, these countries are often listed as Central American nations. In the nineteenth century, however, Panama was a part of Colombia, a South American nation. Belize (before 1981, British Honduras) lies *in* Central America but its social, cultural, racial, and political character bespeaks a Caribbean nation.

1

The World of the Banana Men

North American opportunists, filibusters, and mercenaries have ravished Central America in three epochs. The first great age of filibustering occurred in the 1850s, when William Walker commanded an invading force of adventurers into Nicaragua, then wrenched by civil war. Walker fashioned a political alliance with Nicaraguan Liberals and, following their victory, used his own army to get control of the country. He lured hundreds of southern slaveowners into Jacksonian America's new tropical empire with promises of land in a slave republic. His contemporary and persistent adversary, Cornelius Vanderbilt, sought domination over the vital Nicaraguan transit route from the pestilential town of San Juan del Norte to the Gulf of Fonseca on Nicaragua's northwestern frontier. Vanderbilt made his fortune. After Central Americans drove him out, Walker became a celebrity in the U.S. South, wrote a book about his exploits in Nicaragua, and in 1860, on the eve of the U.S. Civil War, launched another invasion of Central America. He perished before a Honduran firing squad in Trujillo, Honduras, the victim of blind ambition and the determination of Central Americans to resist the intruder.

The second epoch of North American intrusion occurred in the first thirty years of the twentieth century. From 1900 until 1930, soldiers of fortune (the modern equivalent of Walker's generation of filibusters) served U.S. entrepreneurs who were taking advantage of opportunities for banana production and marketing and who needed muscle as well as capital and talent to operate in Central America—men like Samuel Zemurrary of Cuyamel and United Fruit Companies. During the 1980s, the third epoch, mercenaries pursued their own goals, though occasionally—as occurred in Nicaragua—they were in the service of powerful isthmian exiles or, marginally, of the U.S. government. Modern foreign companies still wield considerable clout in Central America, especially in Honduras, but they no longer need mercenaries.

Despite the undeniably admirable work of some private U.S. organizations and citizens who have committed themselves to bettering the lot of the ordinary Central American, these soldiers of fortune and mercenaries, however mitigated their records may be in individual cases, served ignoble causes: the expansion of slavery, the pursuit of wealth, or activity based on warped convictions about what was necessary to preserve isthmian democracy. In none of these three eras of filibustering were Central American aspirations and needs of primary concern to the intruding North Americans. The driving impulses in these interventions had their origins in U.S. society and the parallel economic, social, and political disequilibrium identified with the industrial revolution. Lee Christmas may have gone off to Honduras in 1894 because he had little future in New Orleans; the banana men, however, knew that Central America was the next great frontier of opportunity.

The industrial revolution, which occurred at different times in different countries, altered the method of production, social relationships, the value of labor (from independent and self-directed worker to dependent employee), relationships within the family, and finally each society's relations with other countries. Though this study focuses largely on the last adjustment, all are relevant to societal interrelationships. Modern transnational tension arising from economic growth and technology grew between core (roughly, metropole, industrialized, "have") societies, between core and the peripheral (roughly, third world, less developed, "have not") societies, and, less commonly, between societies on the periphery. This tension was closely related to the rise of the industrial order. In addition to material accumulation, the core powers pursued the intellectual, social, and cultural authority and influence that shaped societal conduct.

Some European states, the United States, and Japan underwent similar experiences of industrial expansion between 1770 and 1930. Industrial activity altered the way wealth was produced, valued, and distributed. Productionism (the belief that material production offered the answer to societal problems, and another byproduct of liberalism's emphasis upon material growth) used technology, science, and the educational system of a society to increase material output. Productionism required an increasing body of consumers and the expansion of raw material sources—including food, even exotic foods—to facilitate the altering demands of the labor force and the values and status of laborers, and to induce them to accept new work relations and values. After brief periods of national internal development, industries strove to reduce labor costs—for example, by using the cheaper labor of the periphery to supply raw materials and food production. On the international level, productionism intensified competition for sources of inexpensive raw materials and food, for areas of potential market expansion, and for control of communication lines or support points. The U.S. government recognized that foreign competition would undermine its capacity to use Latin America to ease its own social and economic crises. Distrustful of foreign penetration into the New World, it staked its claim to a privileged position with the Monroe Doctrine and its self-serving version of pan-americanism.[1]

U.S. officials expected their privileged position in the New World to include a priority stake in isthmian interoceanic transit and access to the Pacific. In particular, U.S. leaders sought better access to East Asia. In the late 1880s the United States confronted Germany and Great Britain in Samoa. A few years later an aggressive U.S. diplomat helped dissident North American planters overthrow the Hawaiian monarchy, and the

Benjamin Harrison administration quickly negotiated a treaty of annexation. For political reasons, this was repudiated by Harrison's successor, Grover Cleveland, but Hawaii was annexed during the Spanish-American War in 1898 and the Philippines and Puerto Rico became U.S. territory in the peace settlement. U.S. strategic concerns in the Caribbean and Central America heightened in the aftermath of that war. Cuban and Panamanian independence in 1902 and 1903, respectively, came at the price of their sovereignty. The United States dominated Cuba for strategic and economic reasons; it created the Panamanian protectorate because it wanted to construct an isthmian canal under the control of the United States. In a sudden but predictable way, Central America's place in the calculations of U.S. leaders was now magnified. The security of the nation, they argued, depended on U.S. domination, given the size of European investment and the dramatic increase in German activity throughout the region. But national security was also linked to internal social and cultural dynamics. In an age when Jacob Riis and other social commentators wrote of the widening gulf between rich and poor, when racist ideologues warned of the "passing of the white race," and when it became manifestly clear to U.S. producers that capitalism could not survive on a domestic market alone, Central America provided a means of exporting not only capital but the cultural and social conflicts that raged within the United States.

In the nineteenth century the major industrializing states— Great Britain, France, Belgium, the United States, Germany, Holland, and Italy—used power and diplomacy to assure themselves of unfettered access to the linkage between the Atlantic and Pacific half-worlds. The North Atlantic metropole nations were motivated by the desire to alleviate internal crises or by apprehension over the alternatives to a liberal economy— "growth versus death or decay"—that intellectuals and theorists from Thomas Robert Malthus to Brooks Adams and Otto Spengler found so threatening and ominous. In Central America the competition generated by productionism from about 1850 to 1930 occurred on two levels: first, between U.S. firms trying to gain access to Central American raw materials, land,

and labor (mostly private firms) and the communications routes (both private and government competition); second, between governments and firms of different nations. Central America, only marginally valued for its resources, was important to any nation wishing to enter the Pacific Basin. Since all industrial, free market powers eyed at least some part of that vast domain, the isthmus attracted their attention.[2]

Metropole countries (those that controlled production and distribution in the world economy) turned to policies of social imperialism (the amelioration of domestic social woes through links to foreign areas) in periphery countries (those that did not control production and distribution in the world economy) in order to preserve the metropoles' well-being and security. In the late nineteenth century the United States government transformed the country from a semiperipheral society into a metropole state, in part by using social imperialist policies to exploit the transit, market, and investment opportunities of the Central American-Caribbean region. Scholars of social imperialism used phrases such as "exporting the social problem" and "exporting the unemployment" to epitomize the transfer of problems, burdens, and injustices of a metropole's political economy to weaker societies. U.S. officials presumed that social imperialism would bring wealth and security to the domestic economy; they rarely gave thought, however, to the impact such programs might have on vulnerable societies of the periphery other than to mention vaguely the transfer of democracy and material progress. More than a hundred years of metropole "uplifting" have not managed to leave many signs of democracy or material progress on the isthmus.[3]

Metropole leaders had to subordinate societies on the periphery in order to coordinate periphery resources effectively with metropole problems. A metropole's desire to apply social imperialism for its benefit required it to restrict the sovereignty and development of the periphery. Metropole policies to ameliorate domestic social and economic policies demanded the extraction of wealth from the land, labor, and capital of the periphery and the domination of import and export trade. All these policies encouraged the preservation of the underdevelopment of the peripheral economy and social order. Thus, social imperialism describes the domestic aspects of metropole foreign policy, and dependency theory focuses on the metropole-periphery relationship.[4]

Liberalism's focus on growth sharpened both internal and external competition. The private and public urge to expand into Central America in the age of the banana men was also rooted in U.S. societal needs to find a place for excess entrepreneurial energy and capital; and expansion served to locate places for the export of U.S. surpluses and to reduce U.S. production costs by supplying food to workers and raw materials to industry. Social imperialism made the Central American nations— which possessed limited resource bases, smaller and less educated populations, and less capital, communication, and technological development—bear some of the burden of metropole unemployment and social disorder in addition to their own. At the turn of the century the internal disorder in Central American societies was related to their ties with metropole states.

During the colonial era and especially under those governments that identified progress with the countries' ties to interests, Central American peoples struggled to retain control of their economies as they exported to acquire investment capital and luxury goods. They met tremendous obstacles in confronting the challenge of modernization. A high mountain range hugs the north and west (or Pacific) coasts. Most Indians and then the Spanish settled chiefly in the mountains along the Pacific coast, and Central America's active ports lay on the Pacific side, although the harbors of Belize and San Juan del Norte on the Atlantic coast were physically more suitable. The coastal plane on the Pacific is narrow and humid; on the Caribbean (or north) coast, wet and humid. The sparse Indian population on the Caribbean littoral lived in the Mosquito area or near Belize, which served the timber people extracting the hard woods from Guatemala to Nicaragua and the overland route for British trade with Guatemala City.

Central America attained independence in 1821. Three years later, the five republics of Nicaragua, Costa Rica, Honduras, Guatemala, and El Salvador formed a political federation—the United Provinces. At the time, independent Central America had about one to 1.25 million inhabitants (Honduras had 100,000; Nicaragua, 160,000). By the end of the century, population had grown to 3.6 million (Honduras's, to 480,000; Nicaragua's, to 450,000) and in the next quarter-century reached 5.8 million. The Honduran population in 1924 stood at 635,000 and the Nicaraguan at 640,000.[5]

Yet despite this impressive growth, old geographic dynamics—environmental, economic, spatial, and cultural—still profoundly affected isthmian development, Central Americans' perceptions of themselves, and their relationships with other cultures. Drought is a recurring problem because the rain generally falls only in one season and then in downpours rather than showers. There are active volcanoes along the mountain chain. Earthquakes are a continual menace. (Managua has been twice devastated by earthquakes in the twentieth century: the first, in 1931, contributed to the rise of the Somoza dynasty; the second, in 1972, to its fall.) Internal communication has always been problematical. The only low spot between the Caribbean and Pacific in Central America (Panama is geographically not a Central American country) lies along the San Juan River (which forms two-thirds of the boundary between Nicaragua and Costa Rica), across Lake Nicaragua, and overland to the Pacific ports of San Juan del Sur and Realejo. In the nineteenth century, however, Nicaragua rivaled Panama as the preferred route for a transisthmian crossing and, in the early twentieth century, as the site for an isthmian canal. This physical feature explains in part why Nicaragua suffered from filibustering and military intervention—Walker's three invasions in the 1850s, the U.S. military intervention and war against Augusto César Sandino from 1909 to the early 1930s, and the subsidizing of a proxy war in the 1980s. Nicaragua and its neighbor Honduras witnessed intense and aggressive foreign intervention in all three eras of filibustering.

Central America opened to the liberal, industrializing states of the North Atlantic about 1850. Commercial magnate Cornelius Vanderbilt's Accessory Transit Company obtained a contract to launch a river, lake, and land route through Nicaragua. A New York group built a railroad across the Panamanian isthmus. Both projects reflected the growing interest in incorporating the Pacific Basin into world trade and, of course, the popularity of the transisthmian route as alternative to the equally perilous overland journey to California. Their success whetted the appetites of transit promoters for even more lucrative concessions. This heightened interest in communications corresponded with the surge of metropole activity in Africa and Asia and an intensified commercial and investment activity in Latin America. U.S. leaders were already voicing a concern of their predecessors, that intensified economic activity in the circum-Caribbean (the "American Mediterranean") might threaten not only the security but the well-being of the nation.[6]

Economic stagnation in the metropoles increased competition between their governments and enterprises and thus prompted vigorous efforts to "guide" the material and ideological restructuring of Central American societies. The influence of the outsider was an explosive issue in isthmian politics. In the early years of independence, isthmian leaders fashioned their confederation (the Provincias Unidas) on liberal, rational notions of governance and economy. Their agenda clashed with the traditional values of the corporatist culture of Hapsburg Central America of the sixteenth and seventeenth centuries, values and traditions that had eroded during the Bourbon era of the late eighteenth and early nineteenth centuries but resonated well with Central America's folk cultures and its patriarchal families. The result was a series of fratricidal wars, conflicts that bespoke social and cultural tensions as much as ideological division, which terminated in the dissolution of the confederation in the 1840s and the appearance of Liberal and Conservative political factions. (These are capitalized for good reason. In the Central American political context, a Liberal can be "liberal" on some issues but "conservative" on others. The same holds true for Conservatives.) Foreign interest and competition over transisthmian commerce and transportation and, especially, the humiliation stemming from the Walker invasions momentarily united Central Americans in the 1850s. Once Walker perished, however, older quarrels revived. One of these had to do with modernization of the economy. Liberals, identified with the foreign intruder, suffered politically after the 1850s. Following a generation of Conservative governments, however, a Liberal resurgence commenced with the transformations of Guatemala under Justo Rufino Barrios and Costa Rica under Tomás Guardia—both dictatorial in their political style but liberal in their approaches to political economy—in the early 1870s. By 1876 the Guatemalan president had assisted Liberal factions in El Salvador in the overturning of Conservative governments suspected of aiding Guatemalan Conservatives. Only Nicaragua resisted the Liberal revival, largely because of the discredited record of Liberal ties to Walker.[7]

Central American Liberals championed material progress. They facilitated the privatization of communal land, advocated policies that hastened the growth of a wage-dependent labor force, freed domestic capital by undermining the *cofradías* (religiously inspired socioeconomic brotherhoods) and other church-controlled sources of capital, and encouraged the formation of banks (especially hypothecary or mortgage land banks). They also offered inducements to foreign settlers and financial interests.[8]

Foreigners took advantage of the new liberalized laws to build isolated centers of extraction, exploitation, and production, which are commonly called enclaves. Before World War II three products—bananas, coffee, and minerals—constituted the bulk of isthmian exports. In the 1880s Costa Rica had enclaves for bananas, Honduras for mining, and Guatemala for coffee. The banana and mining enclaves (located mostly near the Caribbean coast of Costa Rica and Honduras, where governmental authority had traditionally been weak) came under extensive foreign control. In addition, a fourth enclave of mixed commercial, agricultural, and mining activity on Nicaragua's Caribbean coast served as an "adjunct colony" to British and later U.S. commerce.[9]

Enclave exploitation required changes in social attitudes and behavior as well as official support because enclave businesses needed land and labor. Indians systematically lost their *ejidos* or communal lands. In addition, a reformed tax structure burdened Indians with cash tax obligations (as opposed to traditional in-kind services), which accelerated their abandonment of subsistence farming and entry into a wage-labor system. Conscript labor took others away from a self-sufficient life. Liberal legislation converted Indians into mobile, seasonal, wage-earning laborers who were thus more useful to foreign employers in the enclave projects.[10]

When peasant societies resisted the loss of communal land and the new labor roles assigned to them, comprador leaders of Central American governments enforced the laws with rural police and a professionalized military organized and trained by metropole experts. These new agencies of authority, with increased loyalty to a central government rather than a local caudillo or cacique, enforced the tax collection (accelerating the trend toward wage labor), and facilitated land privatization. (In the colonial and especially early national history of Spanish America, caudillos were strongmen who rose to political prominence and wielded considerable power because they commanded the loyalty of other men. Sometimes, as in the example of Rafael Carrera in Guatemala, they organized resistance to Liberal programs. Caciques were men of local power and authority in traditional Indian communities. Their presence antedated the Spanish conquest.) The armed forces managed peasant attempts to occupy unclaimed or unused land: because peasants who settled on vacant lands became less dependent on wage labor and thus frustrated business operations in the enclaves, the military generally drove peasants away from these lands when their labor was required.[11] Foreign entrepreneurs profited from a system that allowed laborers to feed themselves when unemployed yet assured that they would be available when needed. The foreigner's image did not suffer, because it was the government that enforced unpopular laws.

In recent years Honduran historians have closely scrutinized the role of the U.S. government in their country during the decades of "liberal reform." Darío Euraque, for one, has bluntly concluded that the laws identified with liberal politics led to the strengthening of neither the state nor the agro-export economy: concessions made to attract foreign investment in order to permit national development prevented Honduran control and yielded precious little benefit to Hondurans. Mario Argueta concurs about the long-term damage wrought by the concessionary system. Cuyamel Fruit Company obtained concessions on the grounds that these would prevent United Fruit from dominating the banana business, but Cuyamel persistently violated its agreements and conducted its operations in a manner that was, in Argueta's estimation, detrimental to Honduran development. Cuyamel took advantage of the north coast's isolation from the capital and the weakness of national authority. It suborned Honduran comprador leaders, paid bribes, and cavalierly ignored Honduran officials because U.S. war vessels patrolled the coast and thus shielded its business. German representatives noted that U.S. fruit companies regularly settled their claims by making periodic payments to the central government, from which they deducted what they considered was due them; businessmen of other nationalities had to appeal to Honduran courts, enlist the aid of their own governments, or try to influence Honduran officials—all of which involved delays or compromises.[12]

Central American states tried to increase their freedom of action by manipulating metropole intrusions. In the early nineteenth century they appealed for U.S. aid when British conduct was aggressive; later they called on France, Austria, Prussia, Italy, Mexico, and even Britain when U.S. entrepreneurs, soldiers of fortune, and officials threatened their sovereignty and well-being. But as the isthmian leaders learned of the material success of the industrializing states, they opted for a plantation cash-crop system that undermined traditional subsistence agriculture.[13] Incorporation into the world economy soon placed severe limitations on their sovereignty and capacity for self-government because foreign entrepreneurs and governments shielded the large capital and intricate distribution mechanism established on the isthmus.

All metropole governments assumed that Central America's role was that of passkey to one of two major world transit systems (Suez was the other) capable of joining two inefficiently linked half-worlds into one unified, more efficient economic unit that would facilitate world-scale accumulation. North Americans had long recognized that their well-being and national security were linked to their presence in the Caribbean-Central American region. The "no transfer" principle (an 1811 congressional resolution designed to frustrate British designs on Spanish Florida) stated that the United States would not recognize any transfer of European territory in the Western Hemisphere to another Old World state. President James Monroe's December 1823 message to Congress, which enunciated the policy that came to be known as the Monroe Doctrine, reiterated that sentiment and warned of U.S. opposition to further European acquisitions in the hemisphere. Though the immediate concern in the 1820s was the stability of the insular Caribbean (which had only one independent state, Haiti), the parallel interest in commerce and transportation and the southern fascination with "tropical empire" made not only the Caribbean but Central America important for other reasons. U.S. interests there were tied to domestic concerns. North Americans were both frightened and fascinated by filibustering expeditions to Cuba and especially Nicaragua in the 1850s. On the eve of the Civil War a gaggle of northern Democrats tried to placate an angry South with a proposal to annex slave Cuba. Before he acquiesced in emancipation for the slaves, Abraham Lincoln seriously considered purchasing their freedom and settling them on foreign shores. One suggested place was Central America.

That bizarre proposal came to naught, but in the 1860s U.S. liberals triumphed in their quest to dominate national economic policy. After 1861 the U.S. government adopted the general principles of individualistic, free market capitalism to encourage the pursuit of material progress. Though the intent was a national economy with sufficient safeguards against the uncertainties that often occur when the "fair price" succumbs to the "market price" for goods and labor, the rational orderliness promised by liberals did not come about. On the contrary, the opening of the economy to national and international forces merely unleashed programs that encouraged speculation, self-interest, and acquisitiveness. Railroad barons benefited from government support and title to land right-of-way. Giant firms swallowed family enterprises. Urban government became synonymous with graft and corruption. Liberal philosophy held that unleashed human energy or the opportunity to capitalize on one's talents made for a better world. In the abstract, perhaps this was so. But the reality could be a society where it was commonly said, "I've got mine, Jack, now you go out and get yours." If the market had an "unseen hand" directing this "human energy," the notion that it would be guided into desirable channels was a matter of faith.[14] Despite this loosening of governmental economic constraints on the private sector and the encomia to progress and individual creativity, the liberalism of theory was scarcely recognizable in reality.

For nineteenth-century liberals, progress meant material advancement and a market economy. Politicians used the law to advance material accumulation among ordinary folk (the Homestead Act of 1862, a federal land-grant program), which ultimately benefited promoters more than settlers. Even as the federal consolidation of power over the currency (validated in Banking Acts of 1862 and 1864) created a paper money supply and undergirded a national economic policy, liberal political ideologues were driving some 3,000 state, local, and private currencies out of the marketplace. The U.S. government encouraged mining, agriculture, and educational improvement (Morrill Land Grant Act of 1862), improved the communications system (transcontinental railroad and telegraph acts of 1862), and funded an interoceanic cable connection. Arguing that they were necessary to pay off Civil War debts, boost national industry, and punish Great Britain for its abuse of neutral rights during the war, Republicans in power rallied to the passage of protective tariff laws, which manifestly contradicted liberal professions about a marketplace economy.

Lincoln touched a responsive chord in the nation's memory when he declared that the U.S. Civil War was about the survival of nation and republic. But, more than any of its predecessors, his administration invoked liberal principle in the service of economic power on a national scale in order to weaken the states collectively by treating them differently in national economic policy. In this sense, as the late George Anderson used to say in his University of Kansas seminar on "national consolidation," the War between the States should be called the "War *against* the States."

The lamentable social legacy of these economic policies was a continuation of the cycle of prosperity and economic slump that had characterized U.S. economic history since the mid-eighteenth century. In 1873 a depression (brought on, it was argued, by market disturbances caused by overproduction) occasioned factory closings, unemployment, strikes, and the calamity so feared by Britain's middle class a generation earlier—social disorder. From 1873 until the end of the century the world and especially (during fourteen of those twenty-seven years) the U.S. economy went through economic crisis and depression. Three major panics—from 1873 to 1878, 1883 to 1885, and 1893 to 1898—alternated with rapid growth spurts. On the eve of the war with Spain, annual domestic unemployment averaged 14 percent of the civilian labor force (including farm population) and more than 25 percent among nonfarm workers. As usually happens in a depression, however, not everyone suffered. Companies that handled foreclosures, supplied legal services for bankruptcies, and conducted auctions brought in handsome profits. Entrepreneurs enjoyed some good years and opportunities even in erratic times. Nonfarm workers lived with uncertainty throughout these years. At the turn of the century the economy improved, especially in agriculture, and nonfarm unemployment dropped to about 10 percent annually. This was markedly better than the years from 1873 to 1898 but still an ominous indicator of what was in store for the country if it did not expand the marketplace.[15]

Nineteenth-century liberals put their faith in capitalism, and capitalism required a vigorous export economy. A few lonely voices, especially in the agricultural sector, had begun saying this as early as the 1870s, but the country had always had an enthusiastic agro-export philosophy. Industrialists were more hesitant. After all, they had a grip on labor costs and, theoretically, could shut down production when the market was saturated. Government shielded their property from the destructive power of strikers, and when the vaunted middle class had to choose between its interests and the rights of all citizens to protest, it would choose the first. Sooner or later, however, the social disorders accompanying downturns and depressions would exact a price—not in the form of an uprising of the oppressed against oppressors but in the gloomy realization that people needed work not only to survive but to participate in a market economy, however little, as producers *and* consumers. In the protean political culture of the United States there would always be ambitious men or outspoken women to come along and persuade them to vote on the basis not of their conscience but of their situation. On the local level a generation of scofflaws and crooks made government "work" by practicing what may be called a logical oxymoron, "honest corruption."

An expanded foreign market and cheaper raw materials for the nation's manufactures began to seem a godsend to those leaders whose public and private efforts had failed to reverse the recurring sharp economic downturns. As the Virginia gentry had learned in the eighteenth century, white indentures and black slaves living in similar economic despair could be a menace to the social structure. Poor whites could be made the social allies of elites, however, if given a stake in the preservation of the social order. The logic of an aggressive foreign economic policy became clear. An expanded domain for the U.S. economy in the world offered not only the prospect of cheaper raw materials and new markets but—just as valuable—a labor force that might be exploited in ways now increasingly risky at home. Unemployment and downturns in the domestic economy would remain problems, but such a policy would help to ease the domestic social tensions rising from internal disorder and instability. A later generation of socialist critics called such a policy "financial imperialism" or "dollar diplomacy," but it deserved the designation of "social imperialism." Given the increased need to find profitable outlets for the agricultural surpluses of the Midwest and the industrial stockpiles of the Northeast, Latin America and particularly Central America offered the United States clear advantages for carrying out social imperialism.[16]

In the late nineteenth and early twentieth centuries, the land of much of the world fell under the effective control of multinational corporations (through their ability to dominate agro-export economies) or metropole states (through colonies or protectorates). Explaining these transnational entities requires definition of a few key terms. "Home country" refers to the nation-state in which a corporation is headquartered, or where its trademarks, logos, patents, licenses, blueprints, and technology are located and fundamental policies are set. The United States was the home country for United, Standard, and Cuyamel Fruit Companies. "Host country" refers to the nation-state in which a corporation operates through affiliated firms, subcorporations ("daughter" corporations), or other licensed enterprises. Costa Rica, Nicaragua, Honduras, and Guatemala were host countries for United Fruit, and Honduras was the sole host for Cuyamel.

These metropole firms controlled land, labor, capital, and distribution factors in such a manner as to drive the economies in societies on the periphery. By the late nineteenth century, Liberal regimes in Central America were encouraging foreign investors and entrepreneurs to stimulate economic growth; for example, Guatemala and Honduras were noticeably active at the 1884 New Orleans Exposition. Large transnational firms dominated the world shipping, transoceanic telegraph cables, maritime services, and marketing operations that served the isthmus. Central America's Liberals sometimes divided over *which* foreign investor or metropole state (U.S. or European) they preferred to do business with, but there is little doubt of the fundamental understanding between leaders of U.S. holding companies and multinational corporations and U.S. officials about the common benefits accompanying penetration of the Central American economies. The communications network serving the U.S. economy—railroads and shipping lines—was spreading into Mexico, the Caribbean, and Central America. In Guatemala and El Salvador, railroad projects laid the groundwork for International Railroads of Central America, a projected monolithic transportation enterprise on the isthmus. The liberal professions of these private and public spokesmen trumpeted individualism and the free market, but the agencies that penetrated Central America were collectivized, planned organizations.

Multinational corporations utilized Central American enclaves of banana plantations, mining sites, railroad construction areas, and port services (wharves, insurance, lighters, import-export firms, shipping, and so forth) to distribute host country production into the world economy. Enclave development facilitated the making of a "comprador" elite, whose function was to support metropole enterprises. The comprador elite, consisting of representatives of the small professional and artisan class as well as the socially prominent, permitted foreign interests to maximize their production of wealth. After the 1870s, metropole influence spread into all areas of Central American life: education, the professions, the military, local administration, and even public service.[17]

Central American compradores were expected to facilitate the entry of metropole business and political influence, and to manage the host society as well, because disorder reduced business opportunities and increased the likelihood that foreign powers other than the United States might become involved on the isthmus. Disorder arose from nationalist disgust with the loss of sovereignty and from worker protest against exploitation. The political repression used to silence nationalist and labor protest often shocked democratic and human rights advocates in the metropole state, but U.S. society was educated to view its well-being, prosperity, and security in terms of stability in Central America and other periphery host societies. Disorder on the isthmus threatened domestic tranquillity and well-being.

Some critics of the U.S. role in Central America pointed out that aggressive penetration and involvement in isthmian affairs actually disturbed the existing social order by introducing alien values into a traditional culture that was changing, undeniably, but was ill prepared for the intrusion of the banana men and their hired guns, whose social philosophy and behavior more befitted the frontier. But business leaders and U.S. officials had little time for glacial adjustment or reflections on cultural relativism. Central America was too vital to U.S. interests. An ordered, "civilized" isthmus (that is, a dominated Central America) required the approach that had proved effective in the "winning" of the U.S. West. Since U.S. businessmen expected to be able to export surplus production freely into the world economy, their government could not very well stand by if European competitors, with official support, stepped up their activities in Central America and perhaps gained control of the Atlantic-Pacific transisthmian links connecting two vast trade areas and lying across U.S. commercial routes to South America.

International economic competition and domestic matters were twin issues prompting the U.S. government to revitalize older policies aimed at limiting competition in the New World on the pretext of "protecting" Latin America from the Old World menace. North American leaders looked southward for markets. There was little incentive, however, to consult in a meaningful way with their Latin American counterparts to fashion an economic union that would serve Latin American as well as U.S. needs. Pan-Americanism, a word touted in the U.S. State Department in the 1880s and 1890s, was a rhetorical flourish scarcely concealing Washington's intent, which was domination. Little wonder, then, that Latin diplomats privately snickered about "Blah Blah Pan-Americanism." By the end of World War II the United States had achieved its goal: it dominated the import, export, and foreign capital markets of Latin America.[18]

The late nineteenth- and early twentieth-century expansionism of the industrial states represented more than a determined search for markets, raw materials, or investment opportunities to alleviate domestic social crises. Advocates of an in-

vigorated foreign economic policy believed that their nation
must control world communications and dominate the factors
of production on a world scale. In the process, their efforts
would enliven a domestic life-style with exotic products. The
circum-Caribbean, valued for transit as well as its resources,
seemed to be an ideal place for carrying out this complicated
plan.[19] By incorporating the "American Mediterranean" into the
U.S. economy, entrepreneurs could establish new labor relations
abroad as their contemporaries reinforced those at home. By fa-
cilitating metropole control over peripheral labor, free market
imperialism effectively shifted that work force to areas of exploitation. In the foreign arena, metropoles could compete for
control over productive resources and wealth without the political and social restraints they confronted at home.[20]

Harsh treatment of labor in industrially advanced countries
was made difficult by complicated production systems requiring workers to pursue considerable educational and technical
training. Social imperialism, it can be argued, increased the
living standard of domestic laborers by allowing them to "profit" from the labor of workers on the periphery. Entrepreneurs
from the metropole were attracted to Central America not
only for its resources but also by their recognition that it
would be easier, and more acceptable to their own compatriots, to squeeze extra profits from alien workers (such as West
Indians) who were poor, were considered racially inferior, and
lacked the intellectual ability and determination to rely on the
family or other kinship groups, the community, or the law for
legitimate protest. Because alien laborers were so vulnerable,
U.S. firms used them extensively in Central America during
the early twentieth century.[21] Class and race were clearly important features of U.S. policy in the region.

In the last quarter of the nineteenth century, both U.S. and
European economic interests developed rapidly in Central
America. By the 1880s, Germans were well established in
Guatemala and were doing business in Costa Rica and Honduras. The British had strong trade and investment positions
throughout Central America. Save for British interlopers cutting hardwoods, foreigners had neglected the Caribbean coast
until the 1880s, when U.S. entrepreneurs began making sizable

investments in gold mining, banana harvesting, and timber. After the United States commenced work on the Panama Canal in 1904, U.S. military and commercial interests began looking more closely at El Salvador and Fonseca Bay, which offered the best harbor facilities south of Mazatlán, Mexico. By then, British, French, and German concerns had developed important economic interests in El Salvador.[22]

U.S. policy in the early twentieth century called for the replacement of non-U.S. interests in areas deemed strategically important or essential to canal security. Nicaragua figured heavily in this strategy. Despite the French selection of Panama as a canal site, the Nicaraguan route had captivated engineers; in fact, as late as 1902, Nicaragua was the preferred choice of U.S. engineers and had strong support in the Congress. When the decision went to Panama instead, Nicaraguan President José Santos Zelaya—a Liberal but one with a driving nationalist spirit who shared Nicaraguans' belief that an interoceanic canal across his country would bring prosperity—chose to resist rather than acquiesce. Nicaragua was a nation; a nation had the right to determine its own destiny. If the United States was not interested in Nicaragua as a canal site, perhaps other governments would be. When Zelaya began making inquiries among German, Japanese, French, and British investors, the State Department expressed initial shock at his defiance, then announced that a foreign-financed canal would threaten U.S. security in the region. "Legitimate" strategic concerns, of course, have limited value in persuading the general public, so the pronouncements on this matter coming out of Washington were increasingly dotted with disturbing comments about threats to democracy and the best interests of the Nicaraguan people. When the State Department tried to insinuate the Costa Rican government into this conflict (using as pretext the long-standing Nicaraguan-Costa Rican border disputes), the Costa Ricans resisted. Along with other Central American political leaders (some of whom had little compassion for Zelaya), they feared the long-term consequences of a unilateral U.S. decision to humiliate and weaken a small state because of its government's defiance.[23]

Hypocrisy, it is sometimes said, is the tribute vice pays to virtue. Put another way, universals acquire their definition according to place. Costa Ricans were not alone in recognizing the contradiction between the ideological appeals and the self-serving conduct of the United States. Inevitably, there would be a price to pay for such high-handed ways, but the generation that crafted "Imperial America" on the isthmus would not have to pay it. Not a few students of U.S. foreign policy have called this and similar episodes a form of tragedy. Perhaps the most articulate exposition of this view is that of William A. Williams. Tragedy, he argued, often results when Americans adopt liberal developmental values in societies deemed important for the U.S. role in the world. The insistence that these societies assimilate U.S. values and institutions negates the fundamental liberal principle of self-determination and weakens domestic political institutions—particularly where comprador elites, who are often subservient to or co-opted by foreign concerns, seem more determined to defend the interests of the foreigner than those of the nation. The U.S. government wanted Central America developed (as did many Central American Liberals) but in accordance with U.S. economic and geopolitical interests. It also enunciated the goal of assisting Central American states in the modernization of liberal institutions and democratic practices. Tragically, as Williams explained, the materialism of the liberal order frequently triumphs over humanitarian and idealistic goals.[24]

Because metropole states generally looked inward to home country issues rather than to host country needs, their slighting of local conditions sometimes stimulated resistance in Central American societies, particularly in situations where political leaders could not avoid taking sides. Persistent (and frequently increasing) opposition in Central America prompted metropole governments to threaten retaliation or to back up their diplomatic pressures with force on behalf of their nationals in the isthmus. A challenge-and-response process ensued: the more determined the resistance, the greater the need to restrict the sovereignty and independence of isthmian states. Metropole entrepreneurs, however, usually sought the assistance of comprador groups, because the use of force could limit their ability to operate profitably in a host country. They needed friends in local high places. Samuel Zemurray turned to Manuel Bonilla to secure a foothold for Cuyamel in Honduras; United Fruit officials looked to Guatemalan President Manuel Estrada Cabrera when they had trouble in the banana zones.[25]

Central American societies struggled to find a secure role in the revised world order, but in a confrontation the enormous imbalances in power between metropole and isthmian governments frequently determined the outcome. Restrictions on the sovereignty of a peripheral state largely determined the success of the metropole state. For example, the United States invoked the Monroe Doctrine to forbid Costa Rica, Nicaragua, Honduras, or El Salvador to transfer their insular possessions to non-Western Hemispheric states. Sometimes, the method of reducing the sovereignty of the periphery was subtly grounded in propositions for "improving" political and economic institutions. By the 1920s, as the United States came to practice "progressive pan-Americanism," Washington was effectively sharing the sovereignty of states in the circum-Caribbean. It collected state revenues and supplied customs commissioners, finance supervisors, revenue and distribution agents, and military personnel to enforce revenue collection and preserve the order necessary to permit business activity. In fundamental disputes between governments over these matters, the metropole states defined what was meant by "democracy" or "freedom" or "financial responsibility" and what had to be done to assure compliance.

Metropole rivalry, linked to home country disorders and fought on a worldwide, highly competitive economic and strategic battlefield, had a profoundly transforming impact on Central American societies. In the late nineteenth century, promoters from metropole countries were already descending on Central America with developmental schemes for the incorporation of the isthmus into a market economy. By the early twentieth century, isthmian states had virtually surrendered control of major elements in their internal communications, public utilities, national debt, currency, state revenue, and other economic activities that generated national wealth. Influenced by a comprador elite, these governments exercised only limited power over their own political economies, but they were often held singularly responsible for any failures that adversely affected metropole firms, individuals, or interests, or for any assertions of sovereignty that appeared to threaten metropole security.

Metropole leaders responded to domestic economic crisis with proposals to heal the malfunctioning laissez-faire system by extending it worldwide. They developed policies such as British free trade, the U.S. Open Door Policy (a special version of free trade which offered equal opportunity rather than the removal of trade barriers), and President Woodrow Wilson's Fourteen Points (the second through the sixth of which described an international free trade system), incorporated in the liberal agenda for settling World War I. Metropole entrepreneurs used the laissez-faire ideology and the weak mechanism of international political, judicial, and social control to produce opportunities for themselves, while the states on the periphery suffered instability and loss of sovereignty. Metropole governments allowed entrepreneurs who went abroad in search of personal wealth to escape any effective control. The banana men certainly benefited from this policy of benevolent neglect.

Real and imagined competition among French, German, British, and U.S. interests remained central to understanding metropole intrusion into Central America. After German unification in 1871, leaders from the landed aristocracy, the military, and the high bureaucracy came to agree with many merchants, manufacturers, and exporters from the Hansa, the Rhine, and the Ruhr areas that external expansion might ameliorate the social and economic turmoil in Germany's industrializing economy. Some German businessmen and politicians expected to benefit from trading opportunities in the Pacific Basin, to direct part of the frustrated and underemployed segments of the German population to the Caribbean-Central American region, and to build market areas and foster German cultural and political influence in a key strategic area.[26]

Given their common convictions about the fundamental relationship between expansion and national survival, the occasional cooperation between Germany and the United States was constrained by each government's political agenda in Central America. German merchants were successful; they actually eliminated the role of British middlemen in Honduran commerce provoking warning signals from U.S., British, and French diplomats in the late nineteenth century. Ultimately, U.S. officials realized that cooperation with German officials hampered U.S. efforts to secure a dominant position in Latin America under the Monroe Doctrine and pan-americanism. The German attraction to Central American transit challenged the United States in an area that it defined as central to its security. While the U.S. government could cooperate with other metropole states to establish the right of foreigners to conduct business abroad, it was unwilling to share control of the chief isthmian transit sites with Old World powers.[27]

In the late nineteenth and early twentieth centuries, German entrepreneurs used investment in public utilities to introduce the technological products of Siemens, Allgemeine Elektrizitäts Gesellschaft (AEG), and other firms on the isthmus. German interests encountered other nations' businessmen whose corrupted laissez-faire ideology and free-trade rhetoric intensified the competitiveness because it contained political, strategic, social, and especially cultural language that reinforced the home country's determination to assure its adversaries minimum access to the vital isthmus.

French aspirations also included access to interoceanic transit at the isthmus, and engineer Ferdinand de Lesseps's Universal Canal Company spent more than a decade (from 1878 to the mid-1890s) in digging a canal across Panama before corruption and mismanagement bankrupted the firm. Nevertheless, from the 1880s until World War I, France was a major capital-exporting country and commercial power, and its policy in Central America reflected its leaders' judgments that French society's well-being and the nation's economic growth and accumulation rates were intimately linked to the world economy. French capital, trade, culture, and residents assumed a dynamic role in the transmission of these goals.[28] U.S. policy, calling for replacement of non-U.S. interests in the area, sought to diminish French influence.

After 1900 the U.S. presence began to overwhelm the European. Twice in the first three decades of the twentieth century, in 1907 and 1923, the United States closely supervised the negotiation of treaties among the Central American states which were intended to establish peace, order, and stability. In both the campaign against Zelaya of 1909-12 and the "Sandino War" of the late 1920s, however, when Washington concluded that these pacts restricted its efforts to manipulate isthmian politics, it acted in defiance of them. In the case of the Central American Court, established as a result of the 1907 treaties, U.S. determination to obtain a canal treaty with Nicaragua (thus effectively eliminating a European-sponsored waterway in that country) proved decisive in killing the court. Insecurity about Nicaragua as site for an alternative canal was a critical factor in U.S. support of Zelaya's enemies and the decision to intervene with a sizable contingent of troops in 1912. The 1923 treaty, which mandated the withholding of diplomatic recognition of anyone assuming executive power through revolution (or anyone related to someone who engaged in revolutionary activity), failed to survive the seizure of power by strongmen in Honduras, Guatemala, Nicaragua, and El Salvador in the early 1930s.

With expanded multinational activity, enclaves, and cultural, scientific, and military agencies, the United States rationalized its imperial purpose in Central America. When World War I disrupted and decimated the European presence, the United States took advantage of the world crisis to undermine German, French, and British activity in Central America and to achieve unparalleled dominance throughout the circum-Caribbean. The aggressive policy initiated earlier in the century offered reassurance to those who argued that economic clout in the 1920s enabled Washington to run isthmian affairs and intimidate Central American governments without sending in the marines. Such logic collapsed before the reality of the Sandino war in Nicaragua a few years later, but in its aftermath U.S. officials found a Nicaraguan client to police the country and protect U.S. investments.

By then, filibustering and the employment of mercenaries to secure the economic objectives of metropole states had subtly changed. In the seventy years after 1850, filibusters, mercenaries, soldiers, and entrepreneurs descended on vulnerable Central America. Most of the filibusters were private individuals, but the "policing" of the tropics or retaliation for alleged maltreatment of foreigners may be considered a form of official filibustering; thus the complete history of filibustering should include the U.S. bombardment of San Juan del Norte in 1854, the landing of German marines at Corinto in 1878 and British marines on the Mosquito coast in 1894, the dispatch of U.S. forces to Honduras in 1906 and Nicaragua in 1911-12 and 1926-32, and the proxy war in Nicaragua in the 1980s. And, if one expands the definition of filibustering to include the activities of those entrepreneurs who financed rebellions to gain advantage, then the catalogue of private filibusters should add Cornelius Vanderbilt, Minor Keith, Jacob Weinberger, the Vaccaro brothers, Samuel Zemurray, and Victor Cutter to the names of William Walker, Henry L. Kinney, Lee Christmas, Guy "Machine-gun" Molony, "Jew Sam" Dreben, Tracy Richardson, and Victor Gordon. And in the 1980s, when soldiers of fortune fought in the contra war in Nicaragua, the sources of their income were not multinational companies but fundamentalist Protestant and conservative paramilitary organizations in the United States.

The mercenaries and entrepreneurs in the half-century we write about were all linked to bananas. Although they also plunged into mining, railroads, shipping, banking, and other businesses—as well as "revoluting"—the name "banana men" is appropriate because bananas were the most visible and dynamic growth sector on the isthmus during these years, and the fruit companies were very profitable enterprises that required control over transportation, the domestic labor supply, and much of the arable land on the Caribbean coast of the two countries we survey. This voracious appetite for domination of the factors of production meant that the banana men interacted even as their companies competed. All sought to influence the political systems in the countries where they did business— with money or muscle, and often with both. U.S. officials, though distancing themselves publicly from clear violations of neutrality by the banana men, often privately acquiesced in what they were doing, even when their activity appeared legally questionable, because these entrepreneurs benefited U.S. strategic interests in areas deemed critical to interoceanic transport. In their own way, the banana men established a beachhead for U.S. interests at what appeared to be an acceptable cost: the tarnishing of the U.S. image.

2

Banana Kingdoms

In 1900, as the U.S. military policed Cuba and brutally suppressed a Filipino insurrection on the other side of the world, ambitious American entrepreneurs were carving out new empires in the tropics of Central America. Northwest of the Panamanian isthmus, where a 2,000-man U.S. military expedition had put down a rebellion of dissident Colombian Liberals in 1885, the five Central American republics and the colony of British Honduras were virtually unknown lands to most North Americans. But vigorous American adventurers, promoters, and runaways were finding new opportunities in the coastal towns. In the interior—in Tegucigalpa, the capital of mountainous Honduras; in the lake country of Nicaragua, where William Walker and his marauding army had ruled almost half a century before—the American remained an intruder in closed societies dominated by landed families. Along the Caribbean coastline, however, from Bocas del Toro, Panama, to Puerto Barrios, Guatemala, a business that in time became a U.S. empire and shaped the course of twentieth-century Central American history was already taking form.[1]

In 1899 a small group of investors in Boston and Costa Rica formed the United Fruit Company (UFCO), the realization of the dream of three men different in every social respect—

Lorenzo Baker, Andrew Preston, and Minor Cooper Keith. Baker was a ship captain who had gone to sea at fourteen. In May 1871, sailing in the *Telegraph*, he had brought the first cargo of bananas into Boston. Bananas were not unknown in the States, but trading in them was extremely risky because they were highly perishable and considered an exotic fruit. A year or so before he delivered Boston's first bananas, he had bought 160 bunches at twenty-five cents per bunch in Jamaica and sold them in Jersey City for a profit of $2.00 per bunch. (The spine of the banana plant is the *stalk*; branches of the stalk are *stems*; and each stem produces several *bunches* of bananas. A bunch can weigh as much as eighty pounds.) Baker went on to found the Boston Fruit Company, one of the largest firms involved in the banana trade in the 1890s, and joined it with UFCO at the end of the decade.

At eighteen, with only five years of formal schooling, Preston had been a produce dealer's assistant. A thoroughly calculating man, he had the New Englander's disdain for the tropics but realized the potential market for bananas. When proper Boston bankers shunned the idea of forming a fruit company as too risky, Preston persuaded nine men to put up $2,000 each and forgo any profits for five years. He raised the capital for Boston Fruit, succeeded Baker as president, and in 1899 consolidated the company into the new United Fruit Company.

Keith had made his mark as the builder of Costa Rica's Caribbean coast railroads. His uncle, Henry Meiggs, who had constructed railroads in Chile and Peru over the most terrifyingly mountainous terrain imaginable, had obtained the task of connecting the coast with Costa Rica's inland cities and the rich coffee region of the Mesa Central (central plateau). Meiggs, preoccupied with business projects in Peru, turned over the direction of this herculean enterprise to Henry Meiggs Keith, Minor's older brother. After asking his brother's help, Henry Keith died, leaving Minor Keith in charge. Costa Rica provided every economic and political consideration, granting Keith authority over an expanse of territory equal in size to Rhode Island. In ten years, at a cost of $8 million and 4,000 lives, Keith had laid seventy miles of track, linking the Mesa Central to the pestilential coast and the town Keith built, Puerto Limón. By 1883, Keith was exporting bananas to the United States from four Central American republics. He married the daughter of a former Costa Rican president. But a New York bank crisis in 1889 plunged his far-flung operation into financial crisis. The Costa Ricans helped, but he began looking elsewhere for aid. The opportunity came when he struck a deal with Preston and Baker.[2] UFCO grew even faster than the most optimistic calculations. When Preston announced the first dividends of $2.50 per share (in December 1899), the company controlled 250,000 acres in Colombia, Cuba, Jamaica, the Dominican Republic, Honduras, Nicaragua, and Costa Rica; more than one hundred square miles—66,000 acres—had producing banana trees. A few years later it acquired banana lands in Guatemala as well. On its vast estates the company employed 15,000 people. It operated eleven steamships, chartered twenty to thirty more vessels, and ran its three hundred boxcars and seventeen locomotives over more than one hundred miles of track laid exclusively for linking the banana plantations with its coastal warehouses.

In 1906 United Fruit erected two radio stations in eastern Nicaragua, one at Bluefields on the coast and the second upriver at Rama. The company already owned a two hundred-foot transmission tower at Bocas del Toro, Panama. When the conservative New England stockholders complained of the expense of operating the stations—each word cost $50 to broadcast— Preston confidently retorted that in the uncertainty of the banana business a word was sometimes worth fifty dollars. As UFCO expanded its operations along the Central American coast, it sought control of all property suitable for banana production and shipping, including land, warehouses, railroads, wharves, and steamships. From the moment the green bunches were whacked from the trees until they were unloaded in the States, UFCO reigned.[3]

In a congressional investigation of shipping combinations in 1912, the House Committee on Merchant Marine and Fisheries reported that United Fruit's only competition in eastern Nicaragua was the Atlantic Fruit and Steamship Company, owned by Joseph DiGiorgio, who testified that UFCO had frustrated his efforts to get financing and effectively controlled its smaller competitors. Even in Honduras, where four companies operated—UFCO, Atlantic Fruit and Steamship, Standard, and Cuyamel—the committee believed that the last three offered little competition to United Fruit.[4] Two years later the American consul at La Ceiba, in a glowing report on the company's operations on the north coast, wrote that UFCO was a "distinctively American concern" whose agents were "clean-cut young men brought out from the states" and not the "American beachcombers employed largely by other companies."[5] In Guatemala, UFCO had no competition at all; it controlled the railroad linking the capital to Puerto Barrios ("an achievement in ugliness in a natural setting of beauty," wrote Carleton Beals in the 1920s, "where people put water-closets in their front yards")[6] and dominated Guatemalan-American trade.

To charges that UFCO's avarice was stifling any effective competition and swallowing up the best properties, Preston said: "The land that we own in the tropics does not monopolize the banana land. There are enormous quantities of it there." Asked by a naive committee member if UFCO's policy was to purchase property that could be made profitable, Preston replied: "We do our business entirely for profit. Whenever we see we can make a dollar we do it."[7] In later life the unrepentant Preston even boasted that United Fruit's policies ably served the United States, which in 1912 had intervened with marines and bluejackets in Nicaragua and was attempting, through Secretary of State Philander C. Knox's policy of "dollar diplomacy," to frustrate European economic influence in Central America. Over the years, however, Preston gained a reputation as a rather grim accountant out of touch with the empire of green and gold over which he ruled. New England lay a world away from the pestilential Central American coast, but with Preston as its financial wizard Boston became the capital of United Fruit's banana kingdom.[8]

There were other banana entrepreneurs, mostly out of the Mississippi Delta, who had the gambler's instinct and readily plunged into a business that remained forever risky. In 1890

Jacob "Jake" Weinberger established Bluefields Banana Company in Galveston, with a capitalization of only $250,000, and shipped bananas from eastern Nicaragua aboard tramp steamers. A legend in the banana trade along the Nicaraguan coast, Weinberger served as the company's president and "tropical manager." An "affable Southerner" who enjoyed gambling and spoke what was known in the tropics as "dog Spanish," he traveled the banana towns of the Central American coast, trading for bananas, coconuts, parrots, and macaws. His ornithological enterprises earned him the sobriquet "the Parrot King."[9]

More durable than Weinberger were three Sicilians out of New Orleans: Joseph, Luca, and Felix Vaccaro. In the harsh winter of 1899 a freeze wiped out their orange groves in the Mississippi Delta. With his son-in-law Salvator D'Antoni, Joseph and the other Vaccaros moved a few years later to the Honduran coast, roughly halfway between El Porvenir and Tela. Under the most primitive conditions they established Vaccaro Brothers Company, the predecessor of Standard Tropical Trading and Transport Company (formed in 1924), one of several small companies on the Honduran coast. Another was Cuyamel, a fledgling enterprise organized by Zemurray in 1912. Cuyamel's operations extended over land developed by William Streich, a Philadelphian who had garnered a concession on the Honduran coast to build a railroad from Cuyamel to Veracruz so that banana farmers would not have to rely on river barges to ship their produce.

Already the small but fiercely independent banana growers of the Honduran north were succumbing to the expansion of American firms. In the 1890s banana ships bound for New Orleans regularly sailed these waters, taking on bunches from the farmers and traders who populated the coastal towns—Tela, Puerto Cortés, and La Ceiba. None had a wharf suitable for oceangoing vessels, so the Hondurans loaded their bananas on shallow-draft lighters or barges and paddled their cargo out to the steamers. Years later, after the big operators had moved in, swallowing the small Honduran banana farms, people recalled the old days in the coastal towns when "the native farmer [re-

ceived] weekly large sums of money for the sale of his produce . . . [and] it was a common sight to see in the streets . . .
farmers carrying their hats brimful of greenbacks. . . . They
were the only banana producers on the coast."[10]

Within a few years the Vaccaros were moving into the interior to open up new plantations. In 1905 the company started
laying narrow-gauge track near Salado, moving south and west
toward Masica and then east to El Porvenir. When El Porvenir's citizens complained, the Vaccaros bypassed the town
and terminated the line in La Ceiba, twenty-five miles from
Masica, and made La Ceiba company headquarters. On April
12, 1908, the first locomotive chugged into the town. Benefit-
ing from an agreement with the Honduran government, which
had declared in 1907 that the company "merits the protection
of the state," the Vaccaros were permitted to import "duty-
free" the materials, including food and forage, necessary for
their operations. Finding their business hampered by the lack
of a bank on the coast, in 1912 the Vaccaros got permission
from the Honduran government to open the Banco Atlántico in
La Ceiba, a bank of issue and discount capitalized at $500,000 in
gold. When the Vaccaros came to Honduras, boasted the New
Orleans-based magazine *Latin America* in 1914, "the North
Coast was a picturesque, lovely, [and] unbroken wilderness." In
the hundred miles from Tela to Iriona the Vaccaros had transformed the jungle into "flourishing banana and plaintain farms,
and lovely gardens of various kinds of tropical fruits" and made
the "little insignificant" La Ceiba into a major port with a
hurricane-proof wharf connected to a 120-mile railroad line to
the Vaccaros' 160,000 acres of banana lands.[11]

UFCO had been the creation of Andrew Preston, Lorenzo Baker, and Minor Keith—a fruit trader and accountant, a ship captain, and a railroad builder; the future Standard was the labor
of the Vaccaros and Salvator D'Antoni out of New Orleans.
The third banana empire of the isthmus represented largely
the labors of one man, a remarkable Bessarabian immigrant

named Z'murri who anglicized his name to Samuel Zemurray—Sam "the Banana Man." Legend has it that Zemurray began with a pushcart in Mobile, one of UFCO's ports of call, where he bought "ripes" (which the company had to sell quickly) and shipped them upcountry to Alabama railroad towns. With Ashbel Hubbard, Zemurray formed the Hubbard-Zemurray Steamship Company, which began operations with one battered banana steamer. His link with the banana lands was the Honduran port of Omoa, across the spacious bay from Puerto Cortés.[12]

Compared with UFCO's broad operations, Zemurray's business in the banana trade before World War I was negligible, but early twentieth-century Mobile port records reveal that it was expanding: 336,000 bunches were sold in 1903, almost 600,000 the following year, and 1.75 million in 1910—the year Zemurray bought out the Cuyamel Fruit Company. Short of funds, Streich agreed to sell out, after Zemurray got financial help from his father-in-law, Jake Weinberger, Adolph "Dolly" Katz, a New Orleans banker, and, surprisingly, United Fruit itself, which saw in Zemurray's dealings no threat, certainly, but a minor competitive irritant that could be controlled and eventually absorbed. So indifferent, apparently, was Preston to Zemurray's plunge into the banana business in Honduras that a few years later, testifying before the House Committee investigating combinations in restraint of trade in the shipping industry, Preston declared that he knew a "Mr. Zemurray" but somewhat disingenuously said there "could be more than one Zemurray." At that time Preston admitted that UFCO had bought 60 percent of the stock in the Hubbard-Zemurray Steamship Company but sold out in 1910 to Zemurray because, in Preston's estimation, "he seemed to be a man of speculative ideas."[13]

Visitors to Central America in the last decade of the nineteenth century inevitably compared the remote capitals with the more lively coastal towns, which owed their prosperity to the banana trade. Richard Harding Davis, his reputation as fearless journalist not yet molded by the war with Spain, traveled down the isthmus in the mid-1890s and chronicled his

journey in *Three Gringos in Venezuela and Central America.*
Comayagua, Honduras's second-largest city and, until 1880,
the capital of the republic, was a "dull and desolate place of
many one-story houses, with iron-barred windows, and a great,
bare, dusty plaza, faced by a huge cathedral." Tegucigalpa, the
new capital, was not much of an improvement. Davis described the "long, dark, cool shops of general merchandize, and
a great cathedral and a pretty plaza, where the band plays at
night and people circle in two rings . . . and there is the government plaza and a big penitentiary, a university and a cemetery. But there is no color nor ornamentation nor light nor life
nor bustle nor laughter. . . . Everyone seems to go to bed at
nine o'clock." Managua, chosen as the Nicaraguan capital between Conservative Granada and Liberal León, Davis continued, was "a dismal city, built on a plain of sun-dried earth,
with houses of sun-dried earth, plazas and parks and streets on
sun-dried earth, and a mantel of dust all over." But Belize, capital of British Honduras, he wrote, was "a pretty village of six
thousand people, living in low, broad-roofed bungalows, lying
white and cool looking in the border of waving coconut trees
and tall graceful palms. . . . A British colony is always civilized."[14]

The banana towns of the north Honduran coast were live-
lier, certainly, but not especially attractive. Banana laborers
and their supervisors lived primitively. Lacking fresh meats
and vegetables, they survived mainly on canned goods brought
in by the tramp steamers from U.S. ports on the Gulf of Mexico. Water had to be filtered through charcoal and given the
"sulphur treatment," and year round there were recurring
bouts with dysentery and the dreaded yellow fever. When the
seagoing vessels appeared one or two times a month, residents
ventured out on barges with buckets, hoping to get ice.[15]

Surprisingly, isthmian coastal towns attracted a remarkably
heterogeneous population. Puerto Cortés had only eight hundred inhabitants and flooded annually during the rainy season,
wrote one New Orleans promoter in the 1880s, but the town
was "remarkably healthy" and boasted a Frenchified community—dominated by names like De Brot, Arnoux, Caron—and a

well-kept hotel run by Mrs. Berard. Greytown and Bluefields in Nicaragua had British and German merchants and business-men. Other ports had residents of various other nationalities, including Syrians, Jamaicans, and Chinese.[16]

By 1900 Puerto Cortés had already become a place of ref-uge for Americans with ambition or with a good reason for hasty flight from the States. It was there that Davis ran into Charles Jeffs, a mining engineer from Minnesota and now an honorary colonel in the Honduran army, who agreed to guide the "three gringos"—Davis and two companions—across the wilds of mountainous Honduras. A New Orleanian, Lee Christ-mas, had just signed on as engineer for the railroad line that ran out of Puerto Cortés to San Pedro Sula; Davis met him when he went forward to ride in the locomotive, a woodburner that Christmas ran "full throttle," making the sparks fly. John Morris of the Louisiana State Lottery, run out of the state by reform elements, had moved the operation to Puerto Cortés. At one time the Louisiana Lottery has been the "biggest gam-bling concern in the world," wrote Davis, conducting its busi-ness from an ornate building that dwarfed the tin-roofed mu-nicipal and national buildings of the town, but by 1900 it had dwindled to the point of collecting receipts in a "single house on a mud-bank covered with palm-trees."[17]

Until 1912 Honduras had no extradition treaty, so Puerto Cortés, the best-known northern port, had more than its share of people on the run—Americans, Chinese, Syrians, and Turks; soldiers of fortune and tropical tramps. Honduras was especially attractive to bank embezzlers. "Cashier" Brown, who wrecked a bank in Kentucky, absconded to La Ceiba, where he became a clerk for a steamship company. Alex Odendahl, a New Orleans grain merchant, bilked several city banks out of $200,000 and showed up in Puerto Cortés wearing a beard and a suit of white duck. The one-time deputy U.S. marshal for New Orleans, Alcée LeBlanc, after being implicated in a scandal, ran off to San Pedro Sula and got a job as a railroad agent. The writer William S. Porter (O. Henry), on the lam from the law, sought refuge in Puerto Cortés and found there not only sanctuary but sufficient material for his book *Cabbages and Kings*. "Not much of a town," he wrote, with its half-dozen two-story houses and mongrel population—and, of course, its "tintype man" and "kodaking tourist" and "hucksters of Germany, France and Sicily." Porter unmercifully satirized the town and the country, which he called "Anchuria," with endless tales of soldiers of fortune and opéra bouffe revolutions. He told of a probably mythical U.S. consul trying to get the attention of his government: "'Twice before,' said the consul, 'I have cabled our government for a couple of gunboats to protect American citizens. The first time the [State] Department sent me a pair of gum boots. The other time was when a man named Pease was going to be executed here. They referred that appeal to the Secretary of Agriculture.'"[18]

But the most notorious of the runaways to Honduras was Maj. Edward A. Burke, a Confederate veteran and prominent Louisianan who had once ventured into mining at Bessemer, Alabama. He had been the successful promoter of the 1884 World's Industrial and Cotton Centennial Exposition in New Orleans, at which President Luis Bográn had promoted Honduras with a 100,000-square-foot map of his country in the garden section. Burke became very interested in Honduran mining, avidly promoted by Bográn's predecessor, Marco Aurelio Soto, whose presidency from 1880 until 1884 was immortalized as the "Golden Age." In those years a mining boom had lured prospectors from the United States, England, France, and Germany to the tick-infested mountains and the placer river region of Olancho. An 1885 tourist guide to New Orleans described Burke glowingly as a "predestined leader" with a "combative instinct" and "affable and winning manners." After the triumph of the exposition Burke became state treasurer. It was in that position, according to friendly accounts, that in order to rescue the financially faltering exposition and save Louisiana's reputation, he transferred state securities and bonds into money markets. Then he was off to Honduras to file a mining claim and from there on to London to get financing from the House of Rothschild. During his return voyage the scandal over the Louisiana bonds broke. When Burke's ship approached the Mississippi Delta passes to New Orleans, several friends went out to meet it; their news about the public hostility aroused by his activities as state treasurer persuaded Burke to change ships in the Gulf and board a vessel bound for Honduras.[19]

In 1890 the *New Orleans Daily Picayune* described Burke as a scoundrel who had left the state "penniless" by squandering a million dollars from the treasury but who, with the support of the Rothschilds, was successfully posing as a baron in Honduras, promoting two mining colleges, two agricultural colleges, and two flour mills—all the while complaining that the people of Louisiana for whom he had "slaved for twenty years" were "hounding" him. Burke is playing, wrote the *Picayune* angrily, "his last scheme." In fact, said one traveler returned from Honduras, Burke was losing money, spending $150 to get $100 in gold and living in continual fear of being kidnapped and brought back to face the wrath of Louisianans.[20]

Nevertheless, in the following years Burke prospered, doubtless because his mining enterprises were enhanced by his willingness to lend military experience to Domingo Vásquez, a Honduran political aspirant who figured prominently in the country's revolutionary turbulence in the 1890s. Two dozen or so American soldiers of fortune—most of them ex-Confederate or ex-Union soldiers such as Fred Budde, Joseph Milner, and Frank Imboden—had signed on with Vásquez, and one Herbert "General Heriberto" Jeffries became their commander. Jeffries, arriving in Central America in 1887 to buy cattle, had come to the aid of some Honduran malcontents then encamped in El Salvador. After he helped them stage a meaningless attack on San Salvador, the group retreated to Honduras. There Jeffries's enthusiasm and martial ability caught the attention of President Bográn, who showered the young American with social honors and military promotions. Jeffries returned the favors by helping Bográn crush a rebellion in 1890. Three years later Jeffries was commanding a special American squad in Vásquez's army, a squad that undertook the most hazardous assignments.[21]

Through his shrewd politicking and his genuine concern for Honduras and its people, Burke eventually became the most popular American in the country. But he was never known as the "king of Honduras"; that accolade fell to a shrewd New Yorker, Washington S. Valentine, who at the age of twenty went with his father, Julius Valentine, to Honduras. In the 1870s Julius had run an export-import business in New York City, but it went under after the crash of 1873. In 1879 the family moved to Honduras, and in the following year Julius formed the New York and Honduras Rosario Mining Company in New York. Washington signed on as geologist and translator with a special obligation to the Honduran army. The mining boom was on in the country, and the Valentine family operation expanded rapidly.[22]

In 1894, Washington Valentine formed a Honduran syndicate in an effort to renegotiate Honduras's embarrassingly high foreign debt—most of it accumulated in imprudent expenditures to railroad concessionaires granted liberal contracts to build a transcontinental line from the north coast to Amapala on the Pacific. Between 1867 and 1870 the country had negotiated four loans to build the line, but only fifty miles of track were laid, from Puerto Cortés inland to just beyond San Pedro Sula. The construction was supervised by an American civil engineer, John Trautwine, who wound the line along the Chamelecón River until the money gave out; then he returned to the States and wrote a textbook for civil engineers. Valentine's syndicate lost out in its bid to take over the renegotiation of the foreign debt, but he did get a concession to use the railroad, provided that he would extend the line to Comayagua, the old capital.

By the 1890s ambitious Honduran *políticos* were looking eagerly to these *yanqui* impresarios to help fight their wars and fatten their purses. The impresarios expected land, timber, mining concessions, and tariff-free importation as payment for their services in funding and organizing weapons and bodies of U.S. soldiers of fortune; the soldiers expected adventure, fame, and fortune. All parties got at least some share of their expectations, though in reality the Central American societies that paid them received precious little in return. The U.S. government was generally unhappy with the periods of disorder but content with the end product—an isthmus under its domination.

In 1892 some 2,000 Americans lived in Honduras—most of them miners in the interior; they were "enterprising" colonists, former President Bográn proudly declared on a visit to New Orleans. But a sufficiently sizable number lingered in the north coast towns to make their presence known in any revolutionary situation. To the venturesome observers from the United States, the Honduran troubles of the 1890s had an opéra bouffe quality—plotting by a disgruntled presidential aspirant denied an honest count in the most recent election, or by a bemedaled general grown weary of dress parades. "Sometimes a revolution takes place," wrote Richard Harding Davis cynically, "and half of the people in the country will not know of it until it has been put down or succeeded."[23] In the meantime, miners and banana hands became soldiers, and small businesses were gouged by warring generals for forced loans. Few in the United States understood that behind the bloody fracases plaguing most of Central America stood ambitious men who dreamed not only of power but of creating nations, or of building fortunes out of land, rivers, ports, and favorable concessions.[24]

Two compelling forces—each with deep roots in Central America's past—sustained the new political turmoil. The first, born in Central America's bloodless independence in 1821, called for restoration of the isthmian union, torn apart a half-century before. In 1885 Guatemalan President Justo Rufino Barrios had tried to reinstitute the union forcibly and had lost his life in the struggle; with his death, Guatemala slipped from its prominence in the struggle for a restored union. The second force was liberalism, which until then had stood as much for social ties and family connections as for principles. But with the rise of a new generation of young *políticos* it had come to mean a commitment to modern, Europeanized plans that looked to diversified economies with schools and roads and, above all, an integrated nation.

Nicaragua and its defiant leader, José Santos Zelaya, moved

to the forefront in Central American interstate politics. Zelaya, who had come into power in the Liberal revolt of 1893,
was dedicated to uniting all Nicaragua under his rule. He dra-
matized his movement by challenging the British in the eastern portion of the country, the broad expanse of thicket and
swamp called the Mosquitia (or Mosquito Coast), where Indians had long paid more fealty to the Union Jack than to the
Nicaraguan banner. Zelaya sent an army into the east and
when the reigning Mosquito king, an Indian who anglicized
his name to Robert Henry Clarence, appealed to the British
vice-consul at Bluefields for protection, Zelaya dispatched an
unambiguous directive to his commanding general: "Occupy
Bluefields, depose the Mosquito king, and leave the consequences to me."[25]

In Honduras, liberalism took the form of a political party
shaped largely by the imposing figure of Dr. Policarpo Bonilla,
a vigorous orator in his mid-thirties when he finally gained the
presidency in 1894. In that year, when Domingo Vásquez and
his *norteamericano* sharpshooters were harassing the capital,
Zelaya recognized Bonilla as the legitimate president of Honduras and dispatched an army, commanded by Honduran exile
Miguel Dávila, to repel Bonilla's enemies in the north. Most of
the violence fell on the isolated capital, Tegucigalpa. In the civil
war of 1894, when Bonilla was fending off political enemies trying to take away the presidential sash that was rightfully his,
virtually every public building in the city crumbled before the
cannon fire from the hills during a six-month siege.[26]

Bonilla was sustained, and in the following years he tried
to restore former president Marco Aurelio Soto's *edad de
oro*—the Golden Age. Soto had been a founder of Honduras's
liberal reform; during his tenure, the Honduran government
had enthusiastically promoted education, transportation, and
commercial agriculture. A banana tax imposed in 1892 (two
cents per stem) and a land law of 1899 attempted to prevent
foreign companies from acquiring large blocks of land. The
U.S. entrepreneurs involved in the banana trade intended to
change Honduras's political order. In the course of things,
however, Bonilla inevitably antagonized other equally ambi-

tious Honduran aspirants who favored his economic activism but looked with suspicion on his relations with Zelaya and considered his confrontation with American entrepreneurs on the north coast unwise. These men busily expanded their operations and believed that they should be allowed to import what they needed from New Orleans without the nuisance of imposts levied by Tegucigalpa. Some entrepreneurs formed alliances with compradores, those domestic leaders eager to ally with foreigners who espoused progress and possessed wealth and power; others lined up hired guns; still others did both. Zemurray pursued both courses with considerable success. His chief comprador ally was General Manuel Bonilla (no relation of Policarpo), who became president twice with the timely aid of the banana men and who revoked the banana tax in 1912. Lawyers and agents for the fruit companies continually circumvented the 1899 land law as they built huge plantations. Policarpo Bonilla, who had once performed legal services for some of the U.S. mining companies, solemnly acknowledged that their activities rarely benefited Hondurans. Moreover, he had a personal reason for his ordinarily politely concealed hostility to Americans: most of the *norteamericano* riflemen in the country had fought for his enemy, Domingo Vásquez.[27]

Lee Christmas did not receive his baptism in this feuding until the spring of 1897, when he was using a diminutive locomotive to ferry bananas and ice between San Pedro Sula and the coast along a small gauge line. A band of disgruntled Hondurans led by General José Manuel Durón, including two less than prominent tropical soldiers of fortune, swept into Puerto Cortés from Guatemala and proclaimed a revolt in favor of Enrique Soto, nephew of the former president. They readily overpowered the undermanned—and underpaid—garrison defending Puerto Cortés and marched inland for a few miles to a railroad siding at Laguna. There they met Christmas's train on the downrun from San Pedro and captured it, commandeering his cargo in the name of the revolution. As he told the story years later, written in his crude scrawl some few months before his death: "A Revolution broke out on the 13 of April 1897 where he [Christmas] was captured by the Revolutionist and forced to handle an Eng at the point of a Bayonet, he applied for Protection from the American consul which of course he did not get. he was then taken to a Drunken General and given to understand that he would be shot. This of course was a Bitter pill for Lee so he said to the Gen. all Right if I have to be made a target of give me a Gun so I may kill som S—B—"²⁸ Certainly, the charm of Christmas lay in his bravado, courage, and sense of humor.

At the time, however, he shifted a flatcar in front of the engine and loaded it with sandbags reinforced with three-quarter-inch boiler iron, providing a mobile fortress for a squad of riflemen—*tiradores*—who planned to ride into glory in a charge on San Pedro Sula. Before Christmas could get up steam to take his commandeered train south, however, Policarpo Bonilla's government at Tegucigalpa had already begun to move against the usurpers. Terencio Sierra, the fiery-tempered minister of war scheduled to succeed Bonilla, dispatched a force out of San Pedro. When news of the advancing party reached the small band at Laguna Trestle on April 14, Durón ordered blocks of ice stacked across the tracks. Christmas, apparently, had every intention of sitting out the battle in the sanctuary of his locomotive cab, but when the soldiers and the rebel *tiradores* began blasting away, he jumped down on the flatcar and joined in the fracas. Their commander seriously wounded, the government troops were beaten off and scurried back toward San Pedro. Behind them the joyous defenders of Laguna Trestle embraced one another after their great victory. Christmas, who had impulsively joined in their fight, was the most celebrated among them and for his daring received a captaincy on the spot.

Before long the revolutionaries controlled the north coast, and within a day or so, when Durón ordered Christmas to take the train south, San Pedro fell as well. But the rebels' glory was short-lived. Zelaya, who had backed Bonilla three years before, dispatched a Nicaraguan gunboat to the Honduran north coast to blockade Puerto Cortés, and another Honduran force marched on San Pedro. On the coast, General William Drummond, one of Durón's mercenaries, resolved he would drive off the hostile Nicaraguan ship. He packed twenty-five pounds of powder and two cannonballs into an ancient Spanish muzzle-loader and set it off with the stub of his cigar. The only memorable damage from this blast was to Drummond himself: he was knocked to the ground, one of his eyes blown out. Inland, the rebels fled aboard two trains; the "Bográn" ran out of fuel on a grade, rolled backward slowly, and struck the "Edna," which had been close behind. The collision and derailment that followed formed a tangled mass of locomotives and boxcars.[29]

On May 2 General Durón, realizing there would be another bloody confrontation at Puerto Cortés in which his small force would be trapped between a larger federal force and the Nicaraguan gunboat, abandoned the struggle and with a few comrades headed across the mountains for Guatemala. Christmas was among them. In time, when the myth of Christmas got bigger than the man, tales of this fearless *gringo* routing an army of frightened Hondurans at the battle of Laguna Trestle assumed legendary proportions. Yet had he not been "impressed" into revolt, Christmas would have watched with indifference what to him and other Americans living in the Honduran tropics was a comical affair.

In all likelihood the shifting fortunes of Honduran liberalism were scarcely as consequential to him in the spring of 1897 as his estrangement from Mamie, the first of his four wives. In February 1897 Christmas wrote to ask for a divorce, adding threateningly: "Of course should you refuse me a divorce should I ever want to marry in this country not being divorced would not interfere in the least."[30] Seven months later he returned to New Orleans (to learn Spanish, he told his daughter, in order "to be promoted to general") and demanded to see his children. Meanwhile, Mamie had acquired a lawyer. "Dear Madam," Christmas began another letter, "you know me well enough to know when I come you nor no one had better interfere. . . . You have listened to a man whom you would not speak to when we were living together. from what I have heard your legal adviser that is Rowdy Bill [is] a *son of a Bitch*."[31]

A severe Victorian code still governed American women, and Mamie has to be admired for her determination to challenge Christmas and even drive him from the country. In this confrontation Mamie apparently won, because in January 1898 Christmas hastily left New Orleans on a banana boat bound for Puerto Cortés. "By the time this [letter] reaches you," he wrote to his daughter, "I will be in the Gulf of Mexico on my way to Central America[.] I did not intend to Leave here but as your mother made up her mind to force me I made up my mind to Leave. I never was made to do anything in my Life nor will I ever."[32]

Six months later, reestablished with the Honduran Railroad in Puerto Cortés, Christmas seemed thoroughly resigned to breaking the remaining ties to his wife: "I just received your letter in reply to the one I wrote you. inclosed you will find a check for $50[.] pay for the divorce and send me my copy[.] I will always send you what I can each month. And may God Bless you and may you Always Live a True Life. I have changed considerable since I seen you Last and will try to Live a Better Life. I would like to visit my children this fall if you will consent. . . . will write when I send you some money. God Bless you and my children are my prayers."[33]

Within a year he had remarried, quit the railroad, and acquired part interest in a store in Choloma. In the years that followed Christmas prospered. Though he had given up his railroad position, he never appeared to lack for funds. Many years later his biographer, Hermann Deutsch, turned up an aged Honduran who had been a treasury official at the turn of the century and recalled that President Terencio Sierra had personally authorized payment of $2,000 to Christmas for a "mission in Guatemala."[34]

The domesticity he was enjoying with his new-found Honduran bride, Magdalena, did not keep him out of trouble, however. For one thing, no sooner was he settled down in his second marriage—a union that produced two children—than he became involved with another woman, Adelaide Caruso. In the small town of Puerto Cortés, of course, their affair could not be kept a secret for very long, and Magdalena had a vengeful brother. Christmas had other local enemies as well. The first of several assassination attempts occurred in 1898 when a man hired by some Hondurans—who were angry over Christmas's investigation of the murder of an American named Maury—tried to poison him. About a year later some of his Puerto Cortés rivals, envious of Christmas's food concession with the railroad, arranged a second assault. This time the assassin caught him with a slug, which left an ugly scar. The third attempt almost killed him: he protected an old man at Choloma from some swindlers, whose hired gunman hit Christmas three times with successive shotgun blasts as he sat drinking in a local saloon. An American doctor in San Pedro saved him with a shot of nitroglycerin to the heart.[35]

As yet, Christmas had not committed his talents to the cause of Manuel Bonilla, the Honduran general who would be his benefactor until Bonilla died in 1913. After Policarpo Bonilla's triumph in the revolt of 1897, the Liberal banner passed to the mercurial Sierra, who knew of the ruddy-faced *norteamericano*'s exploits in the battle of Laguna Trestle. In May 1902 Sierra appointed Christmas a colonel and the police chief of Tegucigalpa because, the president declared, he is "known for his honor, energy, impartiality. . . . [and he knows] how to bring about a good organization in the said police force, developing it into a safeguard for the community and the public peace."[36] But within a year the Liberal bonds forged in the campaigns of the 1890s had broken, and Christmas had to choose sides in a civil war.

As police chief of the capital he was, more important, director of police of the entire country, but his immediate command counted less than two hundred men. In a crisis Sierra did not expect his *jefe de policía* to maintain a neutral stance. In the ensuing political contest, when Manuel Bonilla achieved a plurality but not a majority for the nation's coveted executive seat,

Sierra—known for his alternating bouts of rage and moodiness—suddenly laid the obligation to govern the country on his ministers. This Sierra accomplished the day before his term legally ended. Already General Bonilla and his faithful were stealing out of the capital for a rendezvous and, if necessary, a military campaign to seat him in the executive palace. Christmas and some of his handpicked gendarmes were among them.[37]

Over the years Bonilla had built a loyal following in the country. He was an orator, he kept his word, and he made friends. Christmas and Manuel Bonilla had known one another for less than a year, having first met when Christmas became police chief and Bonilla minister of war in Sierra's cabinet. When Sierra, despite the persistent efforts of Policarpo Bonilla to prevent it, ordered Manuel Bonilla to the commandant's post at Amapala as a way of preserving harmony in the Liberal party, Manuel had dutifully accepted. His rise to minister of war was a sign, apparently, that Sierra intended to pass the presidential sash to him, as Policarpo Bonilla had transferred it to Sierra. But just as abruptly the quixotic Sierra changed his mind. Manuel and his followers, like so many frustrated office-seekers in isthmian history, persuaded themselves that a revolt was necessary to put their man in power.

On the way to the coast Manuel had himself sworn in as provisional president, but he was willing apparently to negotiate with Sierra and his political enemies in the capital for the seat that was rightfully his. When Sierra discovered that Christmas had taken off with a goodly portion of the police force to join the rebellion, he went into one of his legendary tirades. His ministers, fearful of disobeying him, promptly named Sierra as general, and the former president departed the capital with a thousand men, bent on putting down the Bonilla revolt. Tegucigalpa was left with virtually no government except for the rump assembly made up of the deputies who had not stolen away with Manuel's army. Those who remained in town, of course, were Bonilla's political enemies, and in the absence of their colleagues and the newly appointed General Sierra, they declared Juan Ángel Arias (who had come in second behind Manuel Bonilla in the presidential balloting) provisional president.

Zelaya's minister to Honduras immediately recognized Arias as the lawful executive of the country.

Lodged at Amapala with an army that daily grew by hundreds, Manuel dispatched a congratulatory message to Christmas for being among the first to take up arms "in order to defend the honor of the country." A few weeks later another dispatch appointed Christmas second in command to Bonilla's general in the department of La Paz and Comayagua. "I count on the vitality and discipline," Bonilla averred, "that you can give to the good fortune of the operations."[38]

Bonilla's move was timely, for less than a week after he assigned Christmas to his new post, the mercurial Sierra attacked near Aceituno. Sierra claimed a great victory, saying later that the enemy had been devastated by the grenades and shrapnel of the federals, but the local U.S. consul probably provided a less biased judgment when he wrote that Sierra "was completely defeated." In any event, Sierra pulled back to Nacâome, where in a bloody three-day battle Bonilla again triumphed. Bonilla had linked up his various armies with an excellent telegraph system. Christmas declared that the information Bonilla's scattered forces were able to share was vital to the success of the revolt, and he confidently expected to take the capital soon. Yet Manuel still appeared conciliatory, quite willing to settle this affair by negotiations through the German consul, whom he entrusted with an overture of peace. The consul returned saying that Sierra had called him a liar and had thrown him out.[39]

In time a legend grew about this war and about Sierra's "communing" with spirits for advice. E.A. Lever, an old New Orleanian promoter in Central America, was probably closer to the truth when he wrote later for the *Daily Picayune* that Sierra was counting on help from Zelaya and especially from Salvadoran President Tomás Regalado, who was bound to him by a treaty signed the previous year. Regalado equivocated when Sierra invoked the pact and, in fact, gave Bonilla's agents rifles and ammunition for 2,000 men and $50,000. Ensconced in Managua, Zelaya brooded about intervening, then decided the risk was too great. Within Sierra's army disaffection was widespread; many of his troops, it was rumored, were avidly pro-Bonilla, and there were reports of ordinary soldiers who actually assaulted their officers rather than follow them into battle.[40]

Christmas, declared a Honduran observer sojourning in New Orleans some weeks after the 1903 rebellion, "was in the fight to the finish and proved himself one of the most skilled fighters on Bonilla's staff."[41] Skill perhaps had less to do with his triumphs than determination. When Bonilla ordered the march on the capital, the division in which Christmas served as second-in-command had already won a victory at a village called Lamini, in a battle that began at sunup on February 24 and went on for twelve hours before the enemy commander, severely wounded, ordered a retreat. The victors were exhausted and down to five cartridges per man. Returning to San Antonio del Norte, they were reprovisioned and set out again for Lamini, which the enemy had seized in their absence. The second battle for the town lasted a third of the time taken for the first, and when it was over the government's forces took flight, abandoning a Gatling gun, a Krupp fieldpiece, and 60,000 rounds of ammunition.[42]

Captured artillery pieces were a mixed blessing, however. In the mountainous and ravine-scarred Honduran landscape they had to be laboriously pulled over hills by men tugging on breech straps tied to the gun. Sometimes even the usually reliable mules had to be dragged through the underbrush; on other occasions, the alert commander of fleeing troops who could not be delayed by a cumbersome fieldpiece would simply remove the breech mechanism and toss it in to a nearby river, rendering the captured artillery useless.

In heavily pro-Bonilla Tegucigalpa the desperate Arias declared a state of siege, suspending constitutional liberties, and proclaimed that his armies were winning one victory after another. In the north, however, his weary commanders turned over San Pedro Sula and Puerto Cortés—and the railroad line connecting them—to Bonilla representatives without firing a shot. Near the Salvadoran border, where he owned a plantation, Sierra chose to fight one more battle with Bonilla. When the smoke cleared, the former president with thirty chosen companions was racing across the river into the sanctuary of El Salvador.[43]

Bonilla immediately sent word to his commanders to rendezvous at Toncontin, just outside Tegucigalpa, for the final siege against the pretender's government. Tegucigalpa fell before any fighting commenced; at the approach of the enemy, and after some frantic appeals from half a dozen or so consuls who wished to prevent the kind of destructive shelling that had occurred a decade before, Arias surrendered his presidency to U.S. Consul Alfred K. Moe in return for a safe conduct out of town. Bonilla graciously agreed, permitting Arias to leave with a guard of fifty soldiers. Only later, when the victors had triumphantly taken over the government's coffers, did they realize that Arias had departed not only with an armed guard but also with $10,000 from the treasury. An enraged Bonilla hastily dispatched a force after him. The pursuers caught up with the fleeing Arias near the Nicaraguan border; they brought him back to Tegucigalpa, and Bonilla threw him in jail.[44]

In helping to retake the capital and place Bonilla in power, Christmas had ably served his new benefactor, and Manuel rewarded his *norteamericano* commander by promoting him to *general de brigada* and restoring his former position as director of police. For all the political and social benefits these positions brought, Christmas felt constrained in isolated Tegucigalpa; he yearned for Puerto Cortés and his amorous pursuit of Adelaide Caruso. But Bonilla had further need of his services. Although the newly reformed assembly dutifully declared that Manuel Bonilla rightfully deserved the presidential chair, a clique of vocal anti-Manuelistas within that body kept up a ceaseless condemnation of his betrayal of the principles of liberalism. Their leader was the distinguished former president, Policarpo Bonilla. Though the two Bonillas were not related, they had once been allies. In 1893, when Policarpo had become president, championing Honduras's liberalism and creating for its expression a party of principles rather than a party representing family interests, Manuel had been a dutiful supporter.[45]

In time another legend grew about the bitter rivalry of the Bonillas, largely fostered by North American observers of isth-

mian politics who could not believe that Central Americans
actually fought over anything except personal animosities or
the spoils of office. Their interpretation of the Bonilla feud
held that two women were at the bottom of the trouble. Policarpo was pure Castilian and quite proper; Manuel, contrast-
ingly, was part Indian, a swarthy man who did not always cul-
tivate the right social circles—which may explain why the
raffish Christmas served him so loyally. In any event, the story
goes, while the two Bonillas were courting two sisters of a
proud old Honduran family, Policarpo informed the mother of
Manuel's mixed ancestry; she promptly terminated the relationship between her daughter and Manuel, who of course
swore to get even.[46] A more likely explanation would juxta-
pose Policarpo Bonilla's conservative approach to Honduran
economic growth with Manuel Bonilla's liberal developmen-
talism. Policarpo viewed foreign entrepreneurs and capital
with caution; Manuel fostered alliances with foreign capitalists and envisioned Honduran development as a partnership of
the country's land and labor with foreign capital and know-
how. The involvement of north coast fruit companies in this
rebellion had been marginal, however. Indeed, according to
Thomas Karnes, historian of Standard Fruit, "most of the
American companies in Honduras were as satisfied with the
administration of Manuel Bonilla as they had been with the
two preceding, and there is no evidence that the banana exporters played any part in his victory."[47]

In February 1904 Manuel Bonilla abruptly dissolved the assembly in a *golpe de estado*, ordering the arrest of nine of his
legislative enemies, including Policarpo, using as pretext the
rumors circulating in the capital of a plot to assassinate the
president. As director of police, Christmas led the soldiers carrying out the president's orders. When Policarpo spied him entering the chamber, Christmas raised his Winchester, and the
Honduran, who was carrying a revolver in his coat, challenged
him mockingly, saying "Christmas, you're a dishonor to your
race and a miserable dog." Back home, these were fighting
words, and Christmas's name had surfaced more than once in
Policarpo Bonilla's philippics. He might have shot Policarpo on

the spot had not a bystander raised an arm, deflecting the rifle barrel.[48]

Manuel Bonilla called a new assembly, which produced a constitution more suitable to his personal style by permitting a presidential term of six years. When the "conspirators" were tried, Christmas, as police chief, sat as one of the trial judges and had the satisfaction of passing sentence on Policarpo. In time Manuel ordered almost all the condemned men to be released from the national penitentiary. Policarpo, however, remained in jail, kept incommunicado without books or paper; according to his biographer, for many months he was not allowed to bathe or even comb his hair. The state confiscated his estates. Only after the passage of several months was he permitted the traditional conjugal visit of his spouse.[49] Two years later, when he finally won release, Policarpo headed straight for the sanctuary of El Salvador, his head churning with plots to bring the usurper in Tegucigalpa to his knees. Christmas had by then returned to Puerto Cortés to carry on his courtship of wife number three.[50]

The turmoil of Honduran society attracted the attention of all its neighbors. North American entrepreneurs, however, especially the banana men, had used the period from the 1890s to 1904 to remove a hurdle in their search for wealth in Honduras. The banana men had not participated in the victory of a Honduran who promised to facilitate U.S. penetration and development of Honduras's political economy, certainly, but they needed to make sure that the defeated factions did not return to power. One thing was clear: they could not afford to remain neutral in Honduras's often violent political culture. The stakes were too high.

3

The Central American Wars

Among the rulers of Central America at the turn of the twentieth century, the most arbitrary, the most ruthless, and certainly the most feared were José Santos Zelaya of Nicaragua and Manuel Estrada Cabrera of Guatemala. Estrada Cabrera, who took power in 1898, directed his attention largely inward, creating within the country an authoritarian rule that surpassed even that of Zelaya. He never forgot that Guatemala had once played a powerful role in the politics of its neighbors, and in a more secretive way than Zelaya, who operated pretty much in the open, Estrada Cabrera employed his network of spies and his government's treasury in the promotion of Central American strife. Both liberal in their politics, the two men were nonetheless bitter personal rivals in a struggle for isthmian domination.[1]

Estrada Cabrera's Guatemala became a police state in which even "kodaking tourists" could be routinely stopped by an illiterate Indian soldier and have their papers thoroughly scrutinized. Along the major routes the president established checkpoints where travelers had to produce identification and sign a register. Though the law was often flouted by wiseacres who signed "Napoleon Bonaparte" or even "Jesus Christ" (and got away with it because the soldiers were ordinarily illiterate), this and numerous other practices Estrada Cabrera instituted made for frightening stories about the country. The president became so obsessed with fears of assassination that he was constantly moving from one house to another, always demanding detailed reports on the movements of his real (and imagined) enemies.[2]

Estrada Cabrera employed lobbyists in Washington to advance his interests and to minimize U.S. interference in Guatemala's domestic order and its efforts to expand its role in the isthmus. In 1908 a disgruntled German, run out of Guatemala, alleged that four years earlier the Guatemalan dictator had given $10,000 to Theodore Roosevelt's presidential campaign. Among the functionaries of the State Department, inexplicably, Estrada Cabrera acquired a reputation as an enlightened despot who cleaned up Guatemala City—probably the most impressive of the isthmian capitals after the turn of the century—and who smiled benevolently on U.S. enterprise in the tropics.[3]

Zelaya embarked on a personal campaign to modernize Nicaragua and make it the leader of a reborn isthmian union. He built 142 new schools, raised professional salaries, and restructured the archaic governmental system he had inherited from the long years of Conservative rule. In June 1895, with Presidents Rafael Gutiérrez of El Salvador and Policarpo Bonilla of Honduras, he fashioned a solidarity pact, the goal of which was Central American confederation. Predictably, Zelaya intended that Nicaragua dominate this union, and he pledged to aid his harassed political allies, most of them Liberals who shared his suspicions of U.S. policy in Central America. After the U.S. government decided in 1903 to build a canal across Panama, a choice that crushed long-standing Nicaraguan aspirations for wealth and glory from a transit route, Zelaya looked beyond the United States for funds and technology to build a canal. U.S. officials resented this assumption of independence.[4]

Within Nicaragua, Zelaya's rule became increasingly arbitrary and capricious. The old commercial elements resented his intrusion into their affairs; on the isolated north coast (which fronts the Caribbean and lies east from Managua) foreign entrepreneurs chafed under new regulations and taxes emanating from the capital because these edicts sought to assert Nicaraguan authority over activity that had been essentially free from any sovereign control. In their frustration these north coast foreigners encouraged the harassed Conservatives to bring Zelaya down in order to restore, as they put it, a "sensible government"—by which they meant one that would favor U.S. and other foreign nationals by requiring little or no contact with Nicaraguan officials and no obligation to pay Nicaraguan taxes or, for that matter, obey its laws. Zelaya responded by cracking down even harder. When his treasury ran low, for example, he would give one of his infamous and feared "Borgia dinners." A prominent merchant would be invited to dine at the president's table, and at the end of a sumptuous meal Zelaya would politely ask for a "contribution to the cause." To refuse meant banishment from the country. By 1897, only four years into his rule, all semblance of constitutionalism, as far as his Conservative enemies were concerned, had vanished. Zelaya employed every protest as an excuse to increase his already formidable military. In 1899 the intendant of Bluefields province "declared" against him, and Zelaya crushed the revolt in a costly campaign. For every uprising there were a hundred rumors of revolution and conspiracy against the president. There were so many rumors, in fact, that in Managua, the dusty unattractive capital, bombs, grenades, and cartridges were secreted in dozens of places in anticipation of the next uprising.[5]

As Zelaya grew more severe in dealing with his internal enemies, he sensed that his influence in Nicaragua's neighboring states was slipping. As always, he believed that the roots of his international troubles lay in Honduras, where Manuel Bonilla's triumph had driven Zelaya's Liberal allies into exile or, in the case of Policarpo Bonilla, into a dank prison cell. Policarpo's fall had been a double blow to Zelaya. The charismatic Honduran Liberal had been an articulate spokesman, if not so forceful an advocate, for the Nicaraguan's brand of economic nationalism. More concretely, Policarpo had rendered Zelaya an inestimable service by allowing Nicaraguan concessionaires to operate in the expanse of thicket and coast between the Segovia and Patuca rivers, in territory under dispute between the two governments. Manuel Bonilla, once ensconced in Tegucigalpa, warily monitored these concessions as choice prizes for *his* friends, Honduran and American, though he could do little to establish direct Honduran supervision over this remote area.[6]

But in February 1906 Policarpo Bonilla got his freedom in a general political amnesty—a common gesture among twentieth-century Latin American governments—that was inspired, it was rumored, by an appeal from the mercurial Salvadoran minister of war (and former president) Tomás Regalado. After two years of mostly grumbling and rumor from the disaffected Liberal camp, the cause against Manuel began to look more promising, and Zelaya took notice. In southern Honduras, in the broad peninsula dividing Nicaraguan and Salvadooran territory, the conspirators closeted themselves with General José María Valladares, an outspoken anti-Manuelista who had condemned the president for his violation of the Liberal constitution and, generally, his "nefarious labors."

The scheme to overturn Manuel suddenly looked promising—and just as quickly went awry. In El Salvador, Guatemala's alienated exiles worked in fevered conspiracies, looking to Zelaya for support. Estrada Cabrera's spies and henchmen were everywhere, however. A prominent figure in the anti-Estrada Cabrera movement was shot down on a San Salvador street in circumstances suggesting the handiwork of the Guatemalan's notorious spy network. Regalado, an avowed enemy of Estrada Cabrera, went on one of his drunken sprees and shot up San Salvador, an act not altogether unprecedented, but on this occasion the inebriated Regalado called out his troops for an invasion across the Guatemalan frontier. In the first engagement he was killed, and in the aftermath the United States entered the affray by mediating a truce aboard a patrolling U.S. warship, the *Marblehead*.

As far as Zelaya was concerned, the intrusion of any outside power into Central American quarrels could only damage Nicaragua's pretensions. Then the Honduran plotters against

Manuel Bonilla were betrayed and promptly expelled from El Salvador. Valladares, who had been readying to join them, suddenly got fresh orders from the capital: he was directed to take his army in the other direction, toward the Nicaraguan border, where Zelaya was massing a sizable force to intervene once his Honduran friends raised the flag of revolt against Bonilla. Along the border three armies—Zelaya's, Bonilla's, and Valladares's—became entangled in a series of skirmishes. At first Zelaya appeared ready for another round of mediation, which the U.S. and Mexican governments were pressing on the warring Central Americans. Then, in December 1906, King Alfonso XIII of Spain, who had been chosen by both governments to arbitrate the Nicaraguan-Honduran boundary dispute, rendered his decision—in favor of Honduras. Although Zelaya sent a soothing note to Bonilla ("a strip of land is worth nothing as compared with good harmony between sister people"), he decided then and there to install a "friendly" regime in Tegucigalpa.

Bonilla in turn dispatched a conciliatory telegram to Managua averring that Honduran "malcontents [as] part of a malefic plan" had intentionally lured pursuing federal troops onto Nicaraguan soil. But Zelaya readied for a full-scale invasion. Abruptly he withdrew his representative from a peace conference then under way in San José, Costa Rica. Throughout the country went a call for every able-bodied Nicaraguan male adult to present himself to the nearest military detachment for service "wherever the exigencies . . . necessitate."[7] To the peacemaker Theodore Roosevelt, Zelaya sent the following explanation for Nicaragua's sudden belligerence: "I recognize and I appreciate the desirability of the American states [in] preserving peace, and consequently I make every effort to maintain it; but the army of Honduras violated Nicaraguan territory, attacking the frontier guard, shedding blood, committing outrages, and plundering. . . . I must say that public sentiment in Nicaragua is in the same state as that of the American people when the S.S. *Maine* was blown up."[8] (The U.S. president did not acknowledge the equation of Nicaragua's "outrage" with the war fever that had swept his country in February 1898, when Assistant Secretary of the Navy Roosevelt, it is said, daily harangued his colleagues in the department with demands for war with Spain.)

Nicaraguans did not eagerly flock to the cause, however, so Zelaya dispatched recruiting squads into the villages and banana plantations to raise an army. In mid-January 1907, having sent a battalion of regulars to the frontier, Zelaya's generals brought their replacements into the capital: frightened country boys marched along the dusty streets with their hands tied and roped to the next in line, forming a human chain. The U.S. minister, watching them pass by his window, remembered the tale of a Nicaraguan recruiter who dispatched his captives from a coffee plantation to his general with the message: "I send you forty volunteers. Please return the ropes."[9]

By month's end the army had swollen to 12,000 on the northern frontier and another 3,000 stationed on the Costa Rican border in case Zelaya had to contend with an invasion of the Nicarguan exiles in that country. A single swoop by Zelaya's recruiters on a railroad construction project at Monkey Point, forty miles from Bluefields, provided 350 new soldiers, though the U.S. consul considered it "a dangerous undertaking to place arms and ammunition in their hands." Even Zelaya's favored Nicaraguan concessionaires got the squeeze: the English-language *Bluefields American* reported that the directors of the tobacco, rum, and beef monopolies, "in their desire to help the government in its troubles with Honduras," lent Zelaya 25,000 U.S. gold dollars and pledged $100,000 a month for the duration of the war. At Corinto, Nicaragua's most important Pacific port, the president's customs official alertly seized an important arms shipment from Hartley and Company, supplier to the Cuban junta before the war with Spain, which had contracted to provision the Salvadoran government in its frantic efforts to ready for combat. Tales of Zelaya's intimidating reached beyond Nicaragua, circulating in every isthmian capital. For example, U.S. representatives in Central America, determined to split a fledgling Zelaya-Estrada Cabrera understanding, noised it about that Estrada Cabrera's spies had stolen the U.S. diplomatic code-book from the legation in Guatemala City. Estrada Cabrera, the story went, sent a copy to Zelaya. The president's brother-in-law even boasted about the incident among Managua's elite.[10] The truth of the matter, as the U.S. minister in Nicaragua correctly surmised, was that Estrada Cabrera was plotting to draw Zelaya into another destructive war. Reluctant to inter-vene directly in Honduras with his own troops, Estrada Ca-brera sensed opportunity in the unstable isthmian political sit-uation. He sent arms to the president-elect of El Salvador and was even prepared to lend the Salvadorans some of the Ameri-can soldiers of fortune who had gathered in the Guatemalan capital. Estrada Cabrera was aware also of the Honduran-Salvadoran treaty of 1878 in which the contracting parties had pledged mutual assistance in the event of an attack by a third party. And for the Salvadorans there existed an additional rea-son for striking at Zelaya: for years the Nicaraguan dictator had provided a haven for disaffected Salvadoran Liberals.[11]

In February 1907 Zelaya struck his Honduran enemies in a two-front campaign. To the northwestern frontier Zelaya dis-patched his main force, which plunged across the border and, on February 21, engaged the Hondurans, who, Zelaya's general reported, "violently attacked [but were] promptly repulsed and pursued, leaving dead, wounded, rifles, and ammunition." Four days later the exultant Nicaraguans took San Marcos from 2,000 defenders, who left behind 200 rifles, 10,000 car-tridges, and a 7½-inch Krupp artillery piece.[12]

From the eastern coast Zelaya's six hundred-man invasion force steamed out of Bluefields on two vessels to seize the ba-nana ports on the Honduran north coast, an important source of Manuel Bonilla's revenue. Bonilla's strength lay in the north among his favored American concessionaires and the banana companies, but to protect them he had only the *Tatumbla*, a weather-beaten warship that constituted the Honduran navy. It was available, wrote the U.S. consul in La Ceiba in a pessi-mistic report, "for getting away." Christmas, whose safety in these perilous times was a matter of concern as far away as

Bluefields, suddenly disappeared into the Honduran interior, in command of a 2,000-man army. The entire north coast was imperiled by the approaching Nicaraguan sea invaders. Just as dramatically a zealous U.S. Navy captain, William F. Fullam, commanding the *Marietta*, dispatched squads of bluejackets and marines ashore at Puerto Cortés, La Ceiba, and Trujillo in the hallowed Navy tradition of policing tropical seaports in which foreigners predominated. Extracting an assurance from the Nicaraguan attackers that the coastal towns—whose buildings could be easily ignited—would not suffer bombardment, Fullam then permitted Zelaya's troops into La Ceiba and Puerto Cortés, arranging the Honduran surrender aboard the *Marietta*. The banana business of course suffered when many workers were drafted into the ranks, but it did not shut down. The Vaccaros, by far the biggest banana growers on the north coast in 1907, lost 50 percent of their business in the spring but rebounded in the summer, and by year's end they had surpassed their 1906 export of ten million stems.[13]

The Nicaraguans, if outnumbered, nonetheless seemed invincible. Zelaya had equipped his invaders with Hotchkiss and Krupp cannon—giving the Nicaraguans a decisive advantage in artillery—and Maxim machine guns, invented in 1884 by Hiram Maxim but not previously used in a Central American conflict. Unlike the Gatling, which had to be handcranked, the Maxim fired continuously with the initial pull of the trigger. Years earlier its devastating firepower had been demonstrated to the Chinese ambassador to Britain, who watched increduously as a Maxim cut through an eighteen-inch-thick tree. This machine gun, frequently in the hands of mercenaries, wreaked havoc among the armies of the isthmus.[14]

Zelaya's anti-American image did not deter some Americans with martial abilities from joining up on the Nicaraguan side. "Adventuresome" Americans, as the U.S. consul called them, had already discovered the opportunity Central American's wars offered. They fought on both sides. The consul in Managua kept a running tally on the ruddy-faced newcomers in town looking for a government commission. Waldemar Harold Bills of New Orleans, aged twenty-five, formerly a captain in the Louisiana field artillery, offered his services and was rejected but came to Nicaragua anyway. Zelaya made him a captain and assigned him to drill duty at the Nicaraguan military academy. Bills arrived with John Hardy, who said he was a graduate of the Danville Military Institute. James Bulger, veteran of the campaign against Filipino rebels in 1899-1902, descended on Managua sporting a cavalry officer's saber and a U.S. Army Colt revolver. Bulger, in Nicaragua on a "hunting expedition," quickly joined a Nicaraguan force that set out to seize Amapala, Honduras.[15] In Bluefields, the *American* proudly noted, Leonard Groce, a prosperous miner from Siuna, "gallantly offered his services" to the Nicaraguan government and even organized a company of American recruits fired with the "Texas fighting spirit of their leader." The Nicaraguans made Groce a lieutenant colonel; he readied for battle with a celebration of American and Nicaraguan officers in the Hotel Cosmopolitan, Bluefields, where the party drank toasts to José Santos Zelaya and Theodore Roosevelt.[16]

In mid-March a 3,000-man Salvadoran army under General José Dolores Preza joined a 1,500-man force dispatched south by Manuel Bonilla, and together they encountered the Nicaraguans at the town of Namasigüe. Having just gotten word (by cable via New Orleans) that the north Honduran ports of Puerto Cortés and La Ceiba had fallen to the Nicaraguan expeditionaries under General Juan J. Estrada, Zelaya threw every Nicaraguan reserve that could be spared into the war in southern Honduras. The battle for Namasigüe lasted for three days, commencing on Sunday afternoon, March 17, with a furious Nicaraguan artillery barrage against enemy encampments in the hills near the village. The artillery fire lasted until 11:00 P.M. and resumed promptly at 5:00 A.M. On the second day the Honduran-Salvadoran forces attacked the Nicaraguan position, but the Nicaraguans brought up reinforcements and used their Maxim guns to lay down a fire so deadly that Namasigüe had the grim distinction of being, in terms of the number killed in proportion to the number engaged, the bloodiest battle in history. The losses were frightful; Nicaraguans declared they had killed 1,000 on the final day. Zelaya described the carnage:

"The number of dead which they left on the field [was] so great that we were unable to bury all." In the midst of the battle, 40 percent of the Honduran forces abandoned their Salvadoran allies and went over to the Nicaraguans.[17]

President Bonilla, who despite illness had come from the capital to take personal command of his army of the south, learned of the disaster at a small cottage some few miles from the battle. Even in the aftermath of such a decisive defeat (Namasigüe took the lives of virtually every cadet from the Salvadoran Polytechnic Academy), Bonilla refused to surrender and fled farther south. On the island of Amapala, Honduras's southern seaport, he gathered five hundred men and occupied the fortress protecting the bay. When his Honduran enemies and the Nicaraguan invaders prepared to lay down a siege, Bonilla, realizing it would mean another bloody fight, agreed to surrender—but not to a Nicaraguan general. So the victors dispatched his old enemy, Terencio Sierra, to assume command of the fort. Bonilla boarded a patrolling U.S. warship, the U.S.S. *Chicago*, and ultimately found sanctuary in the British Honduran port of Belize.[18]

When the war began, Christmas was enjoying the spoils of office that came with the *comandancia* of the northern port of Puerto Cortés. Bonilla, before his abrupt departure from the capital, dispatched a hasty wire to his trustworthy *general de brigada* to join the command of Sotero Barahona, the minister of war, who was marshaling an army to protect the plain of Maraita against the anticipated invasion of the capital from the south. Sending Adelaide and Lee, Jr., out of the country on a steamer for Puerto Barrios, Christmas rode to the battlefield—and to unexpected new glories.

At Maraita, General Barahona's small ragtag army of teenage cadets and Indians from the mines was quickly surrounded. The attackers, led by the mercurial Honduran General José María Valladares, could not dislodge them, however, and decided to wait for reinforcements. Barahona soon realized the cause was hopcless. At Christmas's urging he gave everybody a chance to break out. A mass charge against Valladares's machine guns would be suicidal, but small groups riding frantically in different directions might so startle the enemy that some would make safety. Barahona did not want to fall into the hands of the vengeful Valladares; neither did Christmas, who had manhandled his hero Policarpo Bonilla and, on another occasion, shut down the general's profitable printing operation. Two others joined their wild charge: Coronel Tejeda Reyes and a jocular American named Fred Mills, who had abruptly skipped out of the dreary routine of a Honduran mining camp to join this fracas.

Mills, who had no personal interest in these sanguinary isthmian wars, had his horse shot from under him. He got up and ran screaming toward a small gulley but was picked off. The two Hondurans, Barahona and Reyes, were shot from their mounts; Reyes was killed, but, miraculously, Barahona survived. Christmas was hit by a volley that simultaneouly struck his horse, and he went down, pinned under the dead animal. Had he not miscounted the cartridges in his Luger before this mad dash began, he would have had one bullet left for himself.

What happened afterward became hopelessly enmeshed in the Christmas legend. Fending off one bayonet thrust by a charging enemy soldier, he was saved from a second by a Nicaraguan officer who promised that Christmas would be properly tried and then executed. By this time what remained of Barahona's defenders had scattered. Sickened by the thought of a firing squad, Christmas decided to provoke the Nicaraguan into finishing him off right there: "Shoot me! But don't bury me." Others from the victorious Honduran-Nicaraguan forces already surrounded him. The attentive Nicaraguan officer who had saved him from the bayonet thrust was taken aback. "Don't bury me, you sons of bitches," Christmas yelled. When the young officer inquired as to his reasons for such an unusual request, Christmas roared: "Because I want the buzzards to eat me, and fly over you afterwards, and scatter white droppings on your god-damned black faces." Then he shut his eyes for the shot to the head. But it never came. The Nicaraguan, startled at first, broke into a hearty laugh, then said: "You are a brave man and shall not be executed at all." The admiring looks on the faces of his captors told Christmas that they agreed.[19]

Within the month, as accounts of the war conveyed by banana boat passengers from the Honduran north coast were picked up by American newspapers, Christmas was reported dead. "Daredevil American Cut to Pieces by Nicaraguan Soldiers," wrote the *New York Times*. (Over the years, Christmas collected clippings of newspaper articles telling of his premature demise in the tropics.) When the rumor was proved false by his abrupt appearance in New Orleans, there were inevitable embellishments of the "Don't Bury Me" tale. Tracy Richardson, soldier of fortune who met Christmas in 1910, included the incident in his 1925 memoirs. As he told the story, the Nicaraguans captured Christmas at Maraita plain, staked him to the ground, took off his shoes, and repeatedly burned his feet with red-hot machetes. Christmas endured the torture, however, cursing his persecutors until he lapsed into unconsciousness. They were so impressed, wrote Richardson, that they decided to let him go.[20] Even more imaginative variations on the incident followed—none believable, but all believed.

The young Nicaraguan officer at Maraita kept his word. Christmas was removed to the hospital in the Honduran capital, by then in the hands of Manuel Bonilla's enemies. Later, he obtained a safe conduct pass from the U.S. consul, who informed the authorities that even though Christmas had fought for Bonilla, he was still a U.S. citizen. Within a short time he had recuperated sufficiently to sit on a mule for the arduous ride north to San Pedro Sula, where Dr. Waller could check his wounds, and then on to Puerto Cortés and Guatemala. In the remote Guatemalan capital he would find Adelaide and new employment as head of Estrada Cabrera's secret service.

Viewed from the serenity of Washington, D.C., these troubles in Central America, which had dragged three republics into another sanguinary war, looked eminently negotiable, especially to the legalistic gaze of U.S. Secretary of State Elihu Root. If only the Central American leaders played the political game the way we do, Root thought, then they would realize that making deals or cutting the pie in equal portions, rather than raising the flag of revolt or invading a neighbor's territory, would bring peace, progress, and, above all, stability. On closer inspection, however, it became apparent—even, eventually, to Root—that in isthmian politics, unlike the U.S. brand, friendships and family ties and political alliances were inseparable values. You did not give your political enemy any of the spoils of office merely to get him off your back or buy his loyalty; nor did you steal an election from him with the implicit understanding that it was permissible for him to try and steal it back the next go-round. In Root's America, politics was business: if you lost one time, you learned a lesson and survived for the next contest. In Central America, politics could be life itself: if you lost once, you might lose everything, even your life.[21]

Through the remainder of 1907, Root nonetheless persisted in trying to find some legal solution to the Central American quagmire. As yet, the U.S. government was not thinking in terms of surrogate dictators, like the fawning Caribbean tyrants of a later era. In fact, had Root looked for a chosen few acceptable isthmian politicians on whom the U.S. government might bestow its blessing, he would have had a welter of conflicting assessments from U.S. diplomatic and military personnel and the scattered American entrepreneurs and soldiers of fortune in the area. About the two Bonillas, U.S. Minister William Merry had observed: "I know Policarpo Bonilla personally. He is more able as well as more Progressive than Manuel Bonilla, who is half Indian and half Negro, uneducated and without much ability." Yet the volatile Captain Fullam said of Policarpo some weeks later: "[He] is an enemy to all foreigners and their interests in this country."[22] U.S. officials and entrepreneurs could seldom agree about which isthmian leaders or factions best served U.S. interests, in part because these varied interests were often in conflict themselves.

So eager was the Theodore Roosevelt administration to fashion a U.S. solution to Central America's debilitating conflicts that Root seized on virtually every diplomatic opportunity, no matter how fragile, to end the fighting. Even before the Honduran war had run its course, proposals for a general settlement were forthcoming. Washington Valentine, sensing the chance to pose as a mediator between the battling isthmian factions, hired a New York law firm to intercede on his behalf to the State Department. The New York lawyers described the American entrepreneur as a man "well informed in regard to the political and commercial situation in Honduras."[23] He had, apparently, also convinced Zelaya that his clout with the U.S. government was considerable. When the State Department evinced interest in his plan, Valentine sent a long analysis of the confusing Central American situation.

Valentine seemed sincere, if self-serving: the biggest building in Amapala, where Manuel Bonilla was still defying his enemies, belonged to Valentine's New York and Honduras Rosario Mining Company, and the "king of Honduras" was fearful that a pitched battle for the town would destroy it. Portraying himself as a "pioneer of enterprise in Central America" and "well acquainted with all the prominent men" in isthmian politics, Valentine characterized Zelaya, the bête noire of the U.S. government, as one who sought peace but trusted no one.[24] The problem was Honduras, wrote Valentine; if Zelaya were permitted to establish a military government in that country, as the United States had done in Cuba the previous year, then Mexico and the United States, as disinterested parties, could lay the foundations for an isthmian peace.[25] The idea of a Nicaragua-imposed military regime in Tegucigalpa was, of course, anathema to Root, and within a short time he cut the impresario out of a broad diplomatic settlement with a curt message to U.S. representatives: "Mr. Valentine has no authority to represent this Government in any way whatsoever, and any action on his part . . . is repudiated and disavowed."[26] Despite Valentine's praise, the U.S. government continued to condemn Zelaya because of his eagerness to draw foreign, non-U.S. investment to the isthmus.

In late 1907, as the Honduran political scene cleared, Root at last got what he wanted. With Mexico as co-sponsor the U.S.

government corralled the war-weary Central Americans in Washington, where they agreed, among other things, to establish an isthmian court, honor Honduran sovereignty, and refrain from extending diplomatic recognition to governments installed by violent means. The rule of law at last governed Central American affairs. But this "rule of law" bore only a slight relationship to the "rules" of the blood feuds raging on the isthmus. The prospect for a pro-Zelaya regime in Tegucigalpa appeared likely. The losers in the latest Honduran battle wanted their revenge. Manuel Bonilla's followers—exiled in Guatemala, in the backwoods of neutral British Honduras, or in the dives and hotels of the Vieux Carré in New Orleans— waited for word from the general about an invasion. Less than a month after the distinguished representatives of the isthmian states had signed the General Treaty of Peace and Amity, rumors of an invasion of Honduras swept the coast.

One of the U.S. Navy's vigilant policemen, patrolling off Puerto Cortés (a likely point of attack), responded in typically militant tones: "Pending instructions, it is my intention to seize and send to the United States for adjudication any armed vessel or transport carrying men and arms for filibustering expeditions which are found navigating these waters, and which cannot show proper authority from the government of a recognized nation. Should a suspected vessel in these waters try to escape, I shall consider it my duty to sink her." Crotchety old Alvey Adee, longtime assistant secretary of state, noted caustically in the margin that the enthusiastic naval officer was doubtless "unmindful" of international law.[27]

It was Christmas, however, not Bonilla, who appeared most active in late 1907 and early 1908 in launching another revolution to reinstall Manuel in the presidential chair in Tegucigalpa. As chief of Estrada Cabrera's secret service, Christmas occupied a position ideally suited for carrying on a clandestine recruitment of volunteers. At Puerto Barrios and at isolated camps in tropical eastern Guatemala, it was said, Christmas began stockpiling supplies and munitions. The local U.S. consul at Livingston noted that an unusual number of Americans had vanished into the jungle along the Río Motagua, which parallels the border with Honduras. Root, hearing of the plot, observed confidently that "no patriotic American" would become involved in another invasion of Honduras.[28]

Christmas always thought himself a "patriotic American," but, as he saw the matter, a little "revoluting" on behalf of his benefactors—Manuel Bonilla and Estrada Cabrera—in no sense harmed the interests of the United States. When prospective recruits expressed some doubts about the wherewithal for such an operation, Lee would matter-of-factly refer them to the president of Guatemala. U.S. envoy William Sands, newly arrived in Guatemala City in early 1908 and a veteran observer of tropical politics from long service in Panama, summoned Christmas ("an old acquaintance") to the legation for a stern warning. Christmas looked robust and eager for a scrap. To the diplomat's knowing query about the current Honduran plot, Christmas replied: "I ain't saying I am and I ain't saying I ain't." Sands was unsatisfied; he began bombarding the Guatemalan government and the British mission with complaints, and shortly the flow of funds to Christmas's camps in the east from mysterious sources in British Honduras ceased.[29]

The planned revolt, frustrated by Sands and the patrolling U.S. gunboats, did not get under way until July 1908. By then, the new Honduran leader, Miguel Dávila, a vacillating man who had been the choice of a bickering Honduran junta in the aftermath of Bonilla's flight, had come almost completely under the sway of the anti-Manuelistas. Learning that Bonilla was still plotting to regain the presidential chair, Dávila gave up all hope of reconciliation with the former president and Christmas, who had been sent from Honduras under Dávila's safe conduct on the pledge that he would never again get mixed up in the armed conflicts of national politics.[30]

There were two rebel incursions. The first occurred near the Salvadoran border, where on July 7 the invaders captured the Honduran town of Gracias without firing a shot and, a few days later, took Choluteca, the most important town in the south. The second was a hastily launched naval invasion of the north coast, the domain of the foreigner, where the Vaccaro brothers were firmly established and the United Fruit Company was just starting operations. Indeed, the State Department, surveying the Honduran political scene, believed that UFCO (which still owned some 60 percent of Zemurray's steamship company) was behind the current troubles. El Porvenir fell on July 17, just as the revolt was collapsing on the Salvadoran border and the rebels—an advance unit for the more formidable force under Christmas and Bonilla that presumably waited to the north—turned toward La Ceiba. The town had fallen on hard times since Dávila had shut down the smuggling of supplies from New Orleans to the banana entrepreneurs in the country, a practice that the gracious Bonilla had understandingly tolerated. Yet the federal garrison was able to repulse the invasion. Back in New Orleans, no less an authority on Central America than the famed "General" E.A. Lever solemnly declared that the rebel cause was hopeless and that Christmas's projected assault was doomed; he is a "bold and enterprising man," said New Orleans's most knowledgeable student of Central America, "but he has no military training whatsoever. Had he in early life been accorded the benefits of a sound military education he would undoubtedly have become a valuable officer." When Lever issued his lofty judgment on the current isthmian strife, Christmas was variously reported as waiting with a strike force on a small island some eighteen miles from Puerto Cortés and lying in his sickbed with pneumonia in Guatemala City.[31]

These wild rumors about Christmas's movements provided a titillating diversion from the real plotter of the invasion of 1908—Estrada Cabrera. The Guatemalan chieftain graciously permitted Bonilla's agents to run off proclamations at the National Printing Office, and he dispatched an army of hirelings to attack El Salvador from across the Honduran border in an effort to lure Zelaya into another costly campaign. Lee Roy Cannon, who gave up his post as police chief of San Miguel, El Salvador, to join in this "merry" affair, was captured, thrown into a Tegucigalpa jail, and thoroughly interrogated by Dávila's generals. Quite candidly, he expressed the belief that Estrada Cabrera would provide support for the rebellion. This and other embarrassing revelations became part of the record when peaceful Costa Rica, in the noblest spirit of the 1907 treaty, demanded that the dispute be handed over to the Central American Court of Justice. In the furor Zelaya and his protégé in Tegucigalpa leveled formal charges against Guatemala and El Salvador for instigating the war. In the course of things the fighting stopped, but when the Court of Justice finally got around to rendering its decision, the judges voted their patriotic convictions: El Salvador was acquitted, and the only legal condemnation of Guatemala came from the jurist representing beleaguered Honduras.[32]

In the aftermath Christmas left his job in the Guatemalan secret service and went back to railroading. For a year or so he vanished into the protective obscurity of Estrada Cabrera's Guatemala. Meanwhile, Groce, Cannon, and sundry other American adventurers in the tropics migrated to eastern Nicaragua, where in the fall of 1909 they joined in the great rebellion against Zelaya. These hired guns were not campaigning against the putative tyranny of Zelaya or for democracy. Groce fought for Zelaya in 1907 and against him two years later. Many of the adventurers in Nicaragua had fought on one side or another in wars in Honduras and El Salvador before they joined Nicaraguan General Juan J. Estrada, the new comprador favorite of U.S. entrepreneurs and officials. This visible alliance of U.S. diplomats and businessmen not only made fighting for one side appear patriotic to the U.S. mercenaries but also went a long way toward defining which side would pay better and more regularly.

Zelaya was predictably irritated by the marked displeasure of Washington toward his conduct in the recent campaign, during which his armies had marched to one triumph after another. His response to this ominous interference, which usually took the form of moral injunctions from the Department of State, was characteristically resentful. A faithful Salvadoran ally, Dr. Eu-

genio Arauz, had warned him that Nicaragua's consent to the
1907 treaties would have "grave consequences" and that Zelaya
would be the "first victim" of U.S. government machinations.[33]

A year later, as Roosevelt triumphantly watched his protégé William Howard Taft sweep to victory in the 1908 elections, Zelaya at last realized that Arauz had been right. The
Diario de Nicaragua, which spoke for the dictator, condemned
pro-American Nicaraguans as naive believers in a U.S. protectorate. The U.S. minister alleged that in Granada, a Conservative stronghold, Zelaya's troops arrested celebrants for wearing
small U.S. flags in their lapels in honor of Taft's victory; in
words doubtless pleasing to the incoming U.S. administration
the minister described Zelaya as "barbarous," adding: "The
only pressure known to this government is force." He over-
looked charges that the crowd was interjecting anti-Zelaya slogans into its praise of Taft and that it was marching toward the
armory. Although these charges may have been distortions, the
crowd was clearly attempting to challenge and test Zelaya behind the cover of the U.S. minister and flag.[34]

As U.S. emissaries dispatched vehemently critical evalua-
tions of his rule back to Washington, Zelaya resolved all the
more to resist. He continued to meddle in El Salvador and to
monitor the administration of the weak and vacillating Dávila
in Honduras. Irritated by Salvadoran President Fernando Figueroa's overtures to Guatemala, Zelaya permitted a band of
Salvadoran exiles, headed by Salvadoran General Prudencio Alfaro and John Moissant, an American adventurer whose family
had moved to El Salvador from California, to organize an expedition in early spring 1909. Moissant, whom the U.S. minister
in Managua described as a "native American citizen now at-
tached to the revolutionary propaganda of Zelaya," had se-
questered 2,000 Remington rifles, 200,000 rounds of ammunition, and four artillery pieces in a small cove on the Pacific side
near the Costa Rican border. Docked securely on Lake Managua
was Moissant's gasoline launch, which Zelaya now allowed the
American to ship on the Nicaraguan railroad to Corinto, from
which it sailed to an inlet on the Gulf of Fonseca.[35]

The plan called for Alfaro to strike out on the railroad rendezvous with Moissant on the gulf, then sail across the short distance to a secluded landing on the Salvadoran coast. Figueroa, however, alerted to Alfaro's conspiracy, publicly charged that Zelaya intended to violate Honduran territory by permitting the invaders to cross the country, an act violating the 1907 treaties guaranteeing Honduran neutrality. In Washington the Salvadoran minister issued a frantic appeal to the State Department and to President Taft, who ordered warships in the region to patrol the gulf and intercept any suspicious vessels. The U.S. vice-consul in Managua, José de Olivares, after a harrowing horseback ride dodging Nicaraguan patrols, found Moissant's launch at its hiding place on the north Nicaraguan shore. Zelaya was publicly embarrassed by the entire affair and even had to send a detachment of Nicaraguan soldiers to Chinandega to escort the Salvadorans back to Managua. Yet while U.S. officials in Washington and Managua were condemning Zelaya's support for Moissant, U.S. officials in El Salvador were protecting the Moissant family and Alfaro's supporters.[36]

Meanwhile, Estrada Cabrera in Guatemala was enthusiastically providing the U.S. diplomatic mission with the most damaging accusations against his fellow dictator. The president of the Guatemalan republic, the U.S. minister wrote in March 1909, would "cooperate with the Government of the United States in any manner desired in order to terminate the perpetual turmoils due to the conduct of Zelaya." As for "neutral" Honduras, the government of Dávila appeared to U.S. diplomatic observers as "divided, weak and demoralized, under the influence of Zelaya, and utterly incapable of enforcing neutrality." In Managua the dictator's newspaper dismissed the anti-Nicaraguan propagandists in San Salvador and Guatemala City as figures characterized by "imbecility" and "perfidy" whose sole intention was to encourage the U.S. government to dispatch its "ships of war which today ply the Central American waters."[37]

But Zelaya's list of enemies was increasing alarmingly. An outspoken Nicaraguan Conservative accused him of having dispatched an army of four hundred "convicted criminals," commanded by a member of his cabinet, to invade El Salvador in 1908.[38] Even more damaging was the conspiracy of Emiliano Chamorro, member of a famous old Granada family prominent in Conservative party politics, who despite his political convictions had helped Zelaya suppress a revolt in 1896. Zelaya evidently forgot the favor and some years later pressed Chamorro for a "loan." Chamorro, a "man of simple tastes" but a "daredevil soldier," had been compelled to flee his country. He went first to El Salvador, where he enjoyed the favor of Figueroa and spent languorous days with his *compañera*, Doña Lastenía, all the time waiting to get even with Zelaya. Figueroa promised much but never delivered, so Chamorro crossed over into Guatemala and headed straight for Estrada Cabrera's palace. The Guatemalan leader was at first guarded in dealing with this outspokenly fearless Nicaraguan, but in time he relented to the persistent Chamorro. "Don Emiliano," Estrada Cabrera told him, "my star is still bright, but that of Zelaya is fading," then asked how much Chamorro would need for the revolt. Ten thousand Guatemalan pesos for provisions, replied Chamorro, and another 10,000 for arms. Estrada Cabrera dismissed him, but the following day a messenger arrived at Chamorro's door with a packet of three envelopes, two containing 10,000 pesos each and a third with a secret code for the military operation.[39]

Predictably, it was in the east, in the broad expanse of tropics that formed the Mosquitia—historically hostile to Spanish and then Nicaraguan control—that the next revolt against the dictator took shape. Here operated some of the republic's most profitable enterprises—lumbering, mining, banana growing—and in the coastal towns the most prosperous citizens were foreigners with names like Joseph Beers, Samuel Weil, and George D. Emery. Isolated from Managua, these coastal residents viewed themselves as ambitious entrepreneurs thwarted by Zelaya's arbitrary tactics. When the dictator transferred this or that concession to one of his cronies, the wrath of the foreign constituency knew no bounds. Its members looked to Europe and, increasingly, to the United States for "civilized authority" and to the patrolling gunboats of the U.S. Navy for law and order. Managua, across more than a hundred miles of thicket and savanna, was seen as a little town "composed of the most sordid sycophants [where] wretchedness prevailed."[40]

The U.S. and other foreign entrepreneurs considered their enclave on the north coast largely independent of Nicaraguan taxes and authority. They arrogantly pretended that the region's economic activity was their doing, overlooking indigenous labor, national resources, and the concessions that assured them of favored treatment. Safeguarding their privileged position was critical. When their will was challenged, they looked to a combination of U.S. naval forces and diplomats, Nicaraguan compradores (Juan Estrada, José Madriz, and later Anastasio Somoza), and U.S. mercenaries to protect their interests. The Mosquitia's U.S. entrepreneurs and banana men jointly relied on domestic compradores, U.S. hired guns, and even U.S. officials for preservation of the order and advantage they required for profitability.[41]

As Zelaya's grandiose plans for an alternative transit route with European or Japanese assistance and a Nicaraguan-dominated isthmus were being thwarted by American meddling, the dictator began cracking down ever harder. To finance his international enterprises, he turned to the privileged and profitable businesses of the coast; in March 1909 tariffs rose by 30 percent. The outcry was so vehement that the government announced an immediate reduction, but in actuality the rates did not come down, and Zelaya's collectors were unrelenting. "Such are Zelaya's methods for extorting money from the public and paralyzing all legitimate efforts," wrote the biased U.S. minister, adding that "wretchedness and abject submission are general." The coast had weathered two hurricanes in two years, wrote the *Bluefields American*, an English-language paper sympathetic to the foreign presence, but Zelaya's economic program was discouraging new investors, and some salaried employees were packing up and heading back to the States. The vice-consul grew so enraged over conditions that he demanded and got a visit from a patrolling warship, the U.S.S. *Dubuque*. But not even its menacing guns could reverse the "wanton maladministration of justice in the courts where foreigners were concerned. . . . An American [has] no chance for justice, no matter how equitable his case."[42] American and British entrepreneurs naturally resented the deterioration of their long-held privileged conditions on the Mosquito Coast.

Zelaya's economic policies had another, largely unanticipated, impact on the coastal communities. The small banana planters living upriver from Bluefields, compelled to pay higher prices for their imports, tried to raise the price of their fruit. UFCO and its subsidiary companies, the Bluefields Steamship Company and Zemurray's shipping line, refused to pay the additional charges, citing "contractual obligations." The planters, most of whom were black descendants of settlers from the West Indies, organized a strike, refusing to load their fruit on the Bluefields barges and even dispatching launches of armed men to patrol the Escondido to seize and cut up any bananas that UFCO tried to ship downriver. The Bluefields Steamship Company had a concession from Zelaya as sole conveyor of bananas on the Escondido, and when the striking planters tried to organize their own river line (the Lala-Ferreras-Cangelosi Steamship Company), Bluefields invoked its privilege. The strike inevitably escalated from economic war to violence as the planters vented their rage in random attacks on foreign-owned property around Bluefields and unruly demonstrations in the town. Since UFCO owned 51 percent of Zemurray's line, Zemurray was obliged to go along with the Bluefields Steamship Company tactics, even when UFCO, angered over the publication of fruit contracts in the *Bluefields American*, boycotted the paper's advertisers. Zemurray, remembered locally as the son-in-law of the "Parrot King" Jake Weinberger, watched his reputation suffer from UFCO's arrogantly insensitive tactics. The next year Zemurray and UFCO dissolved their partnership, and the Bessarabian immigrant with "speculative ideas," as Preston would later characterize him, began looking toward Honduras as domain for a new banana company. Interestingly, however, in this banana conflict Zelaya sided with the U.S. firms against the small, independent fruit producers who should have been his natural allies against U.S. interests. His decision, argues historian Benjamin Teplitz, may have been motivated as much by class as by national interests.[43]

As a result of the local unrest, the *American* wrote angrily in July 1909, the Bluefields Steamship Company had gone "yelping like a whipped cur to Washington for help, and Washington sent a man-of-war and two diplomatic agents." The commander of the U.S. warship, F.K. Hill, steeped in the naval tradition of policing the tropics, had politely informed Juan J. Estrada, Zelaya's governor in Bluefields, that he would be held "responsible" for destruction of American property and arbitrary treatment of U.S. citizens. It was then that Estrada, who had served Zelaya in the Honduran military campaign of 1907, decided that Zelaya was "ruining" the country.[44]

Estrada soon found eager supporters among the old Conservative Party families who had suffered Zelaya's humiliating social persecutions and whose sons had been hounded into exile. Of these the Chamorros were the most visible opponents of the dictator. In the violent spring of 1909, "The General," Emiliano, returned from exile and settled in Bluefields to recruit an army. His uncle, Pedro Joaquín, departed for Guatemala City to make arrangements for shipping the arms and munitions that Estrada Cabrera had pledged to the revolutionary cause. That assignment fulfilled, Pedro Joaquín, "Financial and Commercial Agent for the Provisional Government of General Juan J. Estrada," took the next steamer for the United States. By early June he had established a revolutionary junta at the Gilsley House in New York City.

Estrada argued that Zelaya was destroying the Liberal party, and his persistent grumbling over the ruinous economic policies that had plunged the east coast into depression and labor strikes drew him into the orbit of the Conservative plotters against the dictator. In addition to the Chamorros, there was the persuasive Adolfo Díaz, financial manager of the American-owned La Luz and Los Angeles Mining Company. Estrada's flirtation with these Conservatives prompted Zelaya to declare his defiant governor an apostate Liberal and ban him from Managua.[45]

Determined to "save" Nicaragua from Zelaya's excesses, Estrada sought the advice of the energetic U.S. consul, Thomas Moffat, whose indignant reports to his superiors detailing Zelaya's sins had already confirmed the assumption of the Washington bureaucracy that the dictator was the incarnation of evil. On his arrival as governor of the north coast in late 1908, Estrada had struck local American observers as a governor from whom "great things of a beneficial nature" could be expected. Estrada cultivated Moffat, telling the American a self-exculpatory tale about Zelaya's doings, how during a banana strike the dictator had squeezed the Bluefields Steamship Company for $15,000 in gold to protect its interests. Estrada even confessed that he personally had received $10,000 from the company; now his conscience compelled him to act. Zelaya was so desperate, he told Moffat, that a revolution would drive him from the country. Estrada would be willing to lead the movement against the dictator if the United States demonstrated its "disinterested moral support" and provided $50,000 and 2,000 rifles. Moffat of course made no commitment, but after Estrada's departure he dispatched an enthusiastic report to Washington aboard the next available vessel.[46]

Moffat became a close observer of Estrada's disaffection and ultimately a confidant of the conspirators, who, according to Nicaraguan political legend, sent a messenger to the consul's bedroom window in the dead of night to warn him of the impending revolution. By late 1909, when the U.S. Navy had a major expeditionary force reconnoitering the west coast, Moffat had slipped so completely under Estrada's sway that an astutely observant U.S. naval commander, Rear Admiral W.W. Kimball, described the Bluefields consul as virtually a revolutionary agent. Moffat's visible encouragement of the revolution opened new sources of support for Estrada. This former Zelaya meat-concessionaire, to whom local American residents had to pay $5.00 every time they slaughtered a steer (inexplicably, Zelaya overlooked pork in the concession, so Bluefields possessed a large swine population), became a champion of competition of a sort. Estrada ultimately got the support of foreign companies by demonstrating that *he*, not Zelaya, had the power to determine their success. He took away the Blue-fields Steamship Company's exclusive right to navigate the Escondido River and gave the privilege to the Nicaraguan Fruit Company. The old rivals in the fruit trade, UFCO and Blue-fields, took note of Estrada's grip on the coastal enclaves; soon loans were coming in from the Caribbean coast foreign companies: $1 million "off and on," declared Estrada in New York three years later, $200,000 from the Joseph Beers house, and another $100,000 from the Samuel Weil Company.[47]

The same United States officials who became so angry over Zelaya's corruption accepted Estrada's sales of privilege. The difference was that Zelaya and his cronies lined their pockets and tried to serve Nicaragua's development, while Estrada's crowd did the same thing but only in response to the interests of U.S. entrepreneurs. Even the ordinarily detached U.S. naval officers policing the banana ports from Puerto Limón to La Ceiba seemed taken with Estrada's friendliness toward Americans. Moffat was unabashedly partisan: when the revolt began in October, he informed the State Department that Estrada "would always be a reasonable man to deal with. His inclinations are strongly American."[48]

The autumn 1909 revolt began, properly, with an orotund *pronunciamiento* against the central authority (in the Hispanic tradition of defiance of the national government from the hinterland) and a denunciation of Zelaya's perfidy (in the tradition of Nicaraguan revolution against the tyrant of Managua). As far as Zelaya was concerned, Estrada was already beyond the pale and overdue for political excommunication, but the outspoken governor and his Conservative associates were out of reach. To the delight of Nicaraguan nationalists, Zelaya had driven the British out of the Mosquitia, but he had not yet united the Caribbean coast with the populous lake regions of western Nicaragua. When Estrada declared against him and on October 10 seized the promontory known as the Bluff, which controlled ocean traffic into Bluefields harbor, the dictator realized that he must launch a major campaign into the inhospitable northeast province.[49]

In late October and early November the conspirators gloried in one triumph after another. Weekly, enthusiastic press reports on the progress of the revolution went out from the revolutionary headquarters in Bluefields, and the itinerant soldiers of fortune hanging around the New Orleans French Quarter at the Hotel Monteleone or "uptown" at the St. Charles began booking passage for Nicaragua. "Half of Nicaragua controlled by rebels," roared the *Daily Picayune*. Estrada, declaring himself provisional president of the country, held an outpost upriver on the Escondido at Rama with a force of five hundred fresh troops ready for Zelaya's army. Rebel dynamiters began laying mines in the San Juan River and cutting the telegraph lines connecting the coast with Managua. On October 22 Emiliano Chamorro, commanding the main rebel contingent, engaged 1,000 Zelayista troops below Boca San Carlos on the San Juan. It was the first meaningful revolutionary victory: one hundred of Zelaya's soldiers were killed and another three hundred captured, along with two Krupp siege guns and four hundred rifles. Soon Estrada had more than 1,500 victorious soldiers in Rama, and as heavy rains pelted the Mosquitia, Moffat cabled an enthusiastic report describing the "orderly" situation on the coast in rebel-held territory and Zelaya's reluctance to risk dispatching his primary army into the east. As if to provoke Estrada into even closer collaboration with his foreign friends, Zelaya issued a proclamation condemning Estrada's links to foreign influence as treasonous.[50]

Back in the United States, observers of this latest anti-Zelaya revolution were already reading about "chaotic" conditions in Managua. A rigorously enforced martial law compelled the capital's weary inhabitants to desert the streets at 6:00 P.M. every day. Zelaya, according to letters smuggled out of Nicaragua by an escaping foreigner, had barricaded himself in the national palace, venturing out only when accompanied by heavily armed guards. Every telegram leaving the country, it was said, had to receive the dictator's personal approval. A trio of his Conservative enemies, safely lodged in the Hotel Varnum in Washington, provided the Department of State with a scathing if sketchy and unsubstantiated assessment: "Despotism Zelaya atrocious. Country turned into jail, penitentiary. Managua den of horrors where thousands . . . are tortured. . . . Prisoners are starved, flogged, slain. Terror beyond description. . . . Zelaya hires adventurers, scum of all nations."[51] Conservatives, apparently, believed that *their* mercenaries were better than Zelaya's.

Their ranks swelling daily with recruits signed up in New Orleans and sent to Bluefields by Estrada agent Richard Sussman, the rebels established an advance base commanded by Chamorro on the San Juan River, twenty-five miles downriver from Lake Nicaragua. Chamorro was "recognized as a desperate infighter," Moffat cabled in one of his partisan assessments, and Zelaya would need 5,000 troops to dislodge him. As things turned out, Zelaya did not need such a large force: he dispatched a scouting party to divert Chamorro from the main government force, which crossed into Costa Rica at Castillo where the San Juan forms the border between Nicaragua and Costa Rica. On November 6 the Nicaraguan army, forced to recross the river by a vigorous protest from the Costa Rican government, defeated the rebels at Colorado Junction after three days of fighting. Although Chamorro had time to prepare for the battle because of the Costa Rican publicity about the location of Zelaya's army, his smaller force took such a pounding that it withdrew to San Juan del Norte, abandoning the river to Zelaya. A few days later, his army having dwindled to only 350 men, Chamorro fled to Monkey Point, halfway up the coast to Bluefields.[52]

On the drive downriver Zelaya's troops captured two Americans—Lee Roy Cannon and Leonard Groce—who were laying mines in the San Juan River to blow up the *Dinamante*, which Zelaya was using to transport his army to the coast. The *Dinamante* was sunk, but Chamorro's artillery may have been responsible. In any case, the trial and execution of Cannon and Groce brought down on Zelaya the fury of the State Department and the scorn of virtually every North American in the tropics. News of their deaths drew attention to the surprisingly large number of U.S. soldiers of fortune who had joined in the latest Central American war.

Neither Cannon nor Groce, adventurers who had little respect for peace or order in Central America, seemed a likely candidate for martyrdom. From adolescence they had been afflicted with a wandering spirit, the kind of mischievous adventuresomeness that had led many soldiers of fortune to these fierce tropical wars, which looked so romantic from afar. Cannon, the son of a Harrisburg, Pennsylvania, butcher, had been an incorrigible high school student who had tried to enlist for the Spanish-American War. Turned down by the U.S. military, he had attended Drexel Institute for a short time but left to join a railway project in Colombia. A few years later he worked for the canal survey being conducted by the U.S. Canal Commission in Nicaragua. Several revolts against Zelaya broke out in those years, and the uprisings against the dictator, who managed to put them down with characteristically harsh efficiency, fascinated Cannon. According to his family, Cannon acquired property in Nicaragua worth $30,000, but Zelaya, alert to potential enemies, banned him from the country.[53]

An eager participant in various isthmian wars, Cannon made the overthrow of Zelaya a personal challenge from the moment he joined his first rebellion until his death in November 1909. A Nicaraguan associate who met him when the American was living in Managua said that Cannon was incensed when he witnessed a squad of Zelaya's soldiers snatch a young woman from the streets and whisk her to prison. That night the distraught Cannon showed up at a secret meeting of anti-Zelayistas and made an enthusiastic impromptu speech: "The land is sucked dry. . . . Men and women are starving. . . . No home is sacred." He vowed to assassinate the dictator, but cooler heads in the group prevailed with stories about Zelaya's incredible luck in surviving assassination attempts. Once, they said, Zelaya was alone on a hill when seven men crept up from behind. Almost instinctively, he turned and felled four with revolver shots, and the others ran off. Another time a bomb tore his carriage apart, but the dictator emerged unscathed. "Zelaya will not die by the hand of man," the Nicaraguans told Cannon. The American's response: "He was lucky."[54]

When war broke out on the Salvadoran-Honduran border in 1907, Cannon was serving as police chief in a small Salvadoran town. He joined the invading Salvadorans who took Choluteca, Honduras, in 1908, and he was captured when the town fell a short time later. The local U.S. consul interviewed him in prison and reported: "His mind did not seem to be as clear as it had been; he did not seem able to fix his attention on one subject and could talk of nothing but his exploits in the three revolutions in which he has participated."[55] The compliant Honduran executive Miguel Dávila was ready to turn him over to Zelaya when U.S. Minister Percival Dodge intervened, so the Hondurans "tied him like a hog," marched him off to Puerto Cortés, and handed him a steamer ticket for New Orleans. When the ship docked in Belize, however, Cannon got off and made his way to Guatemala, where the conspiring Estrada Cabrera was already receiving Zelaya's enemies.[56]

In Guatemala, Cannon renewed his friendship with Christmas, whom he had met in the 1907-8 war and who, like Cannon, had come perilously close to facing a firing squad, only to be rescued by an interfering U.S. diplomatic emissary and banned from Honduras. Christmas was recruiting Americans for the next campaign against Zelaya. "I can't go to Nicaragua," Cannon wrote a boyhood friend in July 1909, "until Zelaya is out of power." A thousand dollars and an opportunity to bring down Zelaya overcame his caution, however, and brought him back to Bluefields.[57]

Neither was Groce a newcomer to Zelaya's Nicaragua. The son of a central Texas physician, he had migrated to Galveston (where his cousin ran a bank) and worked in a cotton firm. In 1893, the year Zelaya took power, he arrived in Nicaragua. Soon he was operating a mine and expanding his business rapidly. He became too successful to escape the attention of Zelaya. Still, in 1903 Groce served as lieutenant colonel in Zelaya's force gathered near Bluefields. He was also the supervisor of mining properties of the La Luz and Los Angeles Mining Company, a principal financier of the revolt and, as a State Department functionary discreetly noted in a memorandum, a firm "financed in Pittsburgh," where Secretary of State Philander Knox had once figured prominently in the city's banking circles. The Fletcher family was a major investor in La Luz; Gilmore Fletcher managed the company, and his brother Henry Fletcher was a career diplomat who possessed considerable influence in the State Department, where he served as undersecretary of state in 1921-22.[58] According to G. Spencer Holland, another American who had large property holdings in Nicaragua, the dictator so constantly persecuted Groce that he joined the Estrada rebellion to protect his interests, which Holland generously estimated at $500,000 in property in Nicaragua and "about as much in Honduras and El Salvador."[59]

The decision of Cannon and Groce to join the rebellion appears, in retrospect, to have been motivated less by monetary consideration—though both had extensive property holdings in Nicaragua, imperiled by Zelaya's arbitrary manner of dealing with foreigners—than by feelings of intense personal distaste for the dictator himself. Estrada's war against Zelaya was rooted in the Nicaraguan traditional blood feud between old political families over national economic development and privileged foreign entrepreneurs and enclaves. Cannon and Groce shared the animosities that arose from such conflicts and had so often plunged the republic into turmoil. Estrada could scarcely have rejected their services, any more than he might have sent back to the States the brawny soldiers of fortune who kept arriving from Guatemala, British Honduras, or New Orleans. Though Cannon and Groce were not machine gunners or born commanders, their experience as miners meant that they knew how to handle explosives. When Zelaya's troops crossed back into Nicaragua, they cut off Estrada's supply line to his army in the interior, and mining the San Juan River offered a way of slowing the enemy advance. It was risky, however, and Estrada's representative in Washington, Salvador Castrillo, stated later that the rebel commander had tried to dissuade the Americans from the operation.[60]

Their capture offered Zelaya, already condemned by the Taft administration as a Central American miscreant, an opportunity to demonstrate to U.S. officials and North American soldiers of fortune that service in Estrada's revolt was not a wise choice. The Nicaraguan president told one of his ministers (a Conservative historian) that he intended "to shoot these yankees." When the minister astutely observed that doing so would only complicate matters, Zelaya responded, "No, my friend, we're going to yank Mr. Taft by the ear."[61]

Cannon and Groce were thrown into jail in El Castillo. Zelaya provided a defender lacking any legal training and gave him three hours to prepare their defense. According to reports in American papers, the prisoners were tortured; both signed written confessions, which Zelaya published in his memoir of the revolution along with the charge that both were "principal chiefs" in the revolutionary movement and thus liable to the extreme penalty of Nicaragua's military code. Their letters were abject pleas for mercy; Groce alluded to his Nicaraguan wife and four children. Cannon and Groce were not heroic figures. They were willingly involved in the indiscriminate mining of waterways, which endangered civilian as well as military traffic, and their long record of service in foreign wars and revolts undermined their right to U.S. protection. Still, the U.S. consul in Managua called on Zelaya's minister of foreign affairs, lying in his sickbed, to ask for clemency. The minister told him that only one person had been executed for a similar act in Nicaragua in fifty years, and six Nicaraguan lawyers consulted independently told the U.S. emissary that the sentence of death was unwarranted.[62]

It was all to no avail. After their convictions, when the Nicaraguan officer appointed to conduct the execution refused, Zelaya had him thrown into jail. The two men were then taken from their cells and shown their graves. In the foreground was a bench. In a pelting rain, they were seated on it, blindfolded, and their hands and feet tied. The firing squad of four men shot them from a distance of six feet; their bodies, still in their wet clothes and boots, were then tossed into the shallow graves.[63]

Zelaya had their confessions photographed and auctioned. He even wrote a letter of self-justification to William Randolph Hearst, the American newspaper tycoon whose papers were fuming over the dictator's conduct.[64] Secretary of State Knox, in his official response to the executions, called Zelaya a "blot on the history of Nicaragua."[65] The Navy dispatched a flotilla of warships that anchored off Corinto in early December. It landed an expeditionary force of marines and bluejackets to map the rail line from the coast to Managua and draw up a Nicaraguan war plan.[66] Determined to unseat an independent head of state who threatened to attract non-U.S. interests to build an alternative canal and thereby create a permanent challenge to U.S. domination of the isthmus and hegemony in the Caribbean, the Taft administration recognized that its surrogates—Chamorro, Estrada Cabrera, and Juan Estrada—were incapable of deposing Zelaya. A more direct role for U.S. forces was necessary.

4

The Campaign for Nicaragua

Zelaya was now beyond the pale in the minds of U.S. authorities, who considered his regime the bane of all believers in moral authority. No less a distinguished, if absolutely biased, official than the U.S. secretary of state declared that the deaths before a Nicaraguan firing squad of two obscure American entrepreneurs and soldiers of fortune constituted the noblest sacrifice for liberty and against tyranny. French, British, and German officials on the isthmus did not regard Zelaya as "beyond the pale." They generally accepted the culpability of Groce and Cannon and considered Zelaya's action unwise only in light of U.S. power and eagerness to depose him.[1]

Elsewhere, from the excavation camps for the canal across Panama to the squalid watering holes in New Orleans frequented by this generation of U.S. adventurers, there were vengeful cries. Those who had not been lured already to Estrada's army with prospects for a quick fortune now appeared eager to join up in the cause against the tyrant. In the Panama Canal Zone the "wildest indignation and excitement" over the killings swept the camps of engineers and overseers of the new century's next wonder of the world. Many were ready to volunteer for Estrada's cause. Cannon, apparently, had interpreted his own difficulties with Zelaya as a personal grudge. His mother, sought out by

Harrisburg journalists, produced one of Lee Roy's letters, received the summer before his death. "Down here," Cannon had written, "whenever an American gets a little money these natives begin to persecute him."[2]

Cannon's and Groce's deaths prompted curious journalistic analyses of the motivations of Americans in the tropics. "Most gringos," wrote a retired tropical tramp and soldier of fortune who had once fought against Cipriano Castro in Venezuela, "are apt to be of a adventurous disposition and fond of fighting," a not atypical characterization of Christmas's generation of adventurers. But, he went on, "most men of Anglo-Saxon or Teutonic descent have an innate hatred for injustice and oppression, especially if these wrongs are inflicted upon them by men of another race." Here was the strong racist assessment of conflicts in the tropics. The deaths of Cannon and Groce, intoned a Bluefields minister, had not been in vain, for their sacrifice had advanced the cause of freedom. In an encomium that made truth the first casualty, he added: "They came to Nicaragua with that full American spirit—the sword in one hand and the banner of liberty in the other."[3]

For their "assassination," the New York Herald stated, Zelaya "must answer."[4] A State Department functionary solemnly declared that the "obstinate, despotic, avaricious, unscrupulous, and cruel" dictator stood "in the path of humanity." He had ordered Cannon and Groce killed not because they fought for the insurgents but because they were Americans, "their execution being not only an act of unwarrantable savagery but expressly calculated to injure and insult the United States."[5] More likely, Zelaya had mistakenly presumed that his action would convince U.S. officials to cease encouraging U.S. soldiers of fortune to make war upon his government and to increase disorder in Central American society. Condemning Estrada as the lackey of U.S. imperialism, he was publicly jubilant about his order to execute the two Americans. In a defiant proclamation, he boasted: "Estrada wishes to open the country to foreigners with his sword. His ambition is to place the country in the shameful condition of being reduced to slavery. It is better to die than to submit being sold to slavery."[6]

Confronted with mounting U.S. hostility, Zelaya resolved to quit, but always the calculating *político*, virtually hand-picked his successor (José Madriz) and made plans for a military confrontation in the east. Sixty miles upriver from the rebel stronghold at Bluefields stood Rama, near the confluence of two rivers, the Mico and Siguia, that flowed out of the Nicaraguan highland to form the mighty Escondido. Between Rama and Bluefields lay the Mosquitia, a vast area of swamps and plantations that became an impenetrable bog in the rainy season. When the Spaniards ruled Central America, they had failed to establish their authority in the Mosquitia, and its Indian inhabitants—the Mosquitos or Miskitos—had for generations paid a stronger fealty to the British influence along the coast. Not until Zelaya's day had the British grip been broken, but not even the dictator and his conscript army had been able to subdue the region. The control of Rama, strategically located between Managua and the coast, was vital for any army driving east or west.

In his last days of power, confronting a U.S. naval force anchored off Corinto on the northwest coast, Zelaya sent a 3,500-man federal army down from the highlands to the west to attack General Luis Mena's troops at Rama. He calculated that Estrada would be compelled to leave his sanctuary at Bluefields and go to Mena's aid; when he did, Zelaya intended to crush this apostate governor who had defied him by allying with the foreign businessmen of the east coast. The American presence on the west coast had heartened the rebels, however, who barricaded themselves in Rama behind huge loops of barbed wire and awaited battle. To combat the inevitable debilitating diseases of the tropics, Estrada had sent them ample quantities of quinine.[7]

To the west of Rama, a few miles beyond the confluence of the Mico and Siguia Rivers, lies the village of Recreo. Here, with fortifications strung out halfway across the peninsula to Tatumbla and a garrison across the Mico, the Zelayista force gathered four artillery pieces and four machine guns—ample firepower for the kind of battle that Zelaya's armies had waged several years before in Honduras. Indeed, its commander, Gen-

eral Roberto González, and his staff were veterans of Namasigüe. Learning of their strength, the rebel generals caucused
and, reinforced by the solicitous presence of the U.S. consul
and Adolfo Díaz, the financial patron of the revolt and now its
chief civilian adviser, decided to attack.

On December 19, 1909, as Zelaya was turning over power
to Madriz, Mena and his staff planned the assault. Mena would
take seven hundred men, including his U.S. machine gunners,
six miles up the Mico, disembarking on the opposite side of
the river from Recreo for a strike at noon the following day
against the government fortification at Tatumbla. Another
five hundred rebels would move against Jalteva. From the
Mico, rebel gunboats would open up on the federal position in
Jalteva at precisely 1:00 P.M. The rebel strategy held that the
Zelayistas would be distracted by Mena's charge on Tatumbla;
believing it the major assault, they would be unable to rush
reinforcements to Tatumbla before the one o'clock barrage
from Chamorro's gunboats.

The following morning, in a mist that obscured the forti-
fied hills in the distance, the invaders piled aboard banana
barges towed by gasoline launches. Shielded by the firepower
of three armored tugs named *Falcón*, *Pioneer*, and *El Rey*, they
inched upriver. By eleven o'clock the force destined for Jalteva
was ashore and in the bush. At the same time, from their base
at the confluence of the rivers, Chamorro's gunboats moved
up the Mico, pausing to send scouts ashore to patrol for a mile
into the interior on the opposite side of the river. An American
reporter from the *New York Herald* caught sight of one scout, a
boy of thirteen, scantily clad and carrying no weapon, who
emerged from the bush to report. "That's our youngest volunteer," explained a rebel officer. "He's too little to carry a
weapon."[8]

An observer sighting from a distance this flotilla of decrepit
barges pulled by tugs might have thought them banana boats
ferrying laborers for a day's cutting. On closer inspection, however, the glint of rifle barrels or the muzzle of a three-pounder
Hotchkiss would have betrayed these blue-blanketed passengers
as invaders readying to seize the hills rising from the river banks
from the red-blanketed Zelayistas awaiting them. From the

maze of green on the hillside a Maxim machine gun opened fire; to the rebels on the barges its location was unknown, but they responded with their Remingtons and Mausers, and suddenly the tropical stillness erupted with the crackling of rifle and machine gun fire. Scouts emerged from the bush to give frantic reports of the battle above them. Jalteva, a cluster of ordinary thatched huts, had fallen. The Zelayistas, desperate, threw themselves at the hastily erected rebel emplacements in a furious five-minute charge. Six miles away, General Mena and his American machine gunners (led by "Gabe" Conrad of New Iberia, Louisiana) raced through Tatumbla, sending the several hundred Zelayistas scurrying before them. By 1:00 P.M. Mena's force was approaching the Recreo fortification.

As dusk fell the government still held Recreo and a strategic lodgment atop a hill opposite Jalteva. The wounded were brought down to the waiting barges. From the thicket the rebels emerged in small groups for the ride downriver to Recreo. Two Americans—Phil Craven and Pat Dolan, veterans of the Spanish-American and Filipino Wars—had several captives in tow. Back in Rama, the *Herald* observer recorded, tales of the day's glories swept through the town, but the dead and wounded—most of them veterans of the two charges on Jalteva—kept arriving at the dock until midnight, "and with each fresh boat load the horror of the hand fighting in the bush grew and grew."[9]

The next day the rebels closed in around Recreo. An artillery battery commanded by Godfrey Fowler, a member of the adjutant general's office of the Texas National guard and grandson of John H. Reagan, postmaster general of the Confederacy, held a seemingly impregnable position atop a hill across from Jalteva. Mena and Gabe Conrad's machine gunners blocked the retreat to Managua. By noon the Zelayistas, with five hundred more men than the enemy, were surrounded. At three o'clock, after furious exchange of artillery and machine gun fire, the federals began moving toward Fowler's "hill," trying to make their rifle fire count. But Mena and his machine gunners were waiting for just this move, and as the Zelayistas advanced on Fowler's artillery placement, Conrad's machine gunners opened up. At dusk the Zelaya commander raised the white flag.

Not until nightfall did a mud-spattered rebel officer, ferried back to Rama on one of Estrada's gasoline launches, burst in on a dozing Estrada to tell his *jefe* of the glorious victory: the entire federal force had surrendered. The unexcited Estrada chewed his cigar, patiently listening to the details. Then he calmly ordered the sentry to tell the citizens of Rama to begin celebrating. Except for a brief mention of the exploits of Conrad and Fowler, the most authoritative Nicaraguan chronicler of this very costly battle (nine hundred casualties, four hundred dead, out of 4,000) paid scant attention to the Americans in the fight. But Conrad, according to the *New York Times*, had "saved the day" by carrying a vital message from Chamorro, whose attack had been delayed, to Mena.[10]

Conrad and other U.S. mercenaries had in fact performed well. In some way Conrad had forced his way through the jungle, with its bogs and tough interlaced vines and trees. His message threw Mena and his men into a frenzy of energy. Brush which it had been deemed necessary for the *macheteros* to cut was ignored; the men simply swarmed over it. Not even waist-deep bog halted them. They were nearly exhausted and perspiring from every pore when the sight of Recreo lent them fresh energy and enthusiasm. This glowing tribute came from a reporter who had credited the Estrada forces with having only half a dozen or so "real" Americans among them! The remaining ones—though they may not have "saved the day"—nonetheless deserve passing mention: Ralph Lees, New Orleans; Pat Dolan, an aging soldier of fortune from the isthmian wars who listed his home merely as Nebraska; Phil Craven, Dalhart, Texas, for fifteen years a demonstrator of trick pistol shots for a firearms company; James Bransfield, the only American wounded in the fight; and James Edwards, who had spent so many years in Central America that he no longer possessed any strong ties to a U.S. town.[11]

The captured Zelayans were herded on barges and shipped downriver to Bluefields. Estrada, of course, had desperately few provisions for his own men, so the defeated were left to the Red Cross, which had dispatched a mission to the coast, and the medical care of a redoubtable doctor from the U.S.S. *Des Moines*, one of the gunboats patrolling off the coast. Zelaya had sent these conscripts into battle with a rifle, blanket, and ammunition; for clothes and shoes they had had to depend on individual resources, and many, the *Herald* reported, were shoeless. Consequently, 2,500 prisoners—"wretched, starved, half-clad, some almost naked, diseased, wounded and fever-wracked"—roamed the sandy streets of Bluefields, begging for food.[12]

Then word came that the U.S. Congress, resolving that Zelaya must be punished, had authorized the president to use the "entire land and naval forces" of the country to ensure Nicaragua a republican government. Just as suddenly, Zelaya became contrite, appealing for a "disinterested commission" to study conditions in Nicaragua and vowing to resign if it found fault with his rule. When Taft and Knox responded with the Nicaraguan Expeditionary Force, the dictator tendered his resignation to the national assembly and named Vice-President José Madriz as his successor. The new Nicaraguan leader inherited the remnants of Zelaya's army and controlled the most populous regions of the country.[13]

In January 1910, from two hundred miles away in Managua, Madriz dispatched a peace overture to the victorious Estrada. The Nicaraguan rebel, hearing that a dozen New Orleans businessmen with dealings in Nicaragua had urged the State Department to recognize his provisional government, promptly rejected Madriz's overture. But Secretary of State Knox, though suspicious of Madriz's ties to Zelaya, showed no sign of rushing into Estrada's arms, despite the latter's presumably decisive victory at Recreo. The predictable conclusion both Nicaraguans inferred from Knox's behavior was that they should shoot it out, and the victor would shortly receive coveted U.S. recognition. In the United States, emissary Salvador Castrillo proudly reported that Estrada had even been proffered loans from American businesses but had refused them.[14]

Halfheartedly, Estrada issued a peace proposal to his enemy, but the bearer of the dispatch—General Fornos Díaz, a friend of Madriz's, who was ferrying the vital document in a sailboat from Bluefields to San Juan del Norte—drowned at sea.[15] Another message finally did get through to Managua, but by then Madriz's confidence had grown, and he announced that acceptance of Estrada's offer would have "illegitimized" his own government. He resolved to prosecute the war, declaring: "It will be better to have one severe battle than an endless season of unconclusive skirmishes."[16]

Although Madriz, in the State Department's eyes just another Zelayista, was no more acceptable than Zelaya, the dictator's fall threw Managua's previously terrified Conservatives into wild celebration; they roamed the dusty streets shouting anti-Zelaya slogans and cheering Mexico and the United States, whose diplomatic efforts had toppled the eighteen-year dictatorship. With Rear Admiral Kimball's solicitous efforts, Zelaya himself slipped out of Nicaragua, boarding a Mexican gunboat at Corinto and surfacing in the Mexican capital a few weeks later. The Mexicans, reflecting their government's polite opposition to U.S. meddling in Central American affairs, greeted him warmly, listened attentively as Zelaya repeated his justification for the Cannon and Groce affair, and condemned Estrada for hiring four hundred American mercenaries.[17]

Christmas, still in the service of Estrada Cabrera, took no part directly in the overthrow of Zelaya, although with the Guatemalan president's blessing he had sent itinerant soldiers of fortune to Estrada's cause and, after Madriz took power, was rumored to be organizing a filibustering expedition in the Gulf of Fonseca. Madriz's takeover in Managua seemed to make little difference to the Americans who had lent their services to the overthrow of the regime. In the first two months of 1910 eager "volunteers" poured into Bluefields; they roamed the streets visibly displaying their weapons or lounged about the Hotel Tropical, which was filling up with new American guests.

Madriz's adversary, however, had the good will of the U.S. public—and the handy services of a fifty-man force hastily put together by one of the most famous of America's pre-World War I soldiers of fortune, Victor Gordon. Unlike Cannon or Groce, Gordon was a professional mercenary, a veteran of the

Boer War and three revolutions. When Estrada had proclaimed against Zelaya, Gordon was in Panama City. A persuasive Nicaraguan Conservative with $500 from a UFCO manager lured Gordon and several of his cronies to Bluefields. Then Gordon sailed for New Orleans, his suitcase laden with money from American merchants sympathetic to Estrada's cause. In New Orleans he had purchased an old steamship, the *Venus*, and loaded it with men and materiel for the rebellion. State Department officials, alerted by Zelaya's agents, had intervened; they compelled Gordon to head back for Bluefields while the *Venus* remained under federal guard in New Orleans. Estrada next sent him to the Canal Zone to recruit machine gunners. "Then you will be of value," the Nicaraguan rebel general told him. More than forty years later Gordon recalled: "That was how I came to organize the nucleus of the army that fought with me for many years and in practically every country in Central America. It wasn't a very impressive looking band of fighters. . . . Some were cutthroats who had fled the United States and were going under assumed names. Others were youngsters who had come down there for excitement. A few were experienced soldiers."[18]

Three of them left their mark on this war: Guy Molony, Samuel Dreben, and Tracy Richardson. Molony was born in New Orleans in 1884. In 1901, aged sixteen, he ran away to South Africa and fought in the Boer War. Then he served a stint with the U.S. Army in the Philippines, where he learned how to operate and repair machine guns when they jammed; his mechanical aptitude earned him the sobriquet "Machine-gun Molony." Next he tried policing in New Orleans but left for the Central American wars—not, like many other of this generation, for money ("I never earned the money I would have been paid for digging ditches") but for a vaguely defined "cause, for adventure, for fame, or for the hope of future material rewards."[19]

Among those he instructed in the art of machine gun operation was "Jew Sam" Dreben. A product of one of the toughest neighborhoods in New York, Dreben looked less a soldier than a comical merchant without a care for the drudgeries of business; he was, wrote Richardson, "a walking vaudeville act."[20]

Yet stories of his daring and soldierly qualities were legion among American soldiers of fortune. He was ever ready to learn something new about weapons and how to use them. A benefactor of the revolution had sent Estrada an old Gatling gun, and Dreben persuaded Molony, whose reputation as an expert on machine guns had preceded him to Bluefields, to teach him how to use it. "Like a fool," Molony obliged. Dreben took the Gatling for a scrap at the Bluff, the promotory shielding Bluefields from the sea. The gun jammed, and Dreben had to abandon it.[21]

Tracy Richardson, had fought under seven different flags, mostly as a machine gunner, for causes he only vaguely comprehended. At twenty-one he had earned $2,000 as a commissary agent for a pipeline company in Arkansas and headed for New Orleans to spend it. With Louis Grimer, who acquired no particular distinction in these affrays, he boarded a Norwegian steamer for South America because, as he put it in his two-page autobiography, he knew nothing about South America. The steamer docked in Bluefields in the midst of Estrada's revolution; with the dozen or so other adventurers sailing on the same vessel, Richardson took up lodging at the Tropical Hotel, where many of Estrada's American recruits boarded. Apparently, the newcomers had not landed with any intention of joining the rebellion, but a suspicious U.S. vice-consul called them to the consulate. "You're a fine lot of bums," the consul yelled, "to come into this country to shoot up a bunch of peaceable people." Grimer, who weighed 220 pounds, was sufficiently provoked to reach over the desk and yank the "withered little man" from his chair. Back at the hotel, they discovered that their luggage and weapons had been sent to the steamer's next port of call. With nothing but the clothes they were wearing and their money belts, Richardson and Grimer signed on as volunteers to Estrada's cause.[22]

While U.S. entrepreneurs bankrolled helpful leaders and factions, their hired guns followed fame, adventure, good times, and the lure of wealth. The U.S. labor market offered them few opportunities in the late nineteenth and early twentieth centuries. Most left U.S. society because they no longer really fit in and saw there only a drab future existence with little material advantage. Yet few soldiers of fortune found much financial reward in these wars. In a strictly moral sense, they were no more culpable for the misery visited upon Central America in these years than those who hired them. They were simply expendable.

General Estrada dispatched these latest *norteamericano* recruits upriver to General Mena's camp at Rama. Deciding that the gasoline launches were impractical, too costly for transporting such a small party, the rebel leader entrusted the safe passage of the Americans to husky Miskito Indians, who ferried their passengers in "pit-pangs," low-slung canoes, fifty feet long, hacked out of mahogany trees. At Rama they met General Mena, "a large, fine looking, and intelligent man," who immediately assigned them to Conrad's American machine gunners.[23]

Daringly, an advance force of 1,600 rebels under the command of Chamorro was penetrating Chontales province to a point only thirty miles from the capital. Mena moved on Acoyapa with a thousand men; a third rebel commander, Benjamín Zeledón, departed Rama on January 17 with another 1,500. But most of Zeledón's army, Moffat reported, was made up of Zelaya deserters whose loyalty had yet to be tested. By month's end the combined rebel strength pressing against Madriz in the populous lake region of the country rose to almost 4,500. In this swollen army the *New Orleans Daily Picayune* mistakenly estimated that there were ten Americans. In fact, the number was considerably larger.

Chamorro's bold thrust held the key to victory for the rebels, and he performed brilliantly: in early February he won the battle of Boaca and advanced on Matagalpa. His army's approach was preceded by wild rumors among the city's hundred or so Americans that government troops, angered over the U.S. government's "neutrality" in this war, would vengefully destroy American property.[24] Already, Mena, whose army included Victor Gordon's sharpshooters and Conrad's Maxim machine gun-

ners, had faced the enemy in two "fierce engagements" at La
Garita and Santa Clara, capturing numerous prisoners, arms,
and even a Maxim gun. But the retreating soldiers took a strong
position in the hills outside Santa Clara. There Gordon's marks-
men and Conrad's machine gunners, sensing victory, danger-
ously advanced to within two hundred yards of the enemy. The
government's Maxim and Hotchkiss guns swept the rebel flank,
cutting down the vegetation that shielded the Americans. Mena
ordered Conrad to pull back, but by then the Americans were
caught in withering fire from enemy guns. Conrad kept firing,
cooling the hot barrel of the Maxim with water, all the while
yelling for help. In the melee a government bullet tore into his
abdomen. Counting his casualties, including the severely injured Conrad, Mena ordered a retreat. In the dusk of early evening, the wounded borne in hammocks lashed to poles, Mena's
rebels stole into the night. Conrad was propped on a mule, his
weakened body held up by a war correspondent from the states.
When he fainted in the saddle, the reporter provided a shot of
whiskey to rouse him. Safely distant from Santa Clara, they
rested; Dreben, ever resourceful, stole a chicken from a peasant
and cooked it for broth to feed the wounded. Because this war
was as much a battle of words—persuasive rhetoric designed to
influence the impassive Admiral Kimball in his reporting on
the Nicaraguan situation—as bullets, each side jubilantly announced a great victory.[25]

In Matagalpa, the rebel cause fared no better. True to his
word, Chamorro seized this important Nicaraguan town, driving its small government garrison into the countryside. Within
a week, however, Madriz brought his artillery within range of
Chamorro's encampment inside Matagalpa and, despite Admiral Kimball's perfunctory warning about "threats to the lives
and property of neutrals," bombarded the town. Chamorro
scurried out under cover of darkness.[26]

Madriz's army, its numbers swollen by the victories of early
February and the quotas of government recruiting squads,
pushed the scattering rebels deeper into the interior. On February 18 the retreating rebels took their stand at Chino. There one
of Gordon's American "scouts," William Wilkins, recruited in

the Panama Canal Zone, miraculously cheated death when a steel-jacketed Mauser bullet was deflected from his heart by a cartridge belt slung over his shoulder; it penetrated only his arm. Another American, G.T. Busby, was struck by fragments when a boulder serving as protection took a direct hit by an artillery shell. The pursuing loyalists and determined rebels shot it out for ten hours in firing so intense that it became difficult to see through the smoke from the weapons and the dust kicked up by bullets and shrapnel. Finally, the government troops, yielding before a vigorous counterattack by Mena, began withdrawing, pursued by six Americans.[27]

At Tisma and Tipitapa, lying strategically between Lakes Managua and Nicaragua, the old Conservative families considered the U.S. persecution of the Zelayistas and the rebel drive into the interior as an opportunity to recover their properties and power. Chamorro, driven from Matagalpa, vowed to take Tisma. He had Godfrey Fowler's artillery battery to pummel the enemy and 1,100 troops to match against four hundred. But on the verge of defeat, Madriz's army turned the battle with reinforcements that had forced marched for twenty miles. Chamorro next struck Tipitapa in a frighteningly costly assault that lasted from midafternoon through the night and witnessed hand-to-hand fighting with machetes. When dawn arrived, Chamorro had only 150 men able to fight, and the surrounding plain, the *Bluefields American* reported, was "strewn with dead and dying, broken guns, and dead horses."[28]

Remnants of the defeated rebel armies stumbled into Rama, where the great invasion of the lake region had commenced only a few weeks before, to soothe their exhausted bodies and wounded pride at J.A. Walker's saloon. Some soldiers of fortune returned to New Orleans. Gabe Conrad arrived several weeks later to a warm reception and promptly managed to impress gaping onlookers as a serious commander of soldiers, and not just a "soft-brained adventurer who follows revolutions."[29]

The rebel leader, in typically calculating fashion, announced from Bluefields that this costly war should properly be settled by U.S. mediation. Madriz, of course, just as promptly rejected the plan as a violation of Nicaraguan sovereignty. The U.S. entrepreneurs in Bluefields who had committed their money to the rebellion perfunctorily reaffirmed their support for Estrada and then castigated him for neglecting their interests in the disastrous drive into the interior. He had yet another problem. Since December and January, when the rebels were winning, U.S. soldiers of fortune and adventurers had been arriving to augment his armies with their special skills. Crammed into Bluefields, however, they frequently brawled and caused so much trouble that Estrada began shipping them back to New Orleans on banana boats.[30]

Some of Estrada's U.S. "volunteers," frustrated by the recent defeats and angry over stories that one of their comrades, the flamboyant Godfrey Fowler, had been wounded and abandoned to the pursuers, departed eagerly enough. Others—fifty, the *New York Herald* counted—were holed up in Rama without pay and unable to leave.[31] The ever confident Gordon descended on New Orleans and made a polite call on Madriz's consul, Francisco Altschuhl, at the Grunewald Hotel, where he brazenly reaffirmed his intention of recruiting more men for the rebel cause. "Money is coming in now," Gordon boasted. Soon Conrad and 150 eager "volunteers" were sailing for Bluefields—via a Guatemalan stopover.[32]

Dispatching a second loftily phrased appeal to Madriz to permit mediation of the war by the U.S. government, "rightly admired in the civilized world for its noble endeavors," Estrada continued to govern Bluefields as a separate fiefdom. He knew that the vigilant U.S. naval commander would not permit the war to endanger the local American population. Consul Moffat made sure that U.S. naval commanders had a list of Americans deserving protection. He generally excluded the transients at the Hotel Tropical, whose legal status was predictably "obscure," but carefully noted that the town's "permanent" and propertied residents—Bluefields Steamship Company, Atlantic Navigation Company, Bluefields Tanning Company, and La Luz and Los Angeles Mining Company—were all benefactors of the revolt. La Luz, the most visible supporter of General Estrada, was especially pleased with the promulgation of a new mining law that permitted it to import supplies duty-free.[33]

Still, the rebellion needed more than U.S. money and fighters. Madriz possessed the capital and was sending a conquering army, flushed with victory, after Estrada's generals as they retreated into the swamps of eastern Nicaragua. But even success on the battlefield had not won Zelaya's former vice-president the approbation of the U.S. government. Secretary of State Knox vacillated between conflicting reports: one from a U.S. rear admiral with decidedly skeptical opinions about the revolt and its private American benefactors; another from a pro-rebel U.S. consul who repeatedly cited the duty of the United States to protect its citizens in the "savage" world of the Central American tropics. Knox would not recognize Madriz because Madriz was a Zelayista; he could not yet recognize Estrada because Estrada ruled only in Bluefields and along the Escondido. Yet even in retreat, Estrada had something of inestimable political value: the professed U.S. policy of neutrality better served his cause than it did that of Madriz.

Some critics of an expansionist United States, interpreting the unusually arcane processes of isthmian revolutions, saw in Washington's beneficent policy toward Estrada the handiwork of J.P. Morgan and Company. To be sure, Knox looked at Nicaragua—indeed, all Central America—as "another Santo Domingo": that is, a medley of compliant financial protectorates beholden to U.S. capital and freed of the shackles of British finance. (In 1905 President Theodore Roosevelt, confronting similar issues in the Dominican Republic or Santo Domingo, had created the model through an executive agreement that two years later was formalized in a treaty. By its provisions the United States collected customs revenues and dispensed a portion to satisfy the Dominican Republic's onerous foreign debt.) But the U.S. government cited hallowed naval traditions to justify its protection of Bluefields in early 1910. Predictably the Code of Naval Regulations—"the Book"—covered the exigencies of tropical politics: "Section 305: Where American lives or property are endangered in violation of international law or treaty rights, the naval officer shall consult with diplomatic representation and take appropriate steps. The responsibility is his [the officer's]." More pertinent to the Nicaraguan situation was Section 306: The naval officer may not use force against a "friendly" state, but he does possess the "right of self-preservation" and the duty to protect U.S. citizens. There followed an important admonition: "Conditions calling for the application of the right of self-preservation cannot be defined beforehand, but must be left to the sound judgement of responsible officers."[34] As Madriz and other Central American leaders correctly sensed, these obscure regulations conveniently served to justify actions that denied the sovereign rights of Central American governments in order to advance U.S. interests—on the pretext of a "civilizing" mission or the sanctity of private property.

Madriz's troops moved on Rama, where three armies totaling 8,000 men fought a bloody encounter.[35] From the sea, the *Venus*, released to Nicaragua by U.S. officials in New Orleans, landed a force that seized the Bluff, which controlled all seagoing traffic in and out of the Bluefields harbor. Estrada stood in imminent danger of being cut off from his supply line to Guatemala, which was kept open by filibustering Americans. But in May, just as the *Venus* and Madriz's army were closing the vise, the commander of the U.S.S. *Paducah* forbade any bombardment of Bluefields and declared the town "off limits" to fighting. Within a few weeks a U.S. Marine battalion out of Panama, commanded by Major Smedley Butler, arrived to "police" the town. Major Butler only vaguely understood the position of the State Department in this affair but surmised correctly that his government wanted the "revolution to come out on top."[36]

Without the protective shield of a U.S. gunboat and Butler's marines, Bluefields would have fallen, and Estrada's grand revolt would have been crushed. But what was happening in the swamps and lagoons of the fetid Nicaraguan coast in early 1910 was no devilishly conceived capitalist conspiracy or crude militaristic maneuver by the great powers. It was more sophisticated and goal-oriented. Washington wanted compliant isthmian governments ruling ordered, stable political economies that would encourage U.S. entrepreneurs to initiate business. The stability would circumvent any need for foreign intervention, thus increasing U.S. security in the circum-Caribbean.

Zelaya's unwillingness to accept the U.S. decision not to develop interoceanic transit through Nicaragua had increasingly exacerbated U.S.-Nicaraguan relations. The U.S. Department of State, evaluating the isthmian situation, had determined that all Zelayista influence must be eradicated from Nicaragua and with it the potential for a European economic rivalry on the isthmus; its sister bureaucracy the U.S. Navy—occasionally endowed with the mission of policing the tropics—was instructed to declare Bluefields as "off limits" to fighting. (Such a decree was permitted because U.S. naval regulations intruded upon foreign, particularly on the periphery, sovereignty.) The local foreign businessmen, many of whom had financed the revolt and imported the hired guns of New Orleans and the Canal Zone to aid Estrada's cause, were merely protecting their investments, not advancing the specific interests of the House of Morgan. If Madriz won the war, they would have to pay more to stay in business. The State Department wanted to remove hindrance to its hegemony and simultaneously facilitate U.S. investment opportunities. Butler, who had sacked Peking in the cause of "civilizing" China during the Boxer Rebellion, evinced no strong emotion toward either side in the Nicaraguan conflict and, indeed, wrote disparagingly about Estrada and his U.S. hirelings to his Quaker parents back in Pennsylvania. His only duty was to clean up Bluefields and police the town, much like a cop on his beat. When local Chinese merchants, hearing of a rumored Madriz assault on their property, raised the U.S. flag, an act imitated by other nationals, they were paying homage not to the Department of State or the House of Morgan but to a flamboyant U.S. Marine who symbolized order in a disorderly world.[37] Of course, it was the State Department and, probably, spokesmen and lobbyists from large firms like La Luz who were responsible for the major's arrival in Bluefields with his battalion.

Even with the marines, Bluefields fell on desperate days. Its poorer residents subsisted mainly on tropical fruits, and its once vigorous business establishments were practically shut down. Consul Moffat, still committed to Estrada, declared that incoming ships must pay duties to the provisional government, an act that noticeably heartened the rebel cause and infringed upon Nicaraguan sovereignty. In another fierce engagement upriver at Rama, Estrada's army beat off a government attack, and the retreating federals abandoned their wounded to the uncertain care of the enemy. The indecisive character of the war, however, placed a strain on both sides. Butler decreed a plague on both camps, writing his father, a powerful politician, that his most troublesome problem was Gordon's American volunteers, who roamed Bluefields complaining that they had been promised $28 per day each if the revolt succeeded. Since they were not winning the war and had not been paid, they had taken to scrapping around town. Butler, the "policeman" on duty, determined to stop any more fighting in his jurisdiction.[38]

In mid-June Madriz's commander in the east struck in a mad attack against Estrada's fortifications outside Bluefields. Estrada's machine gunners, led by twenty-two-year-old Christian Sands from Seattle, held the town. The casualty total, as in most of these isthmian wars, was disgustingly high. The captain of a U.S. gunboat, the *Paducah*, walked over the battlefield where arms and legs of hastily buried troops protruded from the sand. Lazily flying buzzards served as guides. He came on a rebel lashed to a tree, stabbed so many times that he was unrecognizable save for the white armband of the revolutionary cause. His tormentors had hung a sign: "Thus should die the bandit Estrada."[39]

Bizarre reports about the revolution kept filtering out of Nicaragua. In early March, George Cannon, Lee Roy's cousin, suddenly surfaced in Central America. He was apprehended in Corinto by Madriz's agents, subjected to what the U.S. press styled "third degree" treatment, and confessed to having been hired by Estrada's people to assassinate Madriz. He could not go through with the deed, Cannon said, because he had learned

that Madriz was a "brother Mason." In still another tale, Godfrey Fowler, the glory-seeking runaway from the Texas adjutant
general's office, was reported slain at Tisma (along with an
unnamed black from Mobile), then miraculously reappeared, a
prisoner of the Nicaraguan military. In a solicitous gesture
Madriz turned over this latest American hero to the vigilant
Admiral Kimball, who spirited him out of Nicaragua. Fowler's
fan mail, generated by news reports in the U.S. press, piled up
in Moffat's office in Bluefields.[40]

Using every resource he could muster (even the dwindling
Nicaraguan reserves banked in the States), Madriz determined
to crush the rebellion and force Knox to recognize his government. The rebels clung desperately to their fragile hold on
Rama and were embarrassingly dependent on Butler's marines
in Bluefields. But at a critical moment for the rebel cause,
Moffat, with the approval of the captains of U.S. warships off
Bluefields, announced that the Nicaraguan government must
not "interfere" with the movement of vessels of the "visible"
authority of Estrada. The rebel cause was thus sustained.[41]

The U.S. press remained attentive to accounts of the war's
numerous injustices. William Pittman (who in his youth had
run away to the Boer War and served there as a water boy), now
in the service of the rebel cause as a "mining engineer," fell
captive to government troops and was tossed into a five-by-
five-foot squalid cell in Managua. American newspapers took
up his cause. His mother back in Boston was hounded by reporters; she told them: "My poor boy is not an adventurer."
Madriz, alert to the rising anti-American feeling in western
Nicaragua, was even more sensitive to U.S. press coverage of
still another obscure *norteamericano* who had fallen into the
hands of Nicaraguan authorities. Pittman would not be executed like Cannon and Groce, Madriz promised. U.S. officials
visited Pittman daily to report on his treatment, but he was
not liberated until Estrada's summer drive on the capital.[42]

Blockaded by Madriz's virtually unenforceable declaration,
Bluefields's isolated rebels persevered into the torrid coastal
summer of 1910. Two European nations, Germany and Norway,
reluctantly recognized the legality of the government's block-

ade, thus "outwitting" Knox's diplomatic maneuvers. In Managua a subservient press castigated the American presence daily in terms so virulent that the excitable U.S. consul warned of the "seizure and summary execution of all Americans in the country unless the forces of the United States are immediately withdrawn."[43]

Back in the United States a suspicious Congress, critical of Knox's financial schemes for turning Nicaragua into a financial dependency, was raising embarrassing questions about the activities of U.S. companies on the east coast of Nicaragua. A member of the House Ways and Means Committee politely inquired whether or not UFCO was behind the troubles in Nicaragua, prompting Francis Huntington Wilson of the State Department to respond publicly that the accusations were "so unjust that they did not seem worthy to be dignified by a denial."[44]

In late July the outlook for the beleaguered Estrada sharply improved. In the interior a rebel army under General José María Moncada engaged Madriz's troops at Comalapa in a ten-hour battle in which the rebels captured 190 rifles, two hundred horses and mules, and "many prisoners," the *Bluefields American* boasted. Almost simultaneously, commanders of patrolling U.S. warships declared Madriz's blockade of Bluefields illegal and pledged to "protect" commerce with their firepower. The Bluefields Steamship Company, now under the management of Jake Weinberger, made Estrada the "loan" of a banana boat for ferrying arms and men up the Escondido River in preparation for a major rebel drive into the interior.[45]

The rebellion's fortunes, so dismal in the spring and early summer of 1910, thus dramatically changed for the better. In early August, Richard Sussman, Estrada's "consul" in New Orleans, outfitted the *Hornet* (soon to play an even more crucial role in the forthcoming Bonilla revolt in Honduras) and sent it south with arms and ammunition for Bluefields, while Madriz's agents tried desperately to get U.S. federal authorities to stop it.

As things turned out, Estrada did not need this latest shipment of weapons for his cause. Midway through the month his advancing army crossed the Tipitapa River. Government troops scurried out of Granada, the Conservative capital, a few days later and on the eastern front they meekly surrendered the Bluff. By the end of August, Estrada was jubilantly ensconced in Managua. Remembering his American friend in Bluefields, he wired Salvador Castrillo in Washington: "Don't forget, when asking for recognition of the revolutionary government . . . to suggest strongly to [the] State Department the appointment of Mr. Moffat as Minister to Nicaragua to perpetuate the confidence existing between the two countries."[46]

With or even ahead of the conquering rebels came the American legionnaires. One of the first to enter Managua was Tracy Richardson, scouting for General Luis Mena. Richardson headed for the house of a prominent American businessman to discuss the local situation. A band of Madriz followers, apparently roaming the town looking for Estrada supporters, burst in on the two Americans and might have shot them on the spot had not Richardson asked to be taken to their commander. There he casually informed the Nicaraguan general that Managua was surrounded. Reckoning that the nonchalant American standing before him could not possibly be idiotic enough to make up such a tale, the Nicaraguan commander surrendered on the spot. It was a bluff, and Richardson dispatched a desperate message to Mena to hurry his advance on the capital. Afterward, he and Dreben, who had stolen an imposing white horse belonging to Estrada's brother, went on a spree. Richardson returned to New Orleans with $19,000.[47]

Gordon, older and presumbably wiser in the enduring lessons of isthmian wars, headed for the national treasury, but, he later recounted sadly, "Estrada had the same idea" and got there first. Gordon received 40,000 gold pesos for his services to the revolution but had to pay most of it to his men. His explanation left no doubt about his motives: "Naturally this small amount was the result of my failure to get to the National treasury first, an oversight I quickly corrected in succeeding revolutions." Gordon enjoyed some revenge less than a year later when the hard-drinking Estrada was forced out of the presidency by the U.S. government and his own bickering generals; Gordon "escorted" him out of the country.[48]

Sussman, Estrada's recruiter in New Orleans, rushed to Nicaragua with other returning Conservative exiles to share in the spoils. Riding the Nicaraguan railroad from Corinto, the party was attacked by a mob when the train stopped in Liberal León, and Sussman was injured in a furious shoot-out between the train's passengers and León's angry citizens.[49]

The *New Orleans Daily Picayune* claimed that the defeated Madriz profited more in defeat than he had as Zelaya's successor. With the aid of H. Nathan Secrest, an American operator of a Nicaraguan rubber plantation, the newspaper alleged, the fleeing president counterfeited 15,000,000 five-peso notes and dumped them in Guatemala for $2,000,000. Anticipating that Estrada would discover the scheme and ultimately recall the notes, the newspaper charged that Madriz "lived high" for several weeks and then sent Secrest to the States with the plates to counterfeit more money. Alerted U.S. Treasury agents arrested the American conspirator as he headed for Chicago to finish the job.[50] There is no corroborating evidence for this story, which seems inconsistent with Madriz's character. One probable explanation is that Secrest merely wished to transfer blame to someone already in U.S. disfavor.

Soon after Madriz's departure Nicaragua's political and economic fortunes tumbled. For four months in 1912, commerce in the populous western districts practically ceased. Adolfo Díaz, former secretary of the La Luz and Los Angeles Mining Company (a benefactor as well as supporter of the Estrada revolt) and after May 1911 president of the republic, fell out with his generals. In the summer of 1912, Secretary of War Luis Mena revolted.[51] For a few weeks the renewed war appeared as savage as the conflict that had erupted against Zelaya; in León the rebels attacked a government garrison and massacred five hundred soldiers, among them two Americans, Phil Craven and Harvey Dodd, a member of the Mississippi bar who had joined Estrada and stayed on after Estrada fled the country.

This time the U.S. government, busy with financial schemes for Nicaragua's "rehabilitation," resolved to rid the government of Zelaya's followers, real and putative. It dispatched 1,100 marines and bluejackets who marched along the Nicaraguan railroad toward the interior and routed all of Díaz's enemies. U.S. officials then honored the Nicaraguan executive in a dignified reception aboard the U.S.S. *California*. The massive intervention of 1912 appeared to confirm Zelaya's stridently critical charge, which he had published in Spain in his 1910 manifesto *La revolución de Nicaragua*, that the U.S. government had ousted him because he had allegedly harassed property owners in eastern Nicaragua. The Department of State officially denounced the tract, and Zelaya dropped out of the news for several years. But in 1913 he dramatically returned from Europe to New York City. Interviewed at the Waldorf Astoria Hotel, he blamed Nicaragua's fall into the clutches of U.S. capital on wily entrepreneurs who wanted extravagant concessions in violation of the republic's constitution and who had persuaded Estrada Cabrera of Guatemala to finance the Bluefields revolt.[52]

The truth was a bit more complicated. As a true believer in the benevolence of "dollar diplomacy," Secretary of State Knox had indeed promoted some discreditable financial schemes to rid Nicaragua of its European creditors and substitute a "Dominican-style" protectorate with compliant Nicaraguan politicians and American customs collectors. The Senate was suspicious of such arrangements and three times defeated a treaty establishing a Nicaraguan customs receivership. Yet through a more circumspect route the big New York banking houses eventually entered the country; their interests, predicated on order, stability, and a healthy system of collection of import duties, did not always square with the "duty-free" thinking of the smaller U.S. entrepreneurs on the Caribbean coast.[53]

When a Democratic administration swept to victory in 1912 because of a divided Republican vote, the new president, Woodrow Wilson, and his secretary of state, William Jennings Bryan, were outspoken critics of dollar diplomacy. Their renunciation of Zelaya's tormentors indicated no sympathy for the dictator, however. He was, in fact, roused from his bed at

Washington Valentine's New York apartment and threatened with extradition under a 1905 U.S.-Nicaraguan treaty for the deaths of two political enemies in Masaya in 1901. The intimidation was effective. Zelaya was never sent back to stand trial, but thereafter he kept quiet about Nicaraguan affairs and was no longer an embarrassment to either Washington or its political surrogates in Managua. Impoverished and obscure, he died in Valentine's apartment in 1919.[54]

While U.S. presidents could rid Nicaragua of leaders like Zelaya and Madriz, their emissaries showed poor judgment in identifying successors with the talent or capacity to govern in the best interests of Nicaragua. Juan Estrada, Adolpho Díaz, and Emiliano Chamorro proved unable to manage Nicaraguan society as well as Zelaya had done. Only Chamorro, who had close ties to Nicaragua's military, demonstrated qualities of leadership, but he used force or the threat of force to construct a political consensus. As the U.S. government would ultimately learn, *keeping* a surrogate in power in Central America was often as problematical as *putting* him in power.

5

The Campaign for Honduras

In the spring of 1909, just as the Estrada rebellion against Zelaya was hatching in Bluefields, "General" Lee Christmas, on leave in New Orleans, received a letter from a clerk for the Southern Express Company in Mobile. The clerk sought "a place" under the command of the famous Christmas. "I know life down in your country is not a bed of roses and am willing to take a chance and can assure you that I am not a 'quitter,'" wrote this latest applicant to Christmas's nonexistent army. He added: "Don't think for a minute that I have been reading a lot of fairy tales."[1] Christmas must have been amused at this naive volunteer for a cause the writer could have only dimly perceived, but the letter was just one example of the Christmas mystique in an era of vanishing folk heroes.

The truth was, in the spring of 1909, Christmas had apparently disappeared into obscurity in Estrada Cabrera's service. The Guatemalan position, however, provided an invaluable link to Christmas's benefactor, Manuel Bonilla, who had been exiled to a farm on Stann's Creek in British Honduras. The Honduran government knew of Bonilla's connection to Estrada Cabrera and fumed about the threat to its security. In 1908 President Miguel Dávila officially condemned the entire U.S. consular corps in La Ceiba for its intercession between government troops and a rebellious faction in the town. The following year he announced that Estrada Cabrera and the deposed Bonilla had plotted an invasion of the north coast, but that the assault had been frustrated by the timely seizure of rebel chiefs in Amapala, Nacâome, Puerto Cortés, and San Pedro Sula.[2]

The nervous Dávila, uneasy over the political troubles of his benefactor Zelaya, faced yet another dilemma. Honduras, more than its sister isthmian republics, labored under the burden of an enormous public debt—$100 million. Dishonest Honduran and European officials and businessmen had pilfered much of this sum. The moneys that did reach Honduras were squandered on the construction of the north-south transcontinental railroad through the rugged Honduran north. By 1910 just over one hundred miles of railroad existed in the entire republic: the much-touted but never completed National Railway, which ran from Puerto Cortés to Pimienta, fifty-six miles inland; and the lines constructed by the banana companies on the north coast to connect their plantations with the wharves at Tela, Puerto Cortés, La Ceiba, and other coastal towns. Of the latter the most impressive was the forty-five-mile network built by the Vaccaros, which terminated in a modern 810-foot wharf of creosoted wood at La Ceiba. In June 1910 the *Bulletin of the Pan American Union* proudly announced that work had begun on Samuel Zemurray's railroad from Veracruz, twenty-five miles west of Puerto Cortés. Though only thirty miles long, the Zemurray line would traverse a "region unsurpassed in fertility for the cultivation of fruits and cotton."[3] Sam "the Banana Man" had come a long way since the days when he peddled "ripes" out of Mobile.

As the U.S. government sought to establish a Pax Americana on the isthmus, other tropical entrepreneurs grew ambitious in light of the privileged and protected opportunities available. From the turn of the century, already financially secure in his isthmian ventures, Washington Valentine had played the role of broker in Honduran politics. Sensing the rising animosity of the new imperial masters of the "American Mediterranean" to the British economic presence in the republic, Valentine had campaigned for the House of Morgan as the creditor of

Honduras. The plan was engagingly simple: he would take on the monumental task of completing the National Railway and refurbishing the dilapidated wharf at Puerto Cortés; U.S. financiers would provide a $30 million loan to clear the republic's debt to British banks. For a while, Valentine even convinced the State Department (and Zelaya) that he could "broker" a peace in the war-torn isthmus.[4]

Yet factious Honduran politicians retained some sense of national pride. It soon became clear, at least to a few of its more prominent statesmen, that there was little gain in exchanging one financial master for another. The British drove a hard bargain and were represented in the region by a veteran diplomat, Sir Lionel Carden, but their willingness to dispatch gunboats to collect their debts had waned. The Americans, by contrast, could almost certainly be expected to police Honduras more closely if the republic were in arrears to J.P. Morgan. A financial protectorate complete with U.S. customs collectors and a budget closely scrutinized in Washington, would inevitably accompany the U.S. plan for "saving" Honduras. Most assuredly, Morgan and his associates would insist on prompt and full collection of import duties, inasmuch as these constituted (as in the Dominican Republic) the larger portion of government revenues. And that would mean higher costs for the banana companies of the north coast because they had to import almost everything that they used except the Honduran laborers who hacked the banana stalks from the trees. The success of the Morgan plan meant a heavier overhead for Zemurray unless he acted quickly to get his friend Bonilla back in office in Tegucigalpa.[5]

The enterprising and resourceful investigator who seeks to entwine Zemurray in the plot to overthrow the fidgety Dávila and install in his place the burly "Manolo" Bonilla must make his case on motive, inference, circumstance, some evidence, and common sense. These he will find in abundance. The Banana Man never held the "smoking gun"; he bought the guns. According to legend and his devoted daughter, the Central American anthropologist and archaeologist Doris Zemurray Stone, Sam left no written evidence of his revolutionary plotting in the old days. Indeed, he reportedly never had a secretary. Even more frustrating for the investigator, Zemurray is always referred to in the random Bonilla letters among the Hermann Deutsch-Lee Christmas correspondence at Tulane University as "El Amigo" (the friend).

Bonilla might have spent his remaining years in the British Honduran backland had not Christmas and "El Amigo" roused him to action. In 1909 Christmas held a lofty position in Estrada Cabrera's Guatemala; in March he attended a banquet hosted by the president of the republic to honor visiting officers of the U.S. Pacific Squadron. And late in that year Bonilla wrote a congratulatory letter indicating that the Honduran business did not look promising for their return: "Though with a small salary, I am glad to hear that you have found an occupation which gives you daily bread; in these days that is not a small matter, and your talents will soon win you a raise in salary. I do not think there will be a change in the situation in Honduras, unless I am the one who promotes it. So strong is my conviction of this, that I am preparing to leave and till the soil of a small property which I bought a few days ago near Stann Crick." Then, obviously enticed by something Christmas had written, Bonilla added: "This, however, does not bar me from esteeming your offer." Christmas's "countrymen" were going to kick out Zelaya, Bonilla had heard.[6] In that event, Bonilla had to believe that Zelaya's protégé Dávila in Tegucigalpa could not survive.

Rumors out of Honduras spoke of a "crazed" Dávila alarmed that every gesture of defiance was a plot to unseat him. In December 1909 an upstart collection of troublemakers shot up the town of Tortuga; though they in no way threatened the government, Dávila declared martial law. Two prominent pro-Bonilla supporters, the Dávadi brothers, surfaced in New Orleans with high praise for Manuel's enlightened rule from 1903 to 1907, a clear indication to the *Daily Picayune* that another revolt was in the offing. Back in Honduras Dávila became even more estranged from his previously compliant congress. He began inviting prominent legislators to the presidential palace for sensible discussions and finished the sessions in vituperative outbursts.[7]

The plot against Dávila was hardly comparable to the machinations of European statecraft, but the Honduras of 1910 was nearing the end of a century of searching for order, stability, prosperity, and nationhood. Vulnerable as feeble Honduras was to every rumor of revolutionary shenanigans in British Honduras or New Orleans and the casual denigrations of its status by the dollar diplomats of President Taft's administration, it could occasionally manifest defiance. When the erratic Dávila heard that a new U.S. minister was arriving at Amapala, the republic's southern port, he ordered the commandant, the fiery José Valladares, to greet him. General Valladares, who had reportedly named his dog "Taft," refused, and the president sheepishly persuaded some local German businessmen to perform the honor.[8]

Christmas had evidently decided that times were propitious for a change of employment and habitat. In January 1910 he abruptly resigned his position of locomotive engineer on the Guatemalan national railroad. "Your services have been most satisfactory," said the company, "and we wish you every success in whatever direction you may seek other employment."[9] Christmas's inquiries of late 1909 and early 1910, coupled with Zelaya's abrupt fall in Nicaragua, had obviously alerted Bonilla to the possibility of another presidential term in Tegucigalpa. His earlier caution had by spring 1910 noticeably altered. "My silence toward you," he wrote Christmas, "is due to the fact that there is nothing definite regarding the revolutionary movement into Honduras. All is prepared—the men are ready and their spirits elevated. The government is unsuspecting and in political, military and economic bankruptcy—the opportunity is propitious; nonetheless I can do nothing to promote the fall of *that* government. Today I am in need of the indispensable *elements*. . . . Without the decided assistance of El Amigo, I do not rise in arms against Gen'l Dávila."[10]

Two weeks later, however, another letter from Bonilla named Christmas to a prominent post in the rebel army "in line with your valor and military enthusiasm." Still, he hesitated: "I do not see clearly how to make the revolution. You will know that without rifles one cannot make war, and rifles I have not got."[11] All the rumors of Bonilla's money to buy guns were "lies." He did not have 100,000 pesos, Bonilla swore: "I have no funds." Only El Amigo could make the revolution succeed, so it was up to him "to proceed when he thinks advisable." Inexplicably, as summer approached, the tone of Bonilla's correspondence grew more confident. He indicated that if El Amigo did not "resolve the issue," then Manuel himself and his former *general de brigada*, Christmas, must surely act. Bonilla grew uneasy over El Amigo's hesitation and began looking elsewhere (he did not indicate to Christmas the names of his alternative sources) for "that which we need." And he became more assertive—"you must not move unless I tell you to do so"—resolving that if the present undertaking were a *fracaso* (a flop), he would retire from public life and sever his "political relations with friends and partisans."[12] On June 23 Bonilla wrote Christmas in despair that he was "losing hope [of aid] from El Amigo" who "will give us nothing." Bonilla had borrowed heavily from Theodore Rössner's German firm to buy his small ranch in British Honduras, and he had a "small fund created by friends for the revolution, but otherwise very little."[13]

But Zemurray had apparently not abandoned the project. In the week before Bonilla wrote the plaintive note complaining of El Amigo's lack of "executive resolution," Christmas had arrived in Puerto Barrios "amply provided with funds" and "well grounded." The U.S. consul, dutifully interviewing Central America's most illustrious soldier of fortune, had Christmas's solemn promise that "he had forever given up being a . . . schemer, filibuster, or politician," but the consul rightly surmised that he was plotting to reinstall Bonilla in Tegucigalpa. On June 30 Bonilla dispatched a hasty message to his *general de brigada* saying that the situation looked favorable for a revolution. A telegram had arrived two days before stating that the guns would be ready on June 30, but Bonilla was not prepared to move or to believe anything until he received those weapons.[14]

Veterans of the Nicaraguan war, lured by rumors of another Honduran fracas, were already stumbling into Guatemala and the isolated coves of British Honduras. "Machine-gun" Molony had quit his job in New Orleans in 1909 to join the Estrada revolt after receiving a note from "Jew Sam" Dreben: "I'm on the hike to Nicaragua. . . . How about it, kid? Want to come along and sit in?" Molony arrived in Belize with Dreben's "card of introduction." Back in Greytown the card had gotten Molony $250 in gold and a steamer ticket to New Orleans. Then he sailed aboard a banana boat for Belize. There he met Bonilla, who spoke little English, but knew enough to ascertain Molony's ability to handle a machine gun. Before long Molony was aboard the *Centinella* (one of three vessels—the other two were the *Brittanic* and the *Emma*—obtained for the revolutionary cause), shaking hands with Christmas.[15]

The plan called for a rendezvous at Glover's Reef, where the arms were divided among the three vessels of the revolutionary armada and a sleek Indian *goleta* that carried a hundred rifles and ammunition for delivery to the conspirators at Tela. Already Bonilla had disturbing reports that Dávila was reinforcing the puny garrisons at Trujillo and La Ceiba. At this moment his principal concern was the Honduran "navy," consisting of the gunboat *Tatumbla*. If the conspirators failed to take Puerto Cortés, then they could expect the *Tatumbla* to chase them back toward Belize and a predictably severe reception from His Majesty's authorities for violating British Honduran neutrality.[16]

The plan might have worked except for a premature call to arms by Bonilla partisan General Ramón Octavio Marín in Puerto Cortés. On July 22, just as the first shipments of arms were arriving off Tela, the general drank himself into a fighting frenzy, roused his comrades, and attacked the local government garrison. In the melee Marín was killed, which would have been little loss to the cause except for the fact that he carried with him plans for the revolt and letters from Bonilla incriminating almost two hundred supporters at Omoa, La Ceiba, and San Pedro Sula.[17]

Consequently, when the rebel ships arrived off Puerto Cortés, they encountered unexpectedly heavy resistance. The *Tatumbla*, ordinarily no match in speed for the lighter vessels of

Bonilla's force, gave chase and in the windless bay caught up with and threatened to sink the fleeing *Centinella*, which possessed no auxiliary power. Just as the *Tatumbla*'s gun began to find the range, the gasoline-powered oyster lugger *Emma*, carrying *el jefe*, appeared in time to tow the endangered ship farther from shore. Christmas and Molony, sailing on the *Centinella*, were still in the mood for a fight, so Christmas suggested a stopover at Utila, one of the Bay Islands off the Honduran coast, where an isolated unit of Dávila supporters was quickly overpowered.[18]

The Americans were prepared for another assault on Puerto Cortés, but word came from Manuel that the expedition had encountered unexpected trouble. He had a report that a British warship—H.M.S. *Brilliant*—had given chase to arrest these *filibusteros* for violating the neutrality of British Honduras. Bonilla called a hasty council of war and decided that the most prudent course lay in surrendering their persons and arms to the benevolent jurisdiction of Estrada Cabrera. When the conquerors of Utila—Christmas and Molony; Emile Fremont, a native Frenchman hailing now from Mobile; LeMann Elliott, a Mississippian; and, among others, Hans Olsen, Olaf Hanson, and Ole Oleson of presumably Scandinavian background but residents of Gulfport, Mississippi—got the word about scrapping the expedition, they were disappointed. Christmas's force, augmented by defecting government troops on Utila, had not lost its spirit for a set-to with the Dávila partisans on the mainland. Molony's machine guns were in perfect working order, and the *Tatumbla*, having pursued the *Centinella* part way to Utila, had headed back to the sanctuary of the Puerto Cortés harbor.

Christmas and Molony held a hasty strategy meeting of their own and elected to continue the row. After all, the message from Bonilla had a tentative flavor, and a strike by the *Centinella*'s machine guns might turn retreat into victory. Christmas bore a personal excuse for waging battle: General Pedro Díaz, an obscenely plump Dávila official known locally as the "Butcher" for his practice of hanging prisoners by their thumbs, had sworn to deal with Christmas and his American cronies. Christmas characteristically accepted this as a challenge and had made it known along the coast that when the Manuelistas took La Ceiba he would hang Díaz. As the situation developed, Christmas decided to bypass the *Tatumbla's* cannon in Puerto Cortés and instead landed his men at Pedro Pentada, about seven miles from La Ceiba. Word of the approaching rebels sent frightened civilians into hiding in the consulates. General Díaz, just as determined as Christmas for a showdown, led his garrison of two hundred troops out to Pedro Pentada. There, with Molony's machine guns raking the coast from barges anchored off shore, the two armies shot it out in a brief engagement that was properly described as a draw.[19]

The standoff with Díaz at Pedro Pentada might just as well have been a defeat, because Christmas could not move swiftly into La Ceiba and frighten the enemy into surrendering or scurrying into the interior. In the meantime he learned that a British warship, H.M.S. *Scylla*, had dropped anchor in La Ceiba, which meant that its captain, obedient to the informal tradition of naval patrol along the tropical coast, had declared the town "off limits" to fighting. Christmas had no spunk to challenge British authority, so he organized a noisy withdrawal to the vessels off shore and gloriously sailed for Three Corners as Molony's machine gunners raked the beach in clattering response to the cursing government troops ashore.

When Christmas and Bonilla reunited, Bonilla was disheartened but not overly despondent, mainly because he knew that El Amigo had no other Honduran *político* who, once installed in power, would be so understanding about the banana men's problems in doing business in Honduras. With $3,000 Bonilla paid the wages of his revolutionary recruits and dispatched them to New Orleans. Then in a few days, accompanied by Christmas and several other North Americans in his command, Bonilla sailed into Puerto Barrios, Guatemala, and "surrendered." Shortly, Bonilla and Christmas were speeding to Guatemala City on a train.[20]

The invasion had produced surprisingly few casualties. In Puerto Cortés two Italians, frightened by General Marín's premature launching of the rebellion, had run from town and been shot by government guards who mistook them for rebels. The remainder of the small Italian community, of course, was immediately endangered and probably saved from vengeful government troops only by the intercession of the town doctor. In San Pedro Sula the consul reported schoolchildren attending rallies (instigated, he wrote, by Policarpo Bonilla) where speakers exhorted them to learn how to fight Yankees. In a few weeks Honduras resumed its usual postrevolutionary tranquillity, and the republic's president, secure in Tegucigalpa and assured that his enemy remained confined in the Guatemalan capital, spoke in reconciliatory tones. In New Orleans, where the defeated Manuelistas had sought refuge, Dávila's consul announced: "No effort will be made to punish Bonilla and Christmas, as we want peace and not bloodshed. It is not likely that [they] will return to Honduras."[21]

The consul had no basis for such optimism. Zemurray would unlikely stop his intrigues until the effective exercise of power in Honduras was in the hands of a leader or faction sympathetic to his banana business. His chosen comprador leader, Bonilla, was eager to exercise power but needed the wealth and resources of his benefactor. Christmas, Molony, and scores of other hired guns were willing to seek glory, adventure, fame, and possible wealth in the service of the banana men and the isthmian compradores. Since isthmian political power often came from bullets rather than ballots, more experienced U.S. and other foreign officials and businessmen expected a renewal of the violence.

In Tegucigalpa it was widely acknowledged that the rebels would soon try again. No one sensed the predicament of the Honduran government more acutely than the presumably mad Miguel Dávila. On every front—even among his Liberal cronies—the harassed Honduran leader had liabilities that foretold his downfall. Zelaya's abrupt departure had not only deprived Dávila of the Nicaraguan's moral support; it also denied him the backing of a reliable military establishment, one that three years earlier had crushed his enemies in the south and had triumphantly installed him in the Honduran presidency. The prospect of a huge loan from Wall Street, solicited at the behest of Taft's dollar diplomats, would merely transfer the republic's considerable debt from British to American control and endanger Dávila's hold on power. He has no chance, the *Daily Picayune* jubilantly observed, when Bonilla's invaders scurried back to Guatemala in August 1910. If he signed a loan treaty with the U.S. financiers, Policarpo Bonilla and his Liberal allies would turn against him; if he rejected the Morgan loan, then Manuel Bonilla would overturn him. Bonilla viewed the overwhelming defeat of the treaty in Honduras as a signal to move against a publicly weakened Dávila.[22]

Along the north coast, where Manuel Bonilla's invasion had aroused the banana towns from their summer torpor, there was continual talk about the inevitable return of "Manolo" and his North American friends. On the Pacific coast, in contrast, public agitation over Wall Street's maneuvering in the republic's financial affairs galvanized anti-American elements. In Amapala the mercurial General Valladares proclaimed a holy war against the foreign devil in their midst. In October, anticipating a visit from a German ship to protect its nationals, the commander of a U.S. gunboat landed a squad of bluejackets "to maintain order." The outspokenly bellicose Valladares repaired to the capital for a discreet conference with the president. Upon his return he confidently announced that President Dávila was "weak and unworthy" and the stooge of foreign interests. When one of his men, doubtless inspired by the general's own tirades against the foreign menace, shot an American telegrapher in the foot, the incensed U.S. gunboat commander compelled Valladares to surrender his arms and stashed them aboard a German steamer in the port.[23]

The real menace to Honduran peace—and to President Dávila—in the fall of 1910 was a "guest" of Estrada Cabrera in Guatemala City. In the wars against Zelaya and in the conspiracy against Zelaya's disciple in Tegucigalpa, the cunning Estrada Cabrera had employed proxies. Manuel Bonilla and Christmas were probably the ablest political and military combination the Guatemalan president could have chosen to support a little "revoluting" in Honduras. But their reputations for political mischief also made them an embarrassment. Although Estrada Cabrera considered Bonilla a friend and political ally, his wish to see Bonilla wearing the presidential sash diminished noticeably when aligned against the Guatemalan's calculated policy of doing nothing to offend the United States.

Since their abrupt return from the summer revolutionary outing, Bonilla and Christmas had become too visible in their Guatemalan "captivity." Once before, when the two had fled Honduras in 1908, Bonilla had exiled himself in the wilds of British Honduras, and Christmas had signed on with Estrada Cabrera's secret service and then taken up his old profession on the national railroad. This time, with Zemurray's money and promises and Estrada Cabrera's protection, the two busied themselves with recruiting American soldiers of fortune, railroad employees, and tropical tramps for another expedition. Before long, everyone in the Guatemalan capital knew of their doings. The U.S. minister dutifully relayed his government's displeasure about revolutions in the isthmus and their pernicious effect on the region's political tranquillity.[24]

Thus, Estrada Cabrera had a major problem. He was meeting with Bonilla regularly (every day, according to the U.S. minister), and it may be assumed that they did not spend their time discussing Mayan antiquities. Yet the prospect of U.S. censure for harboring (and supporting) Honduran rebels concerned him, because a violation of Guatemalan neutrality (as if *any* Central American government could be neutral in the isthmus's fratricidal wars) might very well bring down on him the wrath of Washington. To complicate matters, President Taft's inquisitive and officious dollar diplomats were already devising schemes to "liberate" Guatemala from the clutches of British finance, and the calculating Estrada Cabrera was not disposed to provide them with an excuse to install in his country the kind of "benevolent" overlordship they were enthusiastically erecting in Nicaragua. To get the Yankees off his back, then, Estrada Cabrera contrived another of his charades: in or-

The founders and operators of the Vaccaro Fruit Company. Starting from the top and moving clockwise: Joseph Vaccaro, Sr., Lucca Vaccaro, Salvador D'Antoni, and Felix P. Vaccaro.

Samuel Zemurray, founder of Cuyamel Fruit Company and president of United Fruit Company. Courtesy of the Middle American Research Institute, Tulane University.

Unless otherwise indicated, all photos are courtesy of the Deutsch Collection, Rare Books and Manuscripts, Tulane University, New Orleans, Louisiana.

Guatemalen president Manuel Estrada Cabrera, about 1910. Courtesy of the Central American Political Ephemeral Collection, Latin American Library, Tulane University Library.

General Don Manuel Bonilla, constitutional president of Honduras, died on March 21, 1913.

Lee Christmas
in military field attire.

Samuel Zemurray's
yacht, *The Hornet*,
used in the 1910
revolution in
Honduras.

Group picture in 1914. Rear row from the left: T.J. McLaurie, Jack Gray, Frank Hershey. Front row from the left: Lee Christmas, Mexican Consul Portio.

In the dark suit, Jew Sam Drebon, behind him Tracy Richardson; the heavy man in the white suit is Pedro Diaz; next to him in uniform with a rifle, Lee Christmas.

Troops on display. The second horseman from the left is Lee Christmas in dress uniform.

"The Victors!" A group of manuelistas, with captured Krupp guns and machine guns after the battle of La Ceiba. The bareheaded Americano in the white shirt is Col. Guy R. Molony.

Aboard a U.S. warship. The center figure is a U.S. naval officer; to the right is Manuel Bonnila.

Lee Christmas at Puerto Barrios shortly before his health turned bad.
Circa 1920.

Salvador D'Antoni
after the heyday of the
filibustering.

Lee Christmas at the height of his career, after the second inauguration of Manuel Bonilla as President of Honduras. In this uniform he was buried, in New Orleans, when he died there more than a quarter century after he had sent to Paris from Tegucigalpa for an outfit that should be in keeping with this newly won magnificence.

der to persuade Washington that he was a stern but progressive ruler who sincerely wanted peace for Central America, to demonstrate that he would preserve Guatemalan neutrality and fulfill the isthmian treaties of 1907, he expelled Bonilla and Christmas to New Orleans.[25]

Although federal agents and Dávila's consul monitored his daily activities in New Orleans, Bonilla acquired the *Hornet* for his naval invasion. Constructed in 1890 by Harlan & Hollingsworth of Wilmington, Delaware, the ship was 160 feet in length, had a twenty-four-foot beam, and, most important for the Honduran plotters, could attain a speed of fifteen knots. In 1898 the U.S. government had requisitioned it for the war against Spain. With three other ships the *Hornet* had taken on nine Spanish gunboats in a naval battle off Manzanillo; disabled by a shell from a Spanish shore battery, it had had to be towed from the battle. After the war the Navy had refurbished the vessel, its rapid fire guns intact, for ferrying officers on inspection cruises. In 1909 the government sold it for $5,100. Before long, despite the vigorous protest of Madriz's consul in New Orleans, it was running guns to rebels in Bluefields. In early December the Honduran legation in Washington officially informed the Department of State that Bonilla had purchased the *Hornet* for a strike on the north shore and that the ship was ready to depart for a rendezvous on the Guatemalan coast. There it would take on arms and ammunition and join the *Centinella*, veteran of the summer raid, lazily masquerading as a fishing vessel off Livingston, Guatemala.[26]

During the next few weeks the Honduran government frantically prepared for the inevitable. At Puerto Cortés soldiers dug trenches and constructed mounts for twelve Maxim machine guns, and Dávila's agents stationed themselves every evening around the local hotel to keep watch on its foreign guests. Each steamer from New Orleans brought someone with a different version of when the attack would come. A *New York Herald* reporter arrived with a tale of "hobnobbing" with Christmas and Bonilla in the dives of the Crescent City; wearied of waiting, he had decided to sail for the Honduran coast ahead of the expedition.[27]

Elsewhere there was military and diplomatic activity designed to forestall Bonilla. The Navy Department, police force of the banana ports on the north Honduran coast, dispatched the *Tacoma* with its menacing guns and authoritative presence to Puerto Cortés. Not to be outdone, the secretary of state pressed upon the vacillating Honduran minister, Juan Paredes, the latest version of a financial treaty that would have transformed Honduras into a U.S. protectorate and made Bonilla's plotting to regain power in Tegucigalpa a profitless endeavor.[28]

Meanwhile, politely denying any connection with the *Hornet*, Bonilla and Christmas provisioned it with food, two hundred tons of coal, and twenty adventurous men captained by Charley Johnson, former gunrunner for the Estrada rebellion in Nicaragua. On December 20, as the harassed Paredes was rejecting Knox's treaty, the *Hornet*, under the close scrutiny of federal inspectors, suddenly received Washington's permission to depart—over the vigorous protest of the Honduran government. Two days later, with a U.S. inspector on board, it cast off Algiers Point.[29]

Christmas and Bonilla were not among its passengers. Nor were Guy Molony, who had abruptly given up his latest "steady work" for this adventure, and Florian Dávadi, Bonilla's Honduran compatriot. Trailed by U.S. Treasury agents, they had discreetly remained in New Orleans, and in the evening after the *Hornet*'s much publicized sailing they repaired to a fashionable bordello operated by Madam May Evans in the city's famed Storyville district. There, with Treasury agents posted outside, they carried on in a suitably revelrous manner until two o'clock the next morning, at which point one of the government men left his station for a nearby phone booth. "It's nothing but a drunken brawl in the District," he reported to his chief, then hung up and went home to bed.[30]

Informed that they were no longer under surveillance, Christmas roared: "Well, compadre, this is the first time I've ever heard of anybody going from a whorehouse to a White House. Let's be on our way!"[31] As the ladies watched admiringly from windows, the men raced away in cars and headed for Bayou St. John, where Zemurray's forty-two-foot yacht waited. Soon they were speeding across Lake Pontchartrain, passing through the Rigolets into Mississippi Sound. At the rendezvous on Ship Island, El Amigo met them, dressed in the garb of a deckhand. Fearful of patrolling Coast Guard vessels, they could not sleep after their frantic escape from New Orleans, so Zemurray cooked them a sumptuous meal. At dawn on December 24 Zemurray took the yacht across the sound to Pass Christian for more supplies, leaving the rebellious foursome playing poker on a case of thirty rifles. Bonilla won big. When Zemurray got back, the *Hornet* had already arrived, and they transferred to it the cases of rifles, 3,000 rounds of ammunition, and a machine gun for Molony. In the bracing winter gusts of the Gulf breeze, the Americans worked methodically. Christmas puffed on one of his favorite tropical stogies. Bonilla shivered in the December wind until Zemurray noticed his champion was suffering, took off his coat, and gave it to the Honduran. "I've shot the roll on you," said El Amigo, "and I might as well shoot the coat, too."[32]

Soon they were heading across the broad expanse of the Gulf. The *Centinella* and the *Emma*, the gasoline-powered launch that had served as Bonilla's command vessel in the aborted invasion the preceding summer, had already taken on arms, ammunition, and forty-five Hondurans in Livingston, Guatemala. The two ships had sailed in broad daylight, under the benevolent gaze of Estrada Cabrera's customs agents and an alert U.S. consul, for Manabique Point. A few days later, the consul reported, another two dozen Honduran "strangers" had slipped into town, obviously waiting for the *Hornet.*[33]

Dávila's garrisons in Puerto Cortés and La Ceiba were preparing frantically for this second invasion of the north coast in less than six months. Their sole naval vessel was the *Tatumbla*, which had engaged Bonilla's ships in the summer, but it had so deteriorated that it was now a source of amusement and ridicule from the American colony in Puerto Cortés. Deep in its hold Honduran natives desperately bailed water; barnacles as large as oysters clung to its rusting bottom. In the previous engagement with Bonilla's flotilla, the *Daily Picayune* sarcastically reported, the *Tatumbla* had shelled four schooners with its one-pounder forward gun and hit nothing but water; this time if it left the pier it would doubtless sink.[34]

The revolt erupted unexpectedly in the interior when an invasion of Honduran exiles from El Salvador managed to overpower Dávila's depleted border garrisons. Half the government's troops, it was reported, deserted. In the meantime, Estrada Cabrera lost no time in dispatching an army to the isolated Guatemalan frontier, where, the dictator announced, it would dutifully "enforce neutrality." On December 29, the day Bonilla's followers crossed over from El Salvador, Honduran refugees spotted the *Hornet* and her sister ships at Manabique Point. Soon Bonilla, Christmas, Molony, and his "crew of crack shots" were sailing gloriously for the Bay Islands.[35]

In desperation Dávila ordered $55,000 in silver bars moved from Puerto Cortés—more vulnerable than its sister coastal towns to a sea invasion—to La Ceiba. In anticipation that the invaders would converge on Puerto Cortés, U.S. and British warships sailed for that port, their captains guided by the Anglo-American maritime policy of preserving their superiors' prescriptions for "order" in the disorderly tropics.

Bonilla and Christmas, anticipating just such a move, abruptly altered their grand war plan and focused their immediate attention on two of the Bay Islands—Roatán and Utila—which were weakly defended and consequently vulnerable. On the last day of 1910 Bonilla's squadron approached Roatán. President Dávila's skeletal force of defenders fired exactly one shot at the invaders, which fell harmlessly into the sea. The "governor" of the island, in no way disposed to wage a pitched battle against Bonilla and his American machine gunners, frantically appealed to the U.S. consul, O.L. Hardgrave, to intercede. The surrendering Dávila official asked only that his life be spared. Bonilla graciously agreed. Soon some seventy-five to one hundred "well-armed" rebels were swarming ashore, Christmas and his "husky" American compatriots among them. "I don't know if I done [sic] the right thing in this affair," the consul reported to his superiors, explaining his interference. "My only excuse if in the wrong is that it perhaps saved life and bloodshed."[36]

Flushed with victory, the invaders settled in on Roatán and made preparations for a New Year's Eve party. Christmas and Molony decided to celebrate by sailing over to Utila and capturing that island in the dead of the night. The *comandante* of Utila, whose command was as grossly undermanned as his colleague's on Roatán, had placed the island under martial law and then decided to celebrate the New Year's arrival by retiring to his bed. Thus Christmas and Molony were able to steal into the harbor virtually unnoticed. It was a heady New Year's frolic for Christmas, as frivolous as any he had celebrated with his cronies back in New Orleans. The supreme triumph of the celebration came with the brawny American dragging the *comandante* of Utila from his bed, kicking him outside, and forcing the humiliated man, still in his underclothing, to yell "Viva Bonilla."[37]

By now, of course, the captains of the U.S. vessels in these waters—the *Tacoma* and *Marietta*—had seemingly indisputable evidence that the *Hornet* was engaging in revolutionary activity and thus violating U.S. neutrality laws. When Christmas and Molony returned with the *Centinella* from their shindig on Utila, a gloomy Bonilla met them. The commander of the *Tacoma* had brought the authority of his menacing guns into the port and (in what was described as a "row") had demanded proof of the *Hornet*'s status; further, he "had laid down the law to Bonilla as to fighting in Puerto Cortés." There would be no firing on the town, declared the U.S. officer. This remark prompted Manuel, who understood little English, to retort in his most belligerent Spanish: "If I had the force the States has I would tell you what I think." When Christmas returned he offered to go aboard the *Tacoma* and clear up the misunderstanding, but Bonilla forbade it, saying the Americans might try to "kidnap" his senior officer.[38]

The truth of the matter was that the U.S. commander had become uncertain about what to do in these circumstances. Rumors were about that if Dávila's minister in Washington signed the financial treaty, the U.S. gunboats would stop the rebellion by seizing Bonilla's flagship. Bonilla had anticipated this brouhaha over the *Hornet*'s status, so after bringing it into Roatán harbor, the captain of the vessel—holding the power of attorney from Joseph Beers, the ship's owner—had sold the *Hornet* to Florian Dávadi for $40,000—$1.00 down and a $39,999 mortgage. The parties signed the necessary papers in the presence of the local U.S. consul.[39]

For the time being, at least, Bonilla and the *Hornet* had escaped the net cast by the hovering U.S. warships. The *Tacoma* remained in Roatán harbor, its captain monitoring the anchored *Hornet*. For a week Bonilla and his invaders made no threatening gestures toward the coast. But the delay was providing time for Bonilla's enemy in Tegucigalpa to reinforce his garrisons in the northern towns. Bonilla decided to attack. An assault on Puerto Cortés was out of the question, given the severe warning from the *Tacoma*'s captain which forbade firing on the town. There had been no similar prohibition about fighting in Trujillo, however, and the day after the *Tacoma* raised anchor and sped away for Puerto Cortés, Bonilla ordered the seizure of Trujillo. He brought the *Hornet* within view of the town's guns early on the morning of January 9, 1911. Characteristically, Bonilla wanted to enter the harbor with the *Hornet*'s guns blazing away at the government *cuartel*, but his Honduran officers politely informed him that they would not accompany him on such a foolhardy enterprise. After a while he relented, accepting the timely advice of Christmas that the *Hornet* should sail about in a provocative fashion, drawing the fire of the Krupp artillery piece that protected the town and permitting Christmas and Ed McLaurie, another railroader turned revolutionary, to land two groups on the shore and advance on the town. To this impromptu tactic Bonilla readily agreed, remaining aboard the *Hornet* and personally tugging on the whistle rope each time one of the enemy's shells plopped harmlessly into the sea. By the time Trujillo's defenders realized that they were being flanked, Christmas, McLaurie, and their followers had swept into town. Dávila's soldiers were soon exchanging their red-and-white armbands for the blue-and-white colors of Bonilla's forces.[40]

Ever the political maneuverer, Bonilla had authorized Christmas to make whatever arrangements seemed necessary with the consuls to facilitate the taking of Trujillo. Furthermore, Bonilla had instructed his American commander to negotiate with Trujillo's *comandante*, offering guarantees of safe passage and employment to his soldiers. Negotiating with the commanders of the U.S. gunboats *Marietta* and *Tacoma* proved more nettlesome. For one thing, the *Hornet's* participation in the attack on Trujillo had removed any uncertainty in the minds of the U.S. commanders as to its status. The only persistent doubt among these Anglo policemen of the north Honduran coast involved the policy of the U.S. government. On the day the Bonilla expedition seized Trujillo—an unmistakable portent of an invasion of the entire north coast—President Dávila's agent in Washington, Juan Paredes, that "slick" diplomat who had flipflopped interminably on the issue of the Morgan loan, penned his signature to the loan treaty. Having anticipated Dávila's move, Bonilla had dispatched a political emissary to Puerto Cortés to inform the U.S. consul that if the State Department "permitted" him to toss Dávila out, he would satisfy the bondholders by reforming Honduras's frail finances.[41]

Nothing was put in writing, of course, and the precise posture of their government was scarcely discernible to the U.S. naval officers skirting the war zones of northern Honduras. Not without some justification then, *both* Dávila and Bonilla believed that the U.S. government supported their respective causes. The roving U.S. troubleshooter in the isthmian tropics, Thomas Dawson, reported that European consuls were beseeching him about protecting foreign property. He relayed the assurances of the *Marietta's* commander that the U.S. Navy would indeed forbid fighting in unfortified towns. Paradoxically, there existed a widespread belief that the United States would sustain the revolution if Bonilla were victorious. Until that happened, its officials maintained a circumspect, if misleading neutrality. "It is perfectly clear that the higher officials of the Honduranean [*sic*] government," Dawson wrote, "from the president down, have taken the position that our government would effectively block all revolutionary activities."[42]

Then, ominously, Bonilla informed Christmas that "we are in difficulty with the captain of the *Marietta*" and ordered him to transfer the *Hornet*'s military supplies to other vessels. The *Marietta*'s commander, George Cooper, still waiting for precise instructions from the Navy Department, had decided to "use his best judgment" in this situation and placed a guard on the *Hornet*. When he told Bonilla his decision, the Honduran was "violent in his protest, abusing the United States Government and saying they knew all about her [the *Hornet*] before he bought her." Commander Cooper related how "patient" he had tried to be with the "old man," saying that Bonilla must await specific instructions from Washington before employing the *Hornet* in further revolutionary activity. Bonilla refused and demanded an immediate decision. When the *Hornet* arrived in Trujillo on the morning of January 17, the *Marietta* awaited her. Cooper dispatched a boat to the *Hornet*. Shortly it returned bearing Christmas. The two Americans had an apparently pleasant conversation:

I found Christmas very good natured and apparently honest and trustworthy. I informed him of my conversation with Bonilla and told him to try to persuade the former to await the decision of the United States as to the *Hornet*'s status before attempting to use her. He told me there would be absolutely no trouble; she would not move. I informed Christmas that in my opinion he was engaging in something his country, the United States, did not wish. He replied that he had never been interfered with in his various revolutionary proceedings but would do what I told him. If I said he must quit he would do so. . . . He informed me that the State Department was well aware of all the plans of the revolutionists before they began and that they were practically encouraged.[43]

Christmas wanted to employ the *Hornet* in a rescue mission for some of his men isolated on the coast. When the U.S. naval commander insisted on accompanying the mission to make sure that the vessel engaged in no hostile activity, Christmas dutifully relayed the demand to Bonilla. The "old man" was too proud to permit it, as Christmas knew. The operation Christmas had discussed turned out to be more than a peaceful rescue effort. He landed a war party in the surf off Iriona and in the affray lost one man. When the *Hornet* returned to Trujillo late that evening, the *Marietta*, reinforced by the *Tacoma*, seized it for violation of the neutrality laws. "It is very possible," Cooper wrote perfunctorily, "that the prevention of the *Hornet* from hostile operations will cause the revolution to collapse."[44]

Cooper underestimated the resolve of Bonilla and the tactical capabilities of Christmas. The frantic efforts of the roving U.S. and British naval officers on the north Honduran coast in January 1911 were indeed curtailing the *Hornet*'s hostile activities, but their alertness had not been able to "discourage that valorous promoter of trouble in foreign land," Lee Christmas.[45]

Midway in the month several hundred Bonilla partisans exiled in El Salvador, learning of the attack on the north coast, slipped across the border and struck several small Honduran towns. Dávila dispatched an army of five hundred that drove the attackers back toward their Salvadoran sanctuary. In Puerto Cortés and La Ceiba, still under his nervous jurisdiction, the president sounded a *llamada general*, a call to arms requiring every Honduran male of military age to report to the local barracks for conscription into the military. In La Ceiba the frightened mayor, anticipating a deadly bombardment on the wooden shacks and houses that constituted this town of 3,000, scurried to U.S. Consul Allen Gard, asking for his intercession. Gard called on the local Honduran *comandante*, General Francisco "Chico" Guerrero, who happened to be an old comrade of Christmas. Guerrero told him that inevitably the rebels would attack the city. Unless ordered to evacuate, he was solemnly obligated to dig trenches around La Ceiba and defend the town.[46]

General Guerrero required no extraordinary perception of events to realize that Bonilla's invasion meant that coastal residents, more vulnerable to conspiracies hatched in New Orleans and Guatemala City than to the authoritative reach of the Honduran executive in Tegucigalpa, were quietly switching sides. The abrupt seizure of the *Hornet*, an act intended to discourage the invasion, had in fact the opposite effect. Among Hondurans resentful of U.S. meddling, the capture of that vessel had dramatically transformed Bonilla into a hero. In Tela the entire garrison of federal troops deserted the town, leaving it defenseless. The sudden nationalism that Bonilla's presence aroused failed to impress the commander of the *Marietta*, however, who complained to the secretary of the navy that if only the "corporations and individuals" providing funds to the revolution could be stopped, the invasion would "collapse."[47]

Commander Cooper could invoke his authority and try to protect La Ceiba. Accordingly, with the gentlemanly concurrence of the captain of H.M.S. *Brilliant*, he called on General Guerrero, demanding the creation of a "neutral zone" in the town that would be "off limits" to any fighting. Christmas received a similar injunction, but the naval commanders, refusing to accord Bonilla a status equal to that of Dávila's *comandante* in La Ceiba, neglected to address a note to Manuel. Incensed at what he considered a snub, Christmas responded angrily. Regarding the neutral zone, he wrote, "I can say nothing because I do not know if *my* gov't has accepted stipulation." The enemy, he continued, "does not seem disposed to come out on neutral ground. . . . Enemy can fire on my forces but I cannot fire on them. So I cordially invited the commander of the port of La Ceiba to meet me out of town. *You can rest assured I shall not endanger the lives of any citizen.*" Honduran officials (and modern Honduran historians) argue that the U.S. intervention favored Bonilla and Christmas because it denied the government forces the option of using the protection of the town. A few days later, as Christmas encamped outside town, another directive from the British and U.S. officers reminded the general that he must formally demand the surrender of unfortified towns.[48] With their note tucked into his pocket, Christmas readied his men for the attack on La Ceiba.

Guerrero was understandably apprehensive about La Ceiba's defense. Many of his men were Bonilla partisans who had been drafted into the hastily created army of coastal defenders, and even the valiant Guerrero himself harbored friendly sentiments toward several of the Americans leading the attack on the town. He had sworn to protect La Ceiba, however, and with the timely declaration of the U.S. and British commanders establishing a neutral zone, he appeared to have the unintended assistance of the great foreign powers of the isthmus. He was relying as well on La Ceiba's seemingly impregnable natural defense, a "virtually impassable" matted jungle lying between the town and the Cangrejal River. Two routes lay open to the invaders. One followed a narrow beach running from the river mouth to the waterfront, a risky choice because this approach led directly into a salt marsh and eight lines of barbed wire strung by the defenders; beyond, a rampart of heavy timbers and sand bags shielded a Krupp gun. The alternative was the dirt road running inland to a ford across the river. Since the first route assured heavy losses to the attackers, Guerrero naturally believed that the main thrust of Bonilla's assault would follow the second. Therefore, Guerrero had dug a trench and placed 350 men in position to cover the ford of the river with a deadly fire. From either approach— along the beach or across the ford—the attackers would have to worry also about firing into the neutral zone, patrolled by British and U.S. bluejackets, and violating the declaration their commanders had issued. On the morning of January 25, obscured by a heavy mist, Christmas held a final conference with his "staff." The night before, he told them, he had sent Guerrero a note formally demanding the surrender of the town. Guerrero of course had gallantly refused. Accordingly, Bonilla had given final approval for the attack plan, which Christmas had drawn up and sent to him a few days earlier.[49]

Christmas, in a pre-battle mood that Machine-gun Molony later described as jovial, directed Molony and Joe Reed to advance along the beach with a Hotchkiss. He sent his second-in-command, General Andrés Leiva, upriver with another group to the fording place. Christmas would follow Molony and Reed with his infantry. Molony was complaining about missing breakfast, so Christmas withdrew a handful of crushed animal crackers from his pocket and gave them to Molony with the comment that the food in town was much better. Molony, Reed, and their Honduran crew started out along the beach. Just then they heard rifle fire from the swamp. Leiva and his men were attacking, and Molony and Reed, not yet detected by La Ceiba's defenders, had an opportunity to set up the Hotchkiss and fire a few bursts across the marsh.[50]

The fight that raged on this January morning on the ordinarily tranquil Honduran coast soon became one of the most celebrated battles of the isthmian tropics. Not as sanguinary as the devastating battle of Namasigüe four years earlier, La Ceiba was fought with fewer combatants but with an intensity combining nineteenth-century bravado with the deadly weaponry of the modern age. The curious bluejackets on the *Tacoma* and *Marietta*, viewing the unfolding scene from the presumably safe decks of their ships, watched as Molony and Reed poured a withering fire into the government's "impregnable" fortification—until an errant shell from the Krupp gun whizzed perilously close and sent their sailors scurrying below deck.

The timbered shield for Guerrero's Krupp gun succumbed to a half-dozen or so bursts from the Hotchkiss, fired from across the swamp at a target the precise location of which had been hastily estimated by Reed, who had sprinted out into the ocean to get around the barbed-wire entanglements for a look. Molony and Reed, followed by the charging Christmas and his infantrymen, plunged through the knee-high surf, dragging Reed's machine-gun. The Hondurans following them got the worst of it. Unprotected from the intense firing, they had fallen along the beach. When Molony and Christmas rushed the Krupp's barricade, expecting a final hand-to-hand battle, they discovered it was empty. A shell from the Hotchkiss had ripped through the top twelve-by-twelve timber, sending the terrified occupants scurrying for safer ground after they had pushed their Krupp cannon into the ocean.

The rest of this battle was over quickly. The timbers that had shielded his enemy became Christmas's defense. Guerrero's fragmented force was caught between Molony's machine gun, set up in the cemetery, and the neutral zone. From around the corner of the town Christmas heard the shouts of running men. Behind the soldiers, riding a mule, was Gue-

rrero, urging his men on with wild flayings from the flat side
of his machete. Instantly the rebels fired at this mounted figure, who lunged crazily amid the scattering troops, then disappeared into the neutral zone. Guerrero collapsed at the door-
step of the British consul and died two hours later. Molony
kept his fire down to avoid firing into the forbidden area, and
with the concentration of a man who has found his calling, he
poured round after round in staccato bursts, sending the enemy
fleeing into the neutral zone. Before long the last of Dávila's
soldiers had stacked their arms under the contemptuous gaze of
U.S. and British officers.

In a boastful tone, Christmas informed the U.S. naval commander, obviously impressed with his tactical prowess, that he
had been "in the right" in this battle. He had played by the
rules of war that regular armies were supposed to follow, and
he was politely requesting these uninvited custodians of peace
in Honduran affairs to carry a message to the remnants of the
government force at the Cangrejal ford: they must surrender or
he would attack them from the rear. This ploy was, like his
famous escape from almost certain death on the Maraita plain
six years before, another of Christmas's grand bluffs. In fact, at
the moment when he was arrogantly dispatching uniformed
messengers from the British and U.S. navies to demand his enemy's surrender, he did not know that his own commander, General Leiva, had become hopelessly stalled in his advance when a
shell devastated his artillery unit. Christmas's emissaries conveyed his threat nevertheless, and by midafternoon La Ceiba
had become another coastal prize for Bonilla. A few days later
the conqueror of the town addressed an eleven-page account of
the battle, mentioning by name the dozens of rebels whose conduct Christmas considered valorous, to "Señor Presidente Provisional de la República, General don Manuel Bonilla."[51]

Bonilla, who had remained in Trujillo during the fight, understood the significance of La Ceiba's capture. The fall of the
coastal towns frequently indicated the approaching end of an
existing government, because the rebel force was no longer dependent upon the largesse of its financial backers. The conquest
of the key ports combined the rebellion's popular support (of

whatever magnitude) with the chief source of revenue—tariff receipts. Simultaneously, the control of the chief ports denied the existing government the funds required to hold its forces together and to retain or attract other caudillos or regional factions.

6

A Different World

La Ceiba's fall brought Bonilla five more machine guns, two Gatling guns, and the ammunition stores of the town barracks. More important, it provided him with the monetary rewards of another coastal customs house, which guaranteed even more defections from the opposition and more eager recruits dispatched south from New Orleans and Mobile by "prominent" businessmen. The capture of La Ceiba did not bring down the government of Miguel Dávila, but Bonilla's and Christmas's victory on the north coast in late January 1911 virtually doomed the Honduran president.[1]

Though he did not know it at this moment of triumph, Christmas was entering the twilight of his career as the "incredible *yanqui*." Manuel Bonilla, his Honduran benefactor, would be dead in a little more than two years. The U.S. government, employing force, guile, and its considerable economic and political power, was systematically incorporating Honduras and Nicaragua into its "stable" of Latin American protectorates. In the year following the great victory at La Ceiba, an articulate U.S. presidential candidate, Woodrow Wilson, would be condemning "dollar diplomacy" and the imperial posturing of his opponent, former President Theodore Roosevelt. Yet in the aftermath of his election victory, Wilson tightened the nation's economic and political grip over its tropical empire, even as he denounced imperialism. At the same time, Christmas's North American sponsor, Sam Zemurray, was busily making Cuyamel Fruit Company into a powerful enterprise in Honduras. No one appeared to have further need for a man with Christmas's talents.

The north coastal towns of Honduras had not one but effectively three groups in charge: Bonilla's invading armies, Dávila's nominal but rapidly disintegrating authority, and the skeletal patrols of U.S. and British bluejackets who policed the ravaged towns in the spirit of Anglo-American paternalism. Inevitably, jurisdictional authority suffered from the lack of precise boundaries. For example, one loser at La Ceiba was the notorious Davilista General Pedro Díaz. Rather than be cut to ribbons by Molony's machine gun, he had fled into the neutral zone and surrendered to the commander of the U.S.S. *Marietta*. Bonilla and Christmas demanded that Díaz be turned over to them. They were not interested in a bloody reprisal against their enemies—indeed, Christmas had headed the funeral procession for the fallen Davilista "Chico" Guerrero—but "because of [Díaz's] reputation," wrote the U.S. naval officer, "he would have [been] killed by the rebels." Even though Christmas promised a fair trial, the *Marietta*'s commander had heard the tale about Díaz's humiliation of Christmas in an earlier Honduran revolution when Díaz had "trimmed Christmas's toe nails to the flesh, cut the skin from the bottom of his feet, and had him led through the streets of Tegucigalpa." The U.S. captain refused to release Díaz, who instead was sent to New Orleans on the next steamer.[2]

Christmas's victory did noticeably quiet public behavior in the town. La Ceiba, wrote the U.S. consul, experienced "no complaints of rowdyism or abuse," despite Christmas's decision—over the vigorous objections of His Majesty's vice-consul—to unlock the jail and turn out its prisoners.[3]

Losing control of the Honduran north coast to his old adversary, Dávila then squandered his last opportunities to preserve his waning influence in Washington and in Tegucigalpa. Desperately, the Honduran executive informed the U.S. minis-

ter that he wanted U.S. intervention and "was ready to deliver
[the Honduran] Presidency to any person designated by the
United States."[4] Six or even two months earlier, this concession might have saved his government; it might have inspired
the United States to greater vigilance over Bonilla's plotting in
New Orleans. In the wake of La Ceiba's surrender, however,
the mood in Washington had noticeably shifted in Bonilla's favor. Even before that decisive battle, his emissary in the American capital, Dr. Alberto Membreño, had publicly testified to
Bonilla's sentiments about the North American colossus. "Is
Bonilla pro-American?" a reporter had queried. "Is he?" responded Membreño, "and would Lee Christmas be his chief of
staff if he were not?"[5]

When Secretary of State Knox discovered that two Honduran lobbyists against the Knox-Paredes treaty were receiving
their hotel expenses from Zemurray, he invited the Banana
Man to his office. El Amigo's candid account of his motive in
the entire affair to Assistant Secretary of State Alvey A. Adee
was recapitulated in a 1933 article by Ernest Baker:

I was doing a small business buying fruit from independent planters,
but I wanted to expand. I wanted to build railroads and raise my own
fruit. The duty on railroad equipment was prohibitive—a cent a
pound—and so I had to have concessions that would enable me to
import that [material] duty free. If the banks were running Honduras
and collecting their loans from customs duties, how far would I have
gotten when I asked for a concession? I told him [Knox]: "Mr. Secretary, I'm no favorite grandson of Mr. [J. P.] Morgan's. Mr. Morgan never
heard of me. I just wanted to protect my little business. Manolo Bonilla and I were working for the same thing. Why shouldn't I help
him?"[6]

In the Honduran capital the beleaguered Dávila, his cred-
ibility virtually exhausted, gloomily roamed the national pal-
ace, his pockets stuffed with banknotes for a quick departure.
The vigorous American community on the coast, only nomi-
nally neutral at the beginning of the war, now stood solidly for
Bonilla—with a notable exception. Washington Valentine, the
"King of Honduras," befriender of Zelaya, proponent of the
Morgan loan, had become a captive supporter of the besieged

Dávila. Valentine hired a former U.S. vice-consul, A.G. Greely, to purchase silver coin in San Pedro Sula and to deliver it to the president.[7]

The "Morgan" treaty, which Valentine believed would save his own financial empire in the country, had aroused even more antipathy in the Honduran legislature than in the U.S. Senate. A few days after the fall of La Ceiba a disconsolate Dávila submitted the document with a request for speedy action. The proposal at once galvanized anti-American feelings. Dávila even pled with the deputies, saying "Providence . . . offered Honduras this opportunity to secure the help of the United States."[8] When he finished his speech, "there was no applause, not a sound, nothing." Two hours later the assembly voted thirty-two to four against the Knox-Paredes convention. The treaty, an assembly manifesto stated, specifically violated the Honduran constitution by permitting the fiscal agent of the nation's creditors to draw up the list from which the customs collector would be chosen and, generally, "constituted an offense against Hondurans" in its presumption of their incapacity to run their own financial affairs. One historian sadly observed: "Honduras had escaped the grasp of the bankers only to fall into the clutches of the banana men."[9]

As the Honduran legislature was rejecting the Knox-Paredes convention, the government was surrendering Puerto Cortés, its last major port on the north coast, to the enemy. The commanders of the U.S.S. *Marietta* and H.M.S. *Brilliant* arranged the transfer, pledging the Dávila commandant a forty-eight-hour reprieve to evacuate his forces and notifying Christmas that he could peaceably occupy the town and take charge of the real prize—the customs house—following the safe departure of the Honduran forces. When the victors at last entered Puerto Cortés's main (and only) street, the "locals"—a curious mixture of Honduran banana laborers and foreign hucksters, runaways, and opportunists—turned out to greet them with lusty shouts of "Viva Bonilla!" "Strange to say," wrote one observer of the makeshift invading army of Honduran peasants and American soldiers of fortune, "many of them wore shoes."[10]

For all practical purposes, the war was over. Christmas set

up headquarters in the Hotel Lafebre and with some funds from the customs house paid his soldiers for provisions—forty cents a day for the Hondurans, $1.20 for the Americans. The presence of U.S. and British bluejackets, who patrolled Puerto Cortés by pumping handcars along the railroad track that ran through town, relieved him of the obligation to provide protection for its citizens. He was confident of victory. Queried by a U.S. correspondent about the war, Christmas declared: "The revolution is won. The evacuation of Puerto Cortés . . . was better than a victory by attack. It shows that Pres. Dávila realizes the sentiment of the people. The last stand of the Government forces will be at the capital. We can surround Tegucigalpa and starve them out. There need be no more bloodshed."[11]

The U.S. government would deny Bonilla and Christmas the final battle for Tegucigalpa: in February 1911, as part of its general plan to pacify the isthmus, it decreed that hostilities cease. The U.S. warships on the turbulent Honduran north coast once more played a decisive role in the political battles of Central America. The crusty Adee bluntly analyzed U.S. policy: "As we cannot take sides against Bonilla, or take any part in setting up a scarecrow to bowl him over, about the only thing left is to do what we have done several times in Central America—call a halt on both parties, inviting an armistice."[12]

Dávila readily agreed, and on February 8, 1911, the shooting stopped. For Christmas, ever solicitous of the approbation of his countrymen, the intervention of the U.S. Navy in his "revoluting" posed no insurmountable problem. He was quite familiar with the traditional American practice, nurtured in New Orleans ward politics, of ending feuds by the simple expedient of dividing the spoils. Bonilla was a very proud Honduran, however, and he was adamant about Hondurans deciding their own destiny. When the commander of the *Tacoma* announced the commencement of negotiations aboard his ship, Bonilla declared: "Who has authorized President Taft to interfere in matters that are the sole province of Hondurans? I have not asked for any intervention from any foreign power to redeem my homeland."[13]

This was the kind of political obstinacy that Thomas Dawson, presiding over the seventeen sessions between Davilistas and Manuelistas aboard a U.S. warship, characterized as an obstacle to the settlement of the conflict. As for Bonilla's Americans, especially Christmas, the U.S. diplomat observed: "The revolutionists have shown themselves to be very amenable to discipline. General Christmas has been exceedingly courteous."[14] Christmas was more than "courteous." He willingly accepted the U.S. peace plan for Honduras—which provided for a provisional president, Francisco Bertrand—and even maintained the American sharpshooters to guarantee a safe transition of power. He habitually read the official telegrams going out of Bonilla's headquarters in Puerto Cortés and kept local U.S. officials informed about his plans.[15]

In the meantime, Christmas dispatched some of his Winchester-bearing American mercenaries into the interior as a precautionary measure to assure the proper transfer of authority from the lingering Davilistas to the provisional government. Charley Jeffs, sometime soldier, railroader, and rancher whose involvement in Honduran revolutions extended back into the 1890s, departed for the capital. There he served as a bodyguard for a Bonilla general encamped in the hills surrounding Tegucigalpa. Tracy Richardson and Sam Dreben, fresh from the Nicaraguan wars against Zelaya, arrived in Honduras in time to get quick commissions and participate in a brief campaign against a Davilista band outside San Pedro Sula. Others, such as Victor Gordon, took their share of the loot with some permissible plundering of the north coast customs houses and then headed back to New Orleans on the next steamer. As part of the U.S. obligation in negotiating the armistice, Minister Fenton McCreery acted as mediator in arranging the surrender of the last of Dávila's commanders. McCreery also received funds from Bonilla to pay off the troops crowding into Tegucigalpa.[16] Christmas remained on the coast for several weeks, basking in the glory of victory and the accolades of his countrymen.

There was still, of course, the troublesome matter of the

Hornet and its alleged violation of U.S. neutrality laws. In February, just as the *Tacoma* negotiations were getting under way, a New Orleans grand jury returned indictments against Bonilla, Christmas, Florian Dávadi, and Joseph Beer for plotting the Honduran invasion on American soil. When Christmas got the news he was furious, vowing, "When the war is over I will return . . . and answer the charges."[17] The State Department, realizing that the government's prosecution of the case would only antagonize Bonilla, who had won the revolution and was clearly going to be the next Honduran president, wanted to drop the matter.[18] Dawson, its mediator on the *Tacoma*, told Bonilla that the indictments would have no effect on the negotiations. After a few months President Taft ordered a nolle prosequi on Bonilla, but the remaining indictments stood, and the Navy announced the formal seizure of the *Hornet*, by then rusting in Puerto Cortés harbor.[19]

Despite his bluster, Christmas was still out of reach and gave no indication he would be returning soon to the States to answer the charges. Beer, who had owned the vessel until its sale to Dávadi, and Charley Johnson, the captain, were twice tried before a New Orleans jury. The government's main witness was Drew Linard, the consul at La Ceiba, who had been a "passenger" on the *Hornet* when it sailed from New Orleans. The first trial ended in a mistrial, and in the second Beers and Johnson were found not guilty after the judge informed the jury that it was not a crime for U.S. citizens to enlist in a foreign military, nor was it unlawful, "if no intent to overthrow a friendly government exists, to send an armed vessel from an American to a foreign port." Following this outcome, the federal attorney in New Orleans decided to nol-pros Christmas and Dávadi.[20]

One casualty in the Honduran revolution was Washington Valentine, the energetic promoter of the national railroad and proprietor of a wharf at Puerto Cortés. Valentine had gambled on Dávila's persuasive abilities to push through the Morgan loan. After the Honduran assembly rejected the treaty, it moved quickly against Valentine's concession, declaring that he had failed to comply with his contractual obligations in the operation of the railroad and the wharf. Provisional President Bertrand, occupying the executive office until Bonilla was elected (in October 1911) and could legally undertake his presidential duties, hesitated to move against the "king of Honduras," and Valentine momentarily protected his interests at Puerto Cortés by persuading the commander of the U.S.S. *Petrel* that as an American he was entitled to the protective shield of his country's navy. In February 1912, as Bonilla formally took power, seventy-five U.S. marines patrolled the wharf, infuriating the local Hondurans who had been roused into a patriotic fury over this issue. The marines staved off the loss of Valentine's concession for a few months, but eventually the Honduran government had its way, and Valentine's career as Honduran railroad promoter rapidly diminished.[21]

Zemurray's maneuvers in Honduran politics and Central American finance during this period were, predictably, almost impossible to decipher. Lobbying against the Knox-Paredes convention (and its attendant Morgan loan), Zemurray ingratiated himself with the State Department's Latin American functionaries as an influential person who understood "local conditions" on the north coast. He apparently even convinced the skeptical Adee that he stood for the "open door" for "legitimate American enterprise" in the tropics. When the Morgan loan fell through, Zemurray labored to put together a consortium of southern banks, under the leadership of the Whitney Bank in New Orleans, to salvage Honduran finance with a $10 million loan (which, unlike the Morgan loan, made no provision for Valentine's claim against the Honduran government). An obstinate Bonilla, not yet elected but exercising de facto power, ordered so many modifications, however, that the Whitney loan, like the Morgan financial package, perished before the outbursts of Honduran nationalism. After Bonilla gained power, however, Zemurray received 10,000 hectares of banana lands on the north coast and a concession to develop Omoa. In 1911, with this and additional land grants, the old Streich holdings, $5 million raised from business associates, and a concession to allow Cuyamel duty-free importation of materials needed for its operations, Zemurray reorganized Cuyamel Fruit Company as a

South Dakota corporation. It grew dramatically over the next two decades.[22]

Zemurray's connections with United Fruit in the years after Bonilla's victory are even more difficult to uncover. In 1911 Bonilla appointed Zemurray fiscal agent to borrow $500,000 to pay the expenses of the most recent revolution, including Zemurray's loan. Zemurray also received the right to select 24,700 acres between the Cuyamel River and the Honduran border with Guatemala, plus other smaller concessions. About 1915 he selected land near the Motagua River. UFCO (which had several banana plantations in the area) and the Guatemalan government challenged Zemurray's move, and the region became embroiled in a twenty-year struggle between the governments and their allied fruit companies. In the first years after the revolution, however, Cuyamel and UFCO seemed to tolerate each other. In 1913 Andrew Preston, representing UFCO before a congressional investigating committee, said that the legal ties had ended in 1910. In June 1912 Zemurray had told essentially the same story to the Latin American Division of the State Department. H.V. Rolston, Cuyamel's vice-president, received a grant to cultivate banana plantations near Tela on lands lying between Zemurray's concession and the Vaccaro brothers' lands. Rolston transferred the concession to Zemurray, who, in March 1913, turned it over to the Tela Railroad Company, a UFCO subsidiary. This transaction may have represented Zemurray's secretive promotion of UFCO interests or, more likely, an astute business deal dictated by Bonilla's untimely death and the failure of the Whitney Bank loan.[23] Zemurray had to wait almost twenty years to make his move against UFCO.

Christmas, on whose martial capabilities Zemurray had staked tens of thousands of dollars, was forty-eight years of age in 1911 and at the height of his popularity and influence. Soldiers of fortune, political opportunists, and even U.S. diplomatic and military functionaries in the isthmian tropics sought his support or solicited his opinion. Christmas possessed, wrote the

Daily Picayune in one of its adulatory accounts of his exploits, "enough suggestion of reserve power in his aspect to cow an entire cabinet."[24]

Yet in his triumph he fell into lapses of boredom and even self-pity. Neglected by Bonilla in the early weeks after the *Tacoma* negotiations (on more than one occasion he complained about his *jefe's* failure to provide funds to pay his men or shoes for his Honduran charges), he had transferred his command to the capital and resumed his old job as director general of police. He pledged to exercise a proper discipline among his subordinates and solemnly announced: "If the law apply equally to all, I shall not allow it to be applied on the basis of partisan politics."[25] His relations with Bertrand never proved as cordially rewarding as those with Bonilla in the old days, and Christmas soon became bored with life in the isolated Honduran capital. In late 1911, citing his difficulties in working with the minister of government, he suddenly resigned. Bonilla interceded, persuading his *general de brigada* to stay on at least until he was safely installed.[26]

For all the unexpected frustrations that can accompany success, Christmas presented to inquisitive reporters the appearance of a "big, broad soldierly man, every inch a soldier, with [a] . . . face bronzed by sun and wind." His method for dealing with Bonilla's scattered and occasionally defiant enemies remained characteristically severe. On one occasion an enterprising reporter, lured by the prospect of a "Sunday-supplement" feature, rousted Christmas from bed. The general had been scouting for rebels all night. He had caught twenty of the twenty-two he pursued and had delivered them to Bonilla with a recommendation that they be shot at the government's earliest convenience. "Which means," growled Christmas, "that they will be out of jail again in three or four days. Bonilla is too tender-hearted."[27]

Christmas remained in the capital until the spring of 1912—long enough to guard the city against an unwelcome intruder bent on disrupting Bonilla's formal accession to office. In early March 1912, several weeks before the inauguration, General Valladares, who had assembled a band of anti-

Manuelistas in El Salvador, swept into Honduras. Pursued by Molony's cadet squad of machine gunners, the invaders sought refuge on Horno Mountain, where, exposed by moonlight against white rocks, they were literally cut to pieces by Molony's guns. Valladares got away but was found and killed two weeks later "while trying to escape."[28]

Bonilla's inauguration should have signaled the success of Christmas's many years of railroading and "revoluting" in the isthmian tropics; instead it brought more bitterness and frustration. In his second presidency Bonilla, reacting perhaps to Liberal criticisms of pro-Americanism, carefully distanced himself from his burly North American general. Before long, Christmas was complaining openly to the U.S. chargé d'affaires in Tegucigalpa that he "had not been sufficiently rewarded" after the triumph of the revolution. His retirement, thwarted by Bonilla's refusal to provide a payoff ($40,000 was the sum mentioned), would have enabled his return to the States, where Christmas evidently wished to clarify his role in the recent revolution.[29]

Instead of a triumphal reappearance in New Orleans, however, Christmas received a sinecure—*comandante* of Puerto Cortés and *subcomandante* of several other northern posts. Still the Puerto Cortés assignment was potentially lucrative, because Christmas could profit not only from the emoluments of office but, more important, from the rewards of illegal enterprise that the port offered to a Honduran officer with personal connections to the president of the republic. The town benefited from the renewed prosperity that Bonilla's administration offered the enterprising banana entrepreneurs of the north coast. In March 1912 a Honduran newspaper boasted that Puerto Cortés produced as much revenue as Amapala, the country's historically important Pacific port. Christmas prospered with the town; his income from sundry activities, according to his biographer, reached impressive proportions for a down-and-out railroader from Louisiana. With Ed McLaurie he acquired a 1,000-acre coconut plantation in a suspicious transaction with the government. Moreover, he expanded his holdings in town by purchasing the tarnished but still serviceable

Palm Hotel, once the fashionable headquarters of the Louisiana Lottery.[30]

The following year Christmas lost his Honduran benefactor
and his third wife. Gravely ill from Gresham's disease, Bonilla
summoned him to Tegucigalpa. On March 20, 1913, the president abruptly relinquished the executive office to Vice-President Francisco Bertrand, and the following day, with Christmas
and Molony at his side, Bonilla died. Then, with dramatic sud-
denness, Christmas's marriage to Adelaide deteriorated, in part
because of his extramarital diversions and Adelaide's refusal to
play the role of betrayed but compliant wife. Instead, she ran off
to Nicaragua with a suitor.[31]

Christmas returned to Puerto Cortés. His relationship with
the new president was outwardly cordial, but it soon was apparent—to Lee no less than the Honduran executive—that the personal link which the American had enjoyed with Bonilla was
not transferable to his successor. Bertrand stripped Christmas of
his *subcomandancias* at Omoa and Cuyamel. Most of the soldiers of fortune who had lingered in Honduras to enjoy the spoils
of Bonilla's victory had already drifted back to the States and
were soon caught up in the great rebellion that had erupted
against the Mexican dictator Porfirio Díaz.

Christmas did not follow them. At fifty he was settling
into prosperous middle age. Reassured by Bertrand that he
could "always fill a post in my government," he returned to
his *comandancia* at Puerto Cortés, where he courted and married Ida Culotta, the demure eighteen-year-old daughter of a
banana plantation manager. The ceremony was celebrated at
the Palm Hotel in a manner befitting the social standards of a
propper wedding in Louisiana. The couple settled into quarters
at the hotel, and Christmas assumed the role of a gentleman
who, having paid his dues in the violent political struggles of
the tropics, had retired to an unhurried private life. Dana Gardner Munro, a young Central American scholar and future State
Department official, remembered visiting Puerto Cortés in
1915 and spying a physically impressive man dressed in a
white suit and wearing a Panama hat, walking along the railroad. He possessed, wrote Munro, "an air of authority that
made it clear he was a person of some importance."[32]

In 1913, as the husband of a socially prominent adolescent bride and a "man of importance," Christmas found his financial needs assured when the government of Honduras designated Puerto Cortés as the republic's sole port of entry for all spirituous liquors and permitted Christmas, as collector of the port, to retain 25 percent of the duties. Honduras also honored its northern provincial *comandante* with another title, Assistant Inspector of the Republic; it was an unsalaried honor but one that enhanced Christmas's reputation.[33] He was already the best known of his generation of mercenaries, sought out by writers angling for a magazine story or perhaps even a biography—a task made difficult by the isolation of Puerto Cortés and Christmas's noticeable reluctance to reveal much about himself to strangers.[34]

Bertrand, though dutifully respectful of his North American ally, surrounded himself with advisers who saw an enemy in Christmas and capitalized on the continuing intrigue that involved his name. Christmas did little to reassure the generals in Tegucigalpa of his loyalty to the republic. At odds with Bonilla's successor, he began looking for other opportunities. The old determination to serve in the U.S. military resurfaced. In April 1914 he volunteered for duty with the U.S. Army in the event of an invasion of Mexico.[35] Early in the following year, facing charges of smuggling, Christmas abruptly resigned his post in Puerto Cortés. His strategy, wrote the U.S. consul, was doubtless to find another Honduran benefactor.[36] To impress the Hondurans with his political usefulness, he journeyed to Guatemala City, where he met with one of Pancho Villa's emissaries. Then he noised it about that he was contemplating "certain propositions made to him by General Villa's agent in the event of his not getting what he wanted at Puerto Cortés."[37]

By summer 1915 he was a virtual house prisoner of Estrada Cabrera, who casually informed the U.S. minister that Christmas was practically penniless. The State Department, anticipating another Honduran revolt, surmised that Christmas somehow would be implicated in it. An inquisitive U.S. minis-

ter, interviewing Christmas in the Guatemalan capital, left
with the distinct impression that the old tropical warrior intended to "side with nobody unless the money is paid down
first."[38] The truth of the matter was that Christmas and his
kind were rapidly going out of fashion even in the turbulent
world of Central American politics.

For several years Christmas vacillated in his commitments
between Honduras and Guatemala, all the while professing his
loyalty to the United States. In Estrada Cabrera's Guatemala, a
police state where all Americans were required to carry two
passports (U.S. and Guatemalan), Christmas occupied a presumably lofty position (Inspector of the Guatemalan Army),
yet he frequently appeared at the U.S. legation to reaffirm his
citizenship and to complain to a weary U.S. minister about his
mistreatment. He was disturbed because rumors out of Honduras implicated him in yet another plot against the government. Such stories, of course, reinforced his reputation as a
decisive force in that country's fragile politics. Fearful that
Christmas was conspiring against them, in September 1917
the rulers in Tegucigalpa offered him another sinecure, Military Inspector of the Departments of Cortés, Atlántida, Colón,
and the Bay Islands, at $300 monthly, payable in receipts from
the Puerto Cortés customs house.[39]

For reasons he never fully conveyed to his correspondents,
Christmas refrained from throwing in his lot with the poten-
tates of Honduran politics. Almost intuitively he sensed an
opportunity to serve—and to benefit from—his own country's
involvement in the European war. Less than two weeks after
President Woodrow Wilson's appearance before Congress asking for a declaration of war against Germany, the "old boy"
network in Central America was busily circulating Lee's name
for service. On Christmas's behalf, Edward Burke wrote a U.S.
official: "Before we're through we'll need his talents here [in
Central America] because for 25 years the German has been
silently but effectively making his way in these countries under your nose."[40] The next month Christmas surfaced in Washington, lodged at the Hotel Dewey, anticipating a visit with
Wilson. The president, apparently, found no time for this aging

soldier of fortune, but Christmas's name jarred the Louisiana delegation in Congress to press his case, and he wrote of two appointments with Secretary of State Robert Lansing. For the moment, at least, he seemed once more a "man of importance." Certainly he felt prosperous, enclosing a $300 check for his young wife in yet another self-congratulatory epistle.[41]

In June he was back in isolated Puerto Cortés with a letter acknowledging him as an "official reference" as his only consolation from the Washington sojourn. Pressed for money, he entered into an agreement with three other U.S. entrepreneurs to apply for a long-term concession from the Honduran and Guatemalan governments for the export of fish oil and "scrap." They intended to issue $100,000 in stock divided equally among the four. This venture (and several others that surfaced in the next few years) never materialized beyond the initial paperwork, and Christmas, fifty-four years old, discovered the obstacles facing an aging mercenary who waits until too late in life to get into a "steady" business.[42]

Then, at long last, U.S. apprehension over isthmian troubles as the country was gearing up for the European war brought renewed opportunities. In truth, the U.S. government, fearful of still another isthmian revolt, purchased Christmas's services. In late 1915 there were rumors of a revolt pending against Bertrand. The logical inference in Washington implicated the banana companies and Estrada Cabrera. The Department of State instructed Christmas, who had special links to both, to exploit every opportunity to prevent a disturbance in Honduras. Christmas played out his role with consummate skill. He journeyed between Puerto Cortés and Guatemala, scarcely concealing his movements and arousing the suspicion of the U.S. consul at Puerto Cortés with a sudden appearance and even more mysterious declaration that he "would just hang around until things looked right and then lend his support where it would do him the most good." A few months later he reappeared at the consulate to announce that he was "loyal" to the country that paid him the most. Christmas, wrote the consul, remained "the same bluff and hearty old locomotive of some years ago."[43]

Christmas's ploy to sell his services to his country, at war in

Europe and fearful of German activity in Central America, at last succeeded. Very cleverly he remained uncommitted in the Honduran troubles of 1916 and 1917, prompting President Bertrand to offer him yet another post in the harassed Honduran administration while the U.S. consuls on the north Honduran coast dispatched premonitory commentaries to Washington about his "mysterious" activities. He suddenly departed for Guatemala, leaving Ida and their child in Puerto Cortés. He arrived in the Guatemalan capital just a few weeks before an earthquake devastated the city, leaving some four-fifths of its 100,000 inhabitants homeless. For eight days the quakes continued, destroying the potable water supply and creating a typhus-infested city. Miraculously only three hundred persons died.[44]

In desperation, President Estrada Cabrera, who had used Christmas's services as railroad engineer and as head of Guatemala's secret police, made the U.S. mercenary "Chief of Sanitary Police." He signed on with an American lumber concern, J.H. Burton & Company, to construct prefabricated housing for the city's homeless. Christmas did not renege on his commitments to Washington, however. Each day he found time to report to the U.S. legation, and in May 1918 he finally received his long-sought appointment: "Special Agent" of the State Department authorized "to make investigations of political and economic conditions in Central America."[45]

Christmas dutifully reported on Central American affairs, as his $200 per month salary and $4.00 per diem travel expense required, yet his long involvement in isthmian politics detracted from his reliability in the estimation of his U.S. benefactors. Still, he did identify a New York arms supplier who had illegally acquired 1.5 million rounds of 30-30 cartridges stolen from the Mexican government; this was the kind of information that only an experienced mercenary could obtain. In the course of little more than a year, however, his usefulness to his country diminished, and in July 1919 the Department of State, pleading financial exigency, devalued his services to only $100 a month. In 1920 his longtime benefactor Estrada Cabrera, isolated by his own madness and surrounded by plotters, was ousted. Christmas fled to Amapala, while General Rafael López Gutiérrez led a sanguinary revolt against Bertrand which ravaged Honduras. Christmas solemnly declared that his sole intention in entering his old war ground was to support his family by exporting cattle.[46] But when the revolution triumphed, Christmas found himself unwelcome at *any* Honduran port, even Puerto Cortés, where he arrived to fetch Ida and was denied entry until the U.S. minister interceded. He received his passports with the admonition that he should not return. In 1920, accompanied by his wife and child, he disembarked in New Orleans, almost penniless, just as he had been twenty-six years earlier when he had shipped out on a steamer for Honduras. About the same time Christmas left Central America, the U.S. Navy established the Special Service Squadron—unofficially designated the "Central American Banana Fleet"—to allow it to supervise Central and South American order and stability.[47]

Central America did advance toward order and stability in the 1920s and 1930s, the decades after the heyday of the banana men. While the mercenaries remained ready to fight, the entrepreneurs who initially hired them could now turn to client governments or, if these proved unreliable, to the U.S. government to maintain order in the banana enclaves. Most of Christmas's generation of Central American soldiers of fortune drifted into other occupations.

Perhaps the saddest experience befell Christmas himself. In his last years he frantically tried to parlay his reputation and limited technical expertise into a share of one financial venture after another: a new design for a rat trap for wharves and ship lines, which received a favorable assessment by the assistant surgeon general; a locomotive throttle-adjusting device, which earned him U.S. Patent No. 1465808; a pathetically tragic venture into Guatemalan oil exploration with some strong financial assurances from a New York City company, Richmond Levering. Christmas returned to Guatemala in 1921, and for a few months he plunged into this petroleum enterprise with his old gusto, persuading himself not only that the venture would reap profits but that the scheme was a patriotic venture. The British, he wrote Sumner Welles, the State Department's chief troubleshooter in Central America, were very interested in Guatemalan oil. A letter of introduction from a member of the Manhattan Club described Christmas as the man who "holds the key to the oil business of [Guatemala]." After two years of operation, however, the Levering firm ceased activities, citing its failure to attract investments for the operation.[48] Here and in other ventures, as one of Christmas's earlier business associates put it years later to his biographer, "the General was not a businessman," despite his martial prowess and Central American political connections.[49]

The first serious indications of the disease that finally took his life occurred in early 1920, when he wrote Ida about "feeling sickly." His malady, ultimately diagnosed as tropical sprue, required hospitalization in a UFCO infirmary three years later, in April 1923. Thereafter he deteriorated rapidly, exhibiting the sickly yellowish appearance characteristic of sprue and related malarial diseases.[50]

Hurriedly he returned to New Orleans. He was still a "man of some importance," a status indicated when the publishing house of Doubleday, Page expressed strong interest in a biography. In the fall, however, the sprue worsened, and Christmas moved to Memphis. He answered a business query with the uncharacteristic response that he had been in "bad shape" for nineteen months, and unless there was a change soon it would all be over. Several of his old comrades, including Guy Molony, then police chief of New Orleans, rushed to Memphis, where Christmas lay in Baptist Memorial Hospital. They offered blood for transfusions and the solace that only fellow soldiers could provide. In January 1924, Christmas died. Among the pallbearers at his funeral were Molony and Richardson. A letter of condolence arrived from Minor Keith, renowned Central American railroad builder and banana baron: Christmas, he wrote, "has been my ideal of manliness and courage."[51]

Lee Christmas's comrades routinely experienced restless lives as they tried to adjust to a different world. Dreben had served with Pascual Orozco, Venustiano Carranza, Francisco "Pancho" Villa, and Álvaro Obregón in the Mexican revolution. Later, after Villa raided Columbus, New Mexico, Dreben joined General John J. Pershing's punitive expedition on its tortuous—and largely unsuccessful—trek after the Mexican rebel through the winds of northern Mexico. When that was over, Dreben settled into the more respectable, and safer, venture of arms merchant in El Paso, until he signed on with Pershing's American Expeditionary Force in World War I. There he won the Distinguished Service Cross, Belgian's Order of Leopold, France's Croix de Guerre with palms and the Medal Militaire, and Italy's Croce di Guerra; Pershing solemnly declared him "the finest soldier and one of the bravest men I ever knew." Returning to El Paso, Dreben again found trouble by impulsively crossing over into Ciudad Juárez with a machine gun to defend a Mexican army friend (General J.J. Méndez) who, confronting a rebellion in the ranks, had fled to El Paso. Dreben bluffed the mutinous soldiers into acknowledging Méndez's authority. Afterwards, Dreben migrated to Los Angeles. He opened a detective agency and plunged into still another international incident, the kidnapping of a petty criminal, "Little Phil" Alguín, who had fled to Ciudad Juárez to escape prosecution on a Los Angeles police charge. Dreben was in the process of literally dragging "little Phil" toward the international bridge when a crowd aroused by Alguín's screaming stopped him. General Méndez repaid his friend by arriving in time to prevent the angry Mexicans from assaulting Dreben.

In March 1925, his sometime associate in the Bonilla revolt, "Jew Sam" Dreben, fell mysteriously ill in Los Angeles and died within a few days. His death was atypical of what pulp storytellers wrote of Christmas's generation of soldiers of fortune—a mistakenly administered fatal overdose from a hypodermic needle in a doctor's office. At his funeral, attended by some two hundred mourners, one aged veteran and comrade of the tropical wars called him "a real man."[52]

Edward Burke found sanctuary and ultimately honor in his adopted nation of Honduras. Pledging to stay out of politics after the defeat of his benefactor, Domingo Vásquez, he settled in Puerto Cortés in 1897. A few years later, legend has it, he dispatched his son Lindsay to Louisiana with funds to pay off his debt, but the son had apparently inherited his father's wanderlust; he gambled the money away, migrated to the Belgian Congo, and died with three other Americans in a fight with cannibalistic pygmies, who, according to Molony, hacked his body to pieces and consumed the edible portions. Burke's involvement in the Louisiana bond frauds had prompted a Louisiana governor to offer $10,000 for his return to the state for prosecution, but in 1912, when Honduras finally entered into an extradition treaty, Burke had become such a celebrity that no Honduran executive dared to deport him. In the 1920s Louisiana dropped all charges, and the governor invited the old Civil War veteran to return, but Burke refused. In early 1928, when aviator Charles "Lucky Lindy" Lindbergh visited Tegucigalpa on his hemispheric goodwill tour, Burke presented him with a basket of gold nuggets on behalf of the Honduran people. Burke died the following September, aged eighty-nine.[53]

Tracy Richardson drifted out of Mexico in 1914, migrated to Canada, and there joined a light infantry unit with the nickname "Princess Patricia's Own." Wounded severely at the second battle of Ypres, May 4, 1915, he spent two years in and out of British hospitals, celebrating his reputation as the "Machine-gun Man of the Princess Pats." He transferred to the British Royal Naval Air Service, then, like Sam Dreben, found a place serving with the American Expeditionary Force, as a training officer at an aerial gunnery school. Richardson's postwar career was a series of diverse employments and scrapes with the law. He worked in mining, in oil, and as a lumber surveyor in Canada, Honduras, Guatemala, and Mexico; as a private detective in New Orleans, a Florida real estate promoter, and a roustabout on an oil rig. On two occasions he ran afoul of the law for displaying a deadly weapon in a threatening fashion, and in 1922 he was charged with killing one John Murphy in New Orleans. A grand jury "no billed" him after Richardson swore Murphy had threatened him. In the 1930s he survived by writing pulp magazine stories about soldiers of fortune. Only World War II resurrected his latent talents; in 1941 he returned to active duty as an intelligence officer and then base commander, Second Air Force, in Colorado. He left the military in early 1946 and died four years later in relative obscurity in Springfield, Missouri.[54]

Edward "Tex" O'Reilly, who glorified Christmas, Dreben, Richardson, and the other soldiers of fortune of his generation, finished his career by promoting his own legend. He published his autobiography (*Roving and Fighting*) in 1918, then almost two decades later sold his life story to Lowell Thomas, who published it as *Born to Raise Hell*. When a Honduran revolt beckoned in the early 1930s, he declined, saying, "I can't figure out any cause down there for me to fight for." He died in 1946, aged sixty-six, in a New York Veterans Hospital, the veteran of ten wars.[55]

Victor Gordon, an early admirer of Christmas and a veteran of tropical campaigns, returned to Central America after service with the U.S. Army in Europe during World War I to find his old "army" dispersed. He took to gunrunning and, in the late 1920s, promoting isthmian aviation schemes. Although the State Department characterized him as an unreliable example of U.S. entrepreneurs in Central America, the Guatemalan government nonetheless awarded him an air mail contract. Over the next twenty years he drifted into virtual obscurity, but surfaced after World War II to tell his life story and warn his countrymen about the international Red menace.[56]

Guy "Machine-gun" Molony, who fought alongside Christmas in Bonilla's Honduran campaigns, found status and respectability in his native New Orleans. In 1920, when Christmas returned penniless from the tropics, Molony was superintendent of city police. During the war reform-minded politicians had removed the protection accorded Storyville, the city's red-light district, and expected Molony to transform New Orleans into a model community. The task was, Molony recalled many years later, an insurmountable one. In mid-1925, shortly after the first anniversary of the death of his old comrade, he abruptly resigned and headed for Honduras, lured by an opportunity to reorganize the national army. Alfred Batson, an observer of isthmian life in the 1920s, found Molony in Tegucigalpa serving as general of the army and bodyguard to Honduran President Miguel Paz Barahona. He was "dressed in khaki and wearing the inevitable pearl-handled [revolver] close to his hip," Batson wrote. "It was difficult to visualize him as one of the greatest remaining soldiers of fortune in the tropics."[57]

Molony prospered, acquiring plantations in the Honduran countryside, an automobile agency in San Pedro Sula, and a managerial post in the national brewery. In 1928, when the U.S. government had 5,000 soldiers pursuing Augusto Sandino in Nicaragua, U.S. officials used Molony to get information on Sandino's contacts in Honduras. Several years later, when a revolution erupted against strongman Honduran President Tiburcio Carías Andino, Molony dutifully left the brewery job to lead federal forces against the rebels. During the campaign he took his machine-gunning talents aloft to fire on enemy positions from a plane piloted by Lowell Yerex, a New Zealand aviator. Hit in the eye by ground fire, Yerex managed to remain conscious long enough to land the plane. His exploits in this rebellion won him a lucrative mail contract from the Honduran government. Later, Yerex became president of TACA, the Honduran national airline.[58]

"Machine-gun" Molony apparently never severed his ties with the ageless New Orleans political machine. When the city endured one of its perennial "irregular" elections in late summer 1934, the city machine pitting its forces against Huey Long's statehouse gang, Molony (accompanied by Yerex) returned from Honduras in order, as he told inquisitive reporters, to vote and settle "business" matters. Long, then a U.S. senator who maintained a firm grip on Louisiana politics, charged Molony with collusion with the New Orleans mayor to steal the election. The governor declared martial law, and Long instigated a legislative inquiry into the situation, which was broadcast on radio. Molony, summoned to testify, indiscreetly boasted that in an earlier mayoralty contest he had stationed thirty-five armed men at the St. Charles Hotel. Asked if he anticipated a similar move in the current election, Molony said "no," then added, "but I will be glad to." "Try and do it!" shouted Long. "Watch us," Molony responded with typical soldier-of-fortune bravado.[59]

Long prevailed, and Molony returned shortly to Honduras to oversee his numerous business ventures. In mid-1941, months before Pearl Harbor plunged the United States into World War II, Molony (as had Christmas in 1917) offered his services as observer and informant on German activities in Central America. His usefulness as an agent is not recorded, though his intimate knowledge of northern Honduras did provide U.S. Army intelligence with an accurate map of that area. After the war he remained in Honduras, operating a successful rice plantation until the early 1960s, when he retired to New Orleans. He lived modestly there for another ten years and died in 1972 at the age of eighty-eight, the last survivor of the plotters of the great Honduran invasion of 1910.[60]

Only one man in the business of "revoluting" reaped really enormous profits in the Honduran tropics—Sam "the Banana Man" Zemurray. After Manuel Bonilla's triumph, Zemurray got a coveted concession in Honduras. Cuyamel Fruit expanded rapidly, even after Bonilla's death in early 1913. This crude entrepreneur who cursed in Spanish with a pronounced Russian accent transformed Puerto Cortés into a modern port, building a wharf to dock his growing fleet of banana boats and constructing an impressive network of rail lines over which his locomotives and cars (imported duty-free) ferried bananas from Cuyamel's irrigated plantations in the interior. His Honduran associates apparently shared his growing fortunes: a glowing tribute in a national magazine declared that if Honduras had more men like Zemurray, the country would certainly prosper.[61]

Political intrigue and payoffs to Central American generals and aspiring presidents remained part of the business of growing bananas in the tropics. UFCO, still the biggest and most powerful of the original triumvirate of banana baronies, was the most brazen. In the López Gutiérrez revolt in Honduras in 1919, UFCO advanced the government $250,000 in U.S. currency in anticipation of the forced loans levied on the fruit companies during the country's political troubles.[62] Several

years later, in the Honduran civil war of 1923-24, when north
coast rebels shot up the Vaccaros' company town of La Ceiba,
the fruit companies—to the dismay of the U.S. representative
dispatched to mediate the war—brazenly financed the rebel
factions. Because Cuyamel, unlike UFCO, operated exclusively in Honduras, Zemurray could afford to promote his
company as a truly national concern. In 1925 he also obtained
a lumber concession in the isolated eastern province of Honduras. The concession, in the territory obtained by the award
of the King of Spain in 1906, covered *one-tenth* of the entire
republic.[63]

By 1925 UFCO was worried about Cuyamel's widening influence. Earlier, the Boston crowd that ran UFCO had looked
upon "the Banana Man" as a small-time freighter and had even
helped to finance his steamship company; now they altered
their assessment. Zemurray anticipated any move on their
part: about 1926, in an imaginatively devised and expertly executed financial ploy, he and several carefully selected friends
began purchasing small but collectively significant shares of
UFCO stock. Then Zemurray initiated a propaganda war, hiring publicists to attack UFCO in print. In 1928 one journalist
reportedly received $100,000 from Zemurray to write a series
of acidly critical stories on UFCO's operations in Costa Rica.
In the same year Honduras and Guatemala came close to war
over disputed territory along the Motagua River. Guatemalan
students, shouting "Destroy Honduras," volunteered for military service. Zemurray championed Honduran claims to the
area, but UFCO, which operated banana plantations in both
countries, had to suffer a self-imposed neutrality, which brought
the company considerable unfavorable publicity. In the end, the
U.S. government virtually compelled the two countries to settle
their differences at the arbitration table. Before the matter was
finally resolved in 1933, UFCO and Cuyamel had merged.[64]

That merger stood as Zemurray's most artful ploy. By 1929,
less than twenty years after its creation, Cuyamel had provided
him with a personal fortune of more than $12 million. He pro-
posed a deal to the Boston banana barons: he offered them the
entire operations of Cuyamel at a price of $2 million more than

their assessment of its worth, correctly calculating that they would nonetheless seize the opportunity to acquire Cuyamel in a merger, which was accomplished through a stock swap. With that stock and the UFCO shares he and his partners had been secretly buying over the years, Zemurray walked away from the transaction as the major shareholder of the largest banana company in Central America. Moreover, he had the reassurance that Cuyamel—its farms, ships, and many of its employees—would remain intact in the merger.[65] Zemurray's only promise was that he would not form a rival banana company. Nothing in the agreement prevented him from taking control of United Fruit.

Triumphant, Zemurray elected retirement. He owned 300,000 shares of UFCO stock, valued at $30 million, a fortune placing him among the nation's monied elite. Boston's social clubs remained closed to this Bessarabian Jewish immigrant, but wealth translated more easily to social status in New Orleans. Zemurray acquired a townhouse in uptown Audubon Place and a dilapidated mansion and 25,000 acres from a lumber company near Hammond. He told friends that he intended to be a gentleman farmer and enjoy the pleasures that come with grandfatherhood. The country estate was one of the few visible manifestations of his wealth, though his choice for unpretentious living had less to do with the animosities most Depression-era Americans held about the nation's wealthy than Zemurray's instinctive reticence. Privately, his generosity was legendary and sometimes benefited reformist causes. He established a chair for women in Radcliffe's English department, bankrolled the Middle American Research Institute at Tulane University with a million-dollar gift, and sponsored a hospital for black women.[66]

In a different era, prospects for a long and unworried retirement for a man who had always been a risk taker would have been virtually assured. By 1932, however, the relentless plunge of the stock market had diminished the value of his UFCO stock to $10 per share, shrinking Zemurray's fortune by 90 percent. The banana trade, surprisingly, remained strong. UFCO shipped a record 65 million bunches to Canada and the United States in 1930. Nevertheless, wary investors disdained the stock.

Throughout the banana domain in sixteen countries and colonies, the company began cutting wages and, even though banana work usually paid more than local wages, precipitated strikes. Despite its power and property, UFCO was in trouble.[67]

Zemurray would have resolved such problems by going into the fields and talking (or cursing) in his accented Spanish. Now he traveled to Boston and politely but directly asked UFCO's directors—among them the chairman of Boston's First National Bank, a former Massachusetts governor, and an eminent Boston lawyer—what they intended to do about the situation. He was prepared to resume work as managing director, not as president. The banker responded with a casual remark about Zemurray's accent. Legend has it that the Banana Man abruptly left the room and shortly returned with his shares of UFCO stock—10 percent of the total outstanding shares, enough to give him control of the company. He dumped the certificates on the table and roared: "You've been fucking up this business long enough. I'm going to straighten it out."[68]

Epilogue

During the first two decades of the twentieth century—in the United States the progressive era, followed by intervention in World War I; in Central America the era of liberal dictators—an expanding U.S. industrial economy commenced a rapid incorporation of Latin America into its production and security networks. In Central America the United States fashioned an informal empire, using its considerable military power directly and, at times, relying indirectly on the growing influence of entrepreneurs and mercenaries. Washington's goal was stability, order, predictability, and efficiency in the U.S. informal empire.

Zemurray, Christmas, and the other banana men were essential to this process. Once the isthmus was enmeshed in the U.S. production and security web, however, the services of the hired guns of the banana men were no longer required to maintain U.S. hegemony. The use of force gave way to more traditional forms of resolving the problems of business expansion and international security: negotiation, diplomatic representation, courts, treaties, international organizations, and (but only if these proved essential to achieve U.S. goals) the marines. In this different world, the entrepreneurs generally adjusted much better than the soldiers of fortune.

Zemurray discovered a different Central American political culture, its leaders chastened by the massive U.S. intervention in Nicaragua in 1927. Under a new generation of dictators—Jorge Ubico in Guatemala, Tiburcio Carías Andino in Honduras, and Anastasio Somoza García in Nicaragua—who suppressed democratic and nationalistic opposition, Central American governments institutionalized the function of the comprador who served foreign investment and achieved a high degree of local stability. Isthmian economics suffered from the world economic crisis, however. As leaders of peripheral regions their presidents had little control over decisions about retrenching, restructuring, or management of foreign company affairs and the specific product sectors of the world economy in which the output of their mines and fields moved.

The man who would run tropical America's most powerful and far-flung transnational company for the next twenty years began "straightening it out" by firing UFCO's president, Victor Cutter, his old adversary. Unlike most of Boston's UFCO executives, Cutter had experienced the banana business firsthand on the Ulua River's right bank and had watched Zemurray develop Cuyamel's properties on the left bank. When Cutter left Central America for Boston, however, he began to think differently about what mattered and what did not matter in the banana business. Like Zemurray, Cutter was a man who followed his own advice, and his undeniably precise assessments of UFCO's situation in these perilous economic times called for slashing wages, maintaining cash reserves, and depending on the strong position of bananas in world agriculture to weather the Great Depression. Banana workers were tough and would accept the verdict. None of this impressed stock traders, and, more consequentially, such arguments offered no reassurance to Zemurray. In the past, UFCO had grown and prospered with rival personalities in command—Lorenzo Baker and Andrew Preston, then Preston and Minor Keith—but in the grim forecasts of 1933 the scenario for the company had no place for such dualities.[1]

In the tropics the news that Zemurray was back prompted barroom celebrations among field managers and banana cowboys, but outside New Orleans few in the United States knew much about him. His name appeared in no financial directory on the U.S. East Coast. Occasionally, in boardroom conversations in Boston or New York, stories circulated about the tall, well-dressed man who appeared at meetings and listened politely until, weary of reports that missed the essential questions, he suddenly blurted out a query that got to the heart of the matter. Such tales, however, told more of Zemurray's personality than of his business strategy. He puzzled Bostonians because he was not one of them; despite his undeniable power and prepossessing appearance, he never fit their image of a corporate baron, although in the banana towns of the north Honduran coast his habits conveyed authority and credibility. Zemurray's personal style permitted him to talk with a Honduran peasant or New Orleans businessman; he had never lost touch with these people. Yet he was not a public man in either culture. He shunned banquets, never gave a public speech, and once failed to show up at a reception in his honor in Havana because he was aboard ship discussing routine manifest documents with the ship's purser. By contrast, Cutter's habits *had* changed as he rose in the UFCO hierarchy. Although both men spoke Spanish, Cutter neglected the managerial duty of inspecting the banana farms and eating a fried chicken dinner with the fieldhands in favor of speaking at the Rotary Club, while Zemurray rode his mule from farm to farm. Such traits made Zemurray's formidable task easier in the 1930s.[2]

The problem was that United Fruit had grown so big that in the process its leaders had become arrogant and had forgotten what Preston had called the company's "git up an' git."[3] A generation earlier, confronted with the prospect that his success in Honduras depended on backing Bonilla's return to the Honduran executive office, Zemurray had shown that he could act. He had mobilized a reliable coterie of adventurers and mercenaries to back him. In the 1930s the challenge facing the Banana Man called for getting control of a vast and complicated banana market, where prices were slipping because of the agricultural losses, plant diseases, neglected maintenance of equipment, and rising transportation costs. He reorganized UFCO's management, bringing together men who had spent years in the banana trade and who thought the same way he did. His decisiveness was a reminder about how he had run

Cuyamel and how he intended to run UFCO: decisions were to be made where they were carried out, by those in the field. The "real" United Fruit was not in Boston but in the tropics.

In the mid-1930s a new plague, sigatoka or Panama disease, struck the banana plantations, forcing the company to abandon old acreage and seek new lands. In Costa Rica, UFCO shifted operations to the Pacific coast, which roused Costa Rican outcries. Already disenchanted with the company's domination of the Atlantic coast, especially UFCO's labor strategy of importing black West Indians and other ethnic workers, Costa Rican nationalists now perceived that the company intended to make the entire country into a banana plantation, driving out the smaller Costa Rican farmers.[4] The company weathered the political storm, and by 1940 it was the largest agricultural enterprise in the hemisphere. In the decade of the 1930s UFCO paid $40 million in taxes to isthmian governments (accounting for 50 percent of the revenue of the governments of Costa Rica and Honduras), $200 million in wages to Central American workers, and $140 million for privately grown bananas and other produce. The company operated eighty-one schools for employees' children, and even as nationalist critics of "El Pulpo" (the octopus) denounced the unsubtle means by which farm managers controlled the work force, it proudly announced that it employed ten Central American laborers to every North American (a deceptive boast, given the company's traditional habits of importing workers from the Caribbean isles, allowing only company stores, fighting unions, and denying nonwhites access to hospitals). To his credit, Zemurray recognized the problem of isthmian dependence on two or three crops; he encouraged diversification and, more important, agricultural education for Central American farmers. Before Pearl Harbor he proposed the creation of a school of tropical agriculture with a teaching faculty of geneticists and biologists and courses in forestry, marketing, health and sanitation, and dairying, among others. With a grant of $800,000 from UFCO, the School of Pan American Agriculture opened in 1943 on a plantation twenty-five miles outside Tegucigalpa. In Honduras and in the "company" Zemurray's name became a legend for his revitalizing of UFCO in the 1930s and his efforts to develop new sources of hemp, quinine, and rubber during the World War II years.[5]

A decade later, when United was justifiably denounced for its propaganda campaign against the reformist Jacobo Arbenz government in Guatemala, stories abounded of the company's highhanded and imperious manner in dealing with isthmian governments. Critics attributed to Zemurray the quip "A mule costs more than a deputy," an unambiguous reference to UFCO's stranglehold. The modern history of the distasteful tradition of the banana men begins with the Guatemalan coup of 1954—in which United Fruit was heavily implicated. Because by then Zemurray had effectively transferred his control over the company, his responsibility for UFCO's transgressions in the following years was at most indirect. Some may argue, however, that Zemurray had shaped United Fruit in the twenty years after his dramatic takeover and, further, that his "style" in establishing his own company earlier in the century involved bribery and the subsidizing of revolution to overthrow a legitimate government in order to place someone more favorable to his interests in the executive office. Unarguably, he stands guilty of this charge—as does the U.S. government in its dealings with isthmian governments in this century.[6]

A decade after Zemurray's death in 1961, United Fruit had become United Brands, a huge and complicated conglomerate, still defying those who sought to control it. Nonetheless, isthmian intellectuals and reformers praised UFCO President Eli Black for his efforts to "humanize" the company known as "the Octopus" among Central Americans. In February 1975, however, Black jumped from the forty-fourth floor of the Pan Am building in New York City. On the heels of his suicide came news that the Securities and Exchange Commission had uncovered evidence that Black had secretly approved a payoff to a high-ranking Honduran in order to effect a reduction in the banana export tax. The scandal eventually drove the Honduran president from office. The company never fully recovered, falling to number 628 in *Business Week*'s top 1,000 companies. "Bananagate" was yet another episode in the sordid record of the United States and, particularly, of United Fruit in Central America.

Zemurray would not have been suprised at such shenanigans. As he had seen things, there was little alternative to operating that way. Central America's political nationalists in the
first decades of the twentieth century, when the banana companies were establishing themselves, offered little solace to
those who subscribed to the imperialist notion that isthmian
governments must accept "reality" and satisfy the American
intruder and U.S. economic and security objectives. Those unwilling to acquiesce in Central America's political traditions,
which derived from the Hispanic, corporatist view of familial
politics, got nowhere. Zemurray entered a culture where status
depended not on wealth but on familial links. He and numerous
other businessmen and officials learned to manipulate isthmian politics. They encouraged or fostered ties with the elite,
middle-class professionals, *políticos*, or the military in an effort to build an effective comprador alliance that would serve
their ends. Some succeeded, others did not. Zemurray had a
close relationship to Manuel Bonilla; Minor Keith married into
the prominent Castro family in Costa Rica; U.S. businessmen
and officials in Nicaragua had warm ties to Adolfo Díaz and
Anastasio Somoza García; and Estrada Cabrera realized that he
could not alienate the U.S. government if he wished to remain in
power. José Santos Zelaya initially allied with U.S. businessmen,
but when Panama received the canal, he resisted serving as a
U.S. comprador and pursued ties with Germany, Britain, France
or Japan. The U.S. government forced him to resign for his mis-
reading of power in the circum-Caribbean. Nicaragua suffered
two and a half decades of civil strife. The metropole-comprador
relationship varied in form, but its essence was the subordina-
tion of isthmian figures to U.S. private or public authority.

This intrusion of U.S. money and power altered but did not
eradicate the familial pattern of Central American political culture. From the Conquest until modern times, those who rule in
the seemingly separate countries of Central America derive
their legitimacy from their blood lines to the conquerors and the
noble families. They may war among one another, but the reasons have little to do with ideology. The "revolutionary frame of
mind" that Theodore Roosevelt ascribed to Central America

early in this century—a debility requiring the intervention of U.S. paternalism, he believed—was actually a violent expression of familial disputes about how best to run an economy increasingly vulnerable to foreign economic penetration. By the early 1950s, certainly, the credibility of the old families had begun to weaken under demands from new social groups such as urban labor and the middle classes, which demanded political as well as economic modernization. Not even Sandinista Nicaragua ended the familial political culture, as more than two dozen high-ranking Sandinistas were descendants of one noble family.

Sam Stone, a social scientist and Zemurray's grandson, perhaps best articulates this view of isthmian political culture in *The Heritage of the Conquistadores: Ruling Classes in Central America from the Conquest to the Sandinistas.*[7] The implications of his thesis for U.S. policy (whether one is looking at the imperial era of the early twentieth century or debating the relative merits of Jimmy Carter's and Ronald Reagan's isthmian policies) are profound. Stone's analysis calls into question both sides of the duality in U.S. policy; forceful or benevolent measures have brought momentary alterations in behavior by Central American leaders but have not changed their thinking about who should rule and to what ends political power should be used. Revolutions change the faces of those in power; they are less successful in changing the political culture. In Nicaragua and Costa Rica the productive forces of the country are subjected to the control of the state; in El Salvador, Honduras, and Guatemala the state is at the mercy of those who control those productive forces. External programs derived from Marxist, Western European socialist, or North American diffusionist models of development have historically foundered in Central America because of this reality. Its ruling elites will accommodate intruders (for example, the banana barons), supplying them with concessions and, up to a point, tolerating the importation of foreign laborers. But these elites have not abandoned their faith that what really matters is familial interest, not ideology or Western precepts about upward mobility. Certainly, metropole and multinational leaders who monitored the incorporation of isthmian states into the world economy were mostly

interested in controlling the land, labor, capital, and communications of the region and in fashioning practical ties with comprador groups. In the familial societies of Central America,
however, universalist beliefs and credos acquired the particular
definition of place.

The modern history of "banana men," entrepreneurs and
soldiers of fortune, continued in an altered form with President Ronald Reagan's support of "contra" forces (who called
themselves the *resistencia*) in their attempt to overthrow the
government of Nicaragua, while he aided three other isthmian
governments in assaults upon their citizenry in a persisting
effort to secure order and stability. United States authorities,
however, commonly seek order and stability as essential objectives. Democracy, self-determination, and social justice are often rhetorical flourishes to conceal patently self-serving goals.
One legacy of this policy was the militarization of tropical
America under the guise of preserving national security interests. President Reagan used the contras to conduct a proxy war
against Sandinista Nicaragua (in defiance of congressional res-
olutions), financed a counterguerrilla campaign in El Salvador,
and transformed the quintessential banana republic, Honduras, into a U.S. base. Predictably, in the myriad assessments
of Washington's reversion to more forceful policies in dealing
with isthmian problems, the phrases "banana wars" and "banana diplomacy" gained renewed currency in the literature.

With Reagan's departure, the collapse of the Soviet Union,
and the retrenchment of Cuba from isthmian affairs, Central
America has lost its immediacy in U.S. strategic calculations.
The Panama invasion of December 1989 (Operation Just Cause)
and the removal of defiant General Manuel Noriega from power,
it can be argued, constituted a reversion to the Big Stick militarism of the Theodore Roosevelt years. Panama, however, remains
a special case in U.S. calculations. Central Americans, as President George Bush made clear after the defeat of Nicaraguan
President Daniel Ortega by challenger Violeta Chamorro in
1990, had demonstrated that they were capable of charting their
own futures. The military's grip on political life lessened a bit in
Honduras, Guatemala, and even in El Salvador, where a dialogue

between government and rebels held out prospects for a resolution of that country's long conflict.

In the old domains of the banana barons, modernizing social and economic currents are dramatically altering political cultures—even in the quintessential banana republic, Honduras. Americans yet venture into these places, but in the 1990s the mercenary is rare, and the multinational company has supplanted the old-style entrepreneur from the States. The most troublesome foreign intruders may be the Protestant evangelicals, who are undermining the traditional order with their appeals to lower-class ladinos and Indians in the countryside and even in the more cosmopolitan cities. Liberal and Conservative political parties still exist in form if not always in name, but other formal political clusters, more ideological, have joined them to compete for power. Debates over economic development, once sharply defined, are now muted by a common agreement among political rivals that none can risk too close an association with a foreign power nor can any Central American government afford to deny entry to those who come to invest and, in the process, to profit. Temporarily at least reliance on the hired gun or the benefactor from the United States is no longer in vogue with Central American political aspirants.

Notes

Introduction

1. Lester D. Langley, *The Banana Wars: United States Intervention in the Caribbean, 1898-1934* (Lexington, Ky., 1983). A paperback edition was published in 1988.

2. Hermann Deutsch, *The Incredible Yanqui: The Career of Lee Christmas* (London, 1931).

3. Ernest Baker, "United Fruit II: The Conquest of Honduras," *Fortune* 7 (March 1933): 25-33.

4. Thomas Schoonover, *The United States in Central America, 1860-1911: Episodes of Social Imperialism and Imperial Rivalry in the World-System, 1860-1911* (Durham, N.C., 1991).

1. The World of the Banana Men

1. Immanuel Wallerstein, *The Politics of the World-Economy* (Cambridge, Eng., 1984); Lester D. Langley, *America and the Americas: The United States in the Western Hemisphere* (Athens, Ga., 1989), 53-132.

2. Thomas Schoonover, "Metropole Rivalry in Central America, 1820s to 1929: An Overview," in Ralph Lee Woodward, Jr., ed., *Central America: Historical Perspectives on the Contemporary Crisis* (Westport, Conn., 1988), 21-46; Paul Kennedy, *The Rise and Fall of the Great Powers* (New York, 1987); Thomas Schoonover, "Germany in Central America, 1820s-1929: An Overview," *Jahrbuch für Geschichte von Staat, Wirtschaft und Gesellschaft Lateinamerikas* 25 (1988): 33-59; Hans-Ulrich Wehler, *Grundzüge der amerikanischen Aussenpolitik: 1750-1900* (Frankfurt, 1983); William Appleman Wil-

liams, *The Roots of the Modern American Empire* (Chicago, 1969); Richard Rubinson, "Political Transformation in Germany and the United States," in Barbara Hockey Kaplan, ed., *Social Change in the Capitalist World Economy* (Beverly Hills, Calif., 1978), 39-73; Tony Smith, *The Patterns of Imperialism: The United States, Great Britain, and the Late-Industrializing World since 1815* (Cambridge, Eng., 1981).

   3. On the world system or world economy theories of international relations, see Fernand Braudel, *Civilisation matérielle, économie et capitalisme, xve-xviiie siècle*, 3 vols. (Paris, 1979), translated as *The Structures of Everyday Life, The Wheels of Commerce*, and *The Perspective of the World* (New York, 1984); Immanuel Wallerstein, *The Modern World System*, 3 vols. (Orlando, Fla., 1974-88); Immanuel Wallerstein, *Historical Capitalism* (London, 1983); Terence K. Hopkins and Immanuel Wallerstein, eds., *World-Systems Analysis: Theory and Methodology* (Beverly Hills, Calif., 1982); essays by Nicole Bousquet, James C. Cronin, Albert Bergesen, Cynthia H. Enloe, and Suzanne Jonas and Marlene Dixon, in Terence K. Hopkins and Immanuel Wallerstein, eds., *Processes of the World-System* (Beverly Hills, Calif., 1980); Christopher Chase-Dunn, "Core-Periphery Relations: The Effects of Core Competition," in Kaplan, *Social Change in the Capitalist World Economy*, 159-76; Theda Skocpol, ed., *Vision and Method in Historical Sociology* (Cambridge, Eng., 1984), esp. chaps. 1, 5, 9-11. See also Charles Tilly, *Big Structures, Large Processes, Huge Comparisons* (New York, 1984); Thomas McCormick, *America's Half-Century* (Baltimore, Md., 1990), 1-42; Bernard Semmel, *The Rise of Free Trade Imperialism* (Cambridge, Eng., 1970); Bernard Semmel, *Imperialism and Social Reform, 1885-1914* (Cambridge, Eng., 1960); Hans-Ulrich Wehler, *Der Aufstieg des amerikanischen Imperialismus* (Göttingen, 1974).

   4. Fernando H. Cardoso and Enzo Faletto, *Dependency and Development in Latin America* (Berkeley, Calif., 1979); André Gunder Frank, *Capitalism and Underdevelopment in Latin America* (New York, 1967); Samir Amin, *Unequal Development* (New York, 1976).

   5. Ciro Cardoso and Héctor Pérez Brignoli, *América Central y la economía occidental, 1520-1930* (San José, Costa Rica, 1977), 225, 230, 232; Ralph Lee Woodward, Jr., *Central America: A Nation Divided*, 2d ed. (New York, 1985), 362; and data compiled by Thomas Schoonover.

   6. Cardoso and Pérez Brignoli, *América Central y la economía occidental*; Ralph Lee Woodward, Jr., "Central America from Independence to c. 1870," in Leslie Bethell, ed., *The Cambridge History*

of Latin America, 8 vols. (Cambridge, Eng., 1982-92), 3:471-506; Woodward, *Central America;* Héctor Pérez Brignoli, *Breve historia de Centro América* (Madrid, 1985); Schoonover, "Metropole Rivalry in Central America," 21-46; Thomas Schoonover, "Imperialism in Middle America: United States Competition with Britain, Germany, and France in Middle America, 1820s-1920s," in Rhodri Jeffrey-Jones, ed., *Eagle against Empire: American Opposition to European Imperialism, 1914-1982* (Aix-en-Provence, France, 1983), 41-58.

7. Ciro F.S. Cardoso, "Central America: The Liberal Era, ca. 1870-1930," in Leslie Bethell, ed., *The Cambridge History of Latin America,* 8 vols. (Cambridge, Eng., 1982-92), 5:197-227; Cardoso and Pérez Brignoli, *América Central y la economía occidental,* 199-320; Pérez Brignoli, *Breve historia de Centro América,* 95-106; Jorge Mario García Laguardia, *La Reforma Liberal en Guatemala: Vida política y orden constitucional* (Guatemala City, 1972), 37-53; Regina Wagner, "Actividades empresariales de los alemanes en Guatemala, 1850-1920," *Mesoamérica* 13 (1987): 93-95.

8. Woodward, *Central America,* 149-202; Alfonso Arrivillaga Cortés and Alfredo Gómez Davis, "Antecedentes históricos, movilizaciones sociales y reivindicaciones étnicas en la costa atlántica de Guatemala," *Estudios Sociales Centroamericanos* 48 (Sept.-Dec. 1988): 388.

9. Paul Dosal, *Doing Business with the Dictator: A Political History of United Fruit in Guatemala, 1899-1944* (Wilmington, Del., 1993); Walter LaFeber, *Inevitable Revolutions: The United States in Central America* (New York, 1983), chap. 1; Karl Berman, *Under the Big Stick: Nicaragua and the United States since 1848* (Boston, 1986), 103-50; Alison Acker, *Honduras: The Making of a Banana Republic* (Boston, 1988), 55-62; Jim Handy, *Gift of the Devil: A History of Guatemala* (Boston, 1984), 57-60; Rafael Menjívar, *Acumulación originaria y desarrollo del capitalismo* (San José, Costa Rica, 1980), 27-57; Craig L. Dozier, *Nicaragua's Mosquito Shore: The Years of British and American Presence* (University, Ala., 1985); Cardoso, "Central America: The Liberal Era," 5:197-227; Thomas M. Leonard, *Central America and the United States: The Search for Stability* (Athens, Ga., 1991), chaps. 2-5.

10. David McCreery, "Debt Servitude in Rural Guatemala, 1876-1936," *Hispanic American Historical Review* 68 (Nov. 1983): 735-59; David McCreery, "Coffee and Class: The Structure of Development in Liberal Guatemala, 1871-1885," *Hispanic American Historical Review* 61 (Aug. 1976): 438-60; Carol A. Smith, *Labor and International Capital in the Making of a Peripheral Social Formation: Economic Transformations of Guatemala, 1850-1980* (Washington, D.C., 1984);

Philippe A. Bourgeois, *Ethnicity at Work: Divided Labor on a Central American Plantation* (Baltimore, Md., 1989); Aviva Chomsky, "Plantation Society: Land and Labor in Costa Rica's Atlantic Coast, 1870-1940" (Ph.D. diss., University of California, Berkeley, 1990).

11. Woodward, *Central America*, 149-202; Cardoso and Brignoli, *América Central y la economía occidental*, 199-320; Handy, *Gift of the Devil*, 65-73; E. Bradford Burns, "The Modernization of Underdevelopment: El Salvador, 1858-1931," *Journal of Developing Areas* 18 (April 1984): 293-316; Héctor Lindo-Fuentes, *Weak Foundations: The Economy of El Salvador in the Nineteenth Century, 1821-1898* (Berkeley, Calif., 1990), 81-185.

12. Darío Euraque, "La 'reforma liberal' en Honduras y la hipótesis de la 'oligarquía ausente,' 1870-1930," *Revista de historia* 23 (Jan.-June 1991): 7-56; Darío Euraque, "Notas sobre formación de clases y poder político en Honduras, 1870s-1932," *Historia Crítica* 6 (Nov. 1991): 59-79; Darío Euraque, "Modernity, Economic Power and the Foreign Banana Companies in Honduras: San Pedro Sula as a Case Study, 1880s-1945," in Edwin J. Perkins, ed., *Essays in Economic and Business History* (Los Angeles, 1993), 11:49-65; Mario Argueta, *Bananos y política: Samuel Zemurray y la Cuyamel Fruit Company* (Tegucigalpa, 1989); José Francisco Guevara-Escudero, "Nineteenth Century Honduras: A Regional Approach to the Economic History of Central America," 2 vols. (Ph.D. diss., New York University, 1983); Marvin Barahona, *La hegemonía de los Estados Unidos en Honduras, 1907-1932* (Tegucigalpa, 1989).

13. Cardoso, "Central America: The Liberal Era," 5:197-227; Cardoso and Pérez Brignoli, *América Central y la economía occidental*, chap. 9.

14. Richard van Alstyne, *The Rising American Empire* (Chicago, 1965); Charles Vivier, "American Continentalism: An Idea of Expansionism, 1845-1910," *American Historical Review* 65 (Jan. 1960): 323-35; Leonard P. Curry, *Blueprint for Modern America* (Nashville, Tenn., 1968); William Appleman Williams, The Contours of American History (Chicago, 1961), 225-342.

15. U.S. Department of Commerce, *Historical Statistics of the United States: Colonial Times to 1970*, 2 vols. (Washington, D.C., 1975), 1:126, 135.

16. Williams, *The Contours of American History*, esp. 225-342; Rubinson, "Political Transformation in Germany and the United States," 39-73; van Alstyne, *The Rising American Empire*, 147-69; Milton Plesur, *America's Outward Thrust: Approaches to Foreign Affairs, 1865-1890* (DeKalb, Ill., 1971), esp. 14-34, 157-81; Thomas Schoonover, *Dollars over Dominion: The Triumph of Liberalism in Mexican-*

United States Relations, 1861-1867 (Baton Rouge, La., 1978); Edward Chase Kirkland, *Industry Comes of Age: Business, Labor, and Public Policy, 1860-1897* (Chicago, 1967), 291-93. Historians have challenged the market expansion perspective: see J.A. Thompson, "William Appleman Williams and the 'American Empire,'" *Journal of American Studies* 7 (April 1973): 91-103; William H. Becker, "American Manufacturers and Foreign Markets, 1870-1900. Business Historians and the 'New Economic Determinists,'" *Business History Review* 47 (Winter 1973): 466-81; David M. Pletcher, "Rhetoric and Results: A Pragmatic View of American Economic Expansionism, 1865-98," *Diplomatic History* 5 (Spring 1981): 93-105.

17. On compradores, see Dale L. Johnson, "Dependence and the International System," and "On Oppressed Classes," in James Cockcroft, André Gunder Frank, and Dale L. Johnson, *Dependence and Underdevelopment: Latin America's Political Economy* (Garden City, N.Y., 1972); Dosal, *Doing Business with the Dictator*; David Healy, "A Hinterland in Search of a Metropolis: The Mosquito Coast, 1894-1910," *International History Review* 3 (Jan. 1981): 20-43.

18. Walter LaFeber, *The New Empire: An Interpretation of American Expansion, 1860-1898* (Ithaca, N.Y., 1964), esp. 102-21; David McCullough, *The Path between the Seas: The Creation of the Panama Canal, 1870-1914* (New York, 1977); Kenneth Hagan, *American Gunboat Diplomacy and the Old Navy, 1877-1889* (Westport, Conn., 1973); Wehler, *Der Aufstieg des amerikanischen Imperialismus*, 74-91; Langley, *America and the Americas*, 93-96; Thomas Schoonover, "Conflicting U.S. and Central American Economic Priorities: From the Open Door to Exploitive Panamericanism, 1881-1899," in Schoonover, *The United States in Central America*, 77-96; Gabriel Kolko, *Main Currents in Modern American History* (New York, 1976), 1-66; Walter Edward Lowrie, "France, the United States, and the Lesseps Panama Canal: Renewed Rivalry in the Western Hemisphere, 1879-1889" (Ph.D. diss., Syracuse University, 1976); LaFeber, *Inevitable Revolutions*, 31-34.

19. Wehler, *Der Aufstieg des amerikanischen Imperialismus*, 24-73; Thomas McCormick, *The China Market: America's Quest for Informal Empire* (Chicago, 1967), 17-52; Williams, *The Contours of American History*, 225-343; Lester Langley, *The United States and the Caribbean in the Twentieth Century*, 4th ed. (Athens, Ga., 1989), 3-62.

20. Charles H. Wood, "Equilibrium and Historical-Structural Perspectives on Migration," *International Migration Review* 16 (Summer 1982): 298-319; Robert L. Bach and Lisa A. Schraml, "Migration, Crisis and Theoretical Conflict," *International Migration Review* 16 (Sum-

mer 1982): 320-41; Magnus Mörner, *Adventurers and Proletarians: The Story of Migrants in Latin America* (Pittsburgh, 1985), 124-29: Alejandro Portes and John Walton, *Labor, Class, and the International System* (New York, 1981), 7-34, 41-49.

21. Woodward, *Central America*, chap. 7; Schoonover, "The World Economic Crisis, Racism, and U.S. Relations with Central America, 1893-1910," in Schoonover, *The United States in Central America*, 111-29.

22. Schoonover, "Metropole Rivalry in Central America," 21-46; Lester D. Langley, *Struggle for the American Mediterranean: United States-European Rivalry in the Gulf-Caribbean, 1776-1904* (Athens, Ga., 1976); Schoonover, *The United States in Central America*, 97-110, 149-65.

23. Schoonover, *The United States in Central America*, 130-48; Berman, *Under the Big Stick*; Richard Millett, *Guardians of the Dynasty* (Maryknoll, N.Y., 1977), 20-24; LaFeber, *Inevitable Revolutions*, esp. 34-49; William Roger Adams, "Strategy, Diplomacy, and Isthmian Canal Security, 1880-1917" (Ph.D. diss., Florida State Univ., 1974), pp. 251-52; 257-60; Charles L. Stansifer, "José Santos Zelaya: A New Look at Nicaragua's 'Liberal' Dictator," *Revista/Review Interamericana* 7 (Fall 1977): 469-71; Charles E. Frazier, "The Dawn of Nationalism and Its Consequences in Nicaragua" (Ph.D. diss., Univ. of Texas, 1958); and esp. John Findling, "The United States and Zelaya" (Ph.D. diss., Univ. of Texas, 1971).

24. William Appleman Williams, "The Frontier Thesis and American Foreign Policy," *Pacific Historical Review* 24 (1955): 379-95; William A. Williams, *The Tragedy of American Diplomacy* (New York, 1972), esp. 1-16; John Chasteen, "Manuel Enrique Araujo and the Failure of Reform in El Salvador, 1911-1913" *Southeastern Latin Americanist* 27 (Sept. 1984): 1-16.

25. Lindo-Fuentes, *Weak Foundations*, 81-185; Argueta, *Bananos y política*, 40-42, 54-60; Barahona, *La hegemonía de los Estados Unidos en Honduras*, 237-42.

26. Schoonover, "Germany in Central America," 33-59; Holger H. Herwig, *Politics of Frustration: The United States in German Strategic Planning, 1888-1918* (Boston, 1976); Holger H. Herwig, *Germany's Vision of Empire in Venezuela, 1871-1918* (Princeton, N.J., 1986), 141-74; Imanuel Geiss, "Sozialstruktur und imperialistische Dispositionen im zweiten deutschen Kaiserreich," in Karl Holl and Günter List, eds., *Liberalismus und imperialistischer Staat: Der Imperialismus als Problem liberaler Parteien in Deutschland, 1890-1914* (Göttingen, 1975), 40-61; Michael Stürmer, *Die Reichsgründung: Deutscher Nationalstaat und europäisches Gleichgewicht im*

Zeitalter Bismarcks (Munich, 1984); Hartmut Pogge von Strand-mann, "Domestic Origins of Germany's Colonial Expansion under Bismarck," *Past and Present* 42 (Feb. 1969): 140-59; Hans-Ulrich Wehler, *Bismarck und der Imperialismus* (Cologne, 1969), 42-135, 454-502.

27. Julio Castellanos Cambranes, *El imperialismo alemán en Guatemala* (Guatemala, 1977), esp. 1-38; Julio Castellanos Cam-branes, "Aspectos del desarrollo socio-económico y político de Gua-temala 1868-1885, en base de materiales de archivos alemanes," *Po-lítica y Sociedad* 3 (Jan.-June 1977): 7-14; Gerhard Sandner, *Zentral-amerika und der ferne karibische Westen: Konjunkturen, Krisen und Konflikte, 1503-1984* (Stuttgart, 1985), 141-80; Euraque, "La 'reforma liberal' en Honduras," 26.

28. Thomas Schoonover, "France in Central America, 1820s-1930: An Overview," *Revue française d'histoire d'outre mer* 79 (1992): 161-97; Cardoso and Pérez Brignoli, *Centro América y la economía occidental*, chaps. 6-9; Pérez Brignoli, *Breve historia de Centro Amé-rica*, chaps. 3-4; Woodward, *Central America*, chaps. 5-7; Joaquín Pé-rez, "El comercio francés en la epoca de la restauracion y el proceso de la independencia americana," *Investigaciones y ensayos* 26 (Jan.-June, 1979): 259-69; Henry Blumenthal, *France and the United States and France: Their Diplomatic Relations, 1798-1914* (Chapel Hill, N.C., 1970), 34-38.

2. Banana Kingdoms

1. On William Walker and pre-Civil War filibustering, see Ro-bert E. May, *The Southern Dream of a Caribbean Empire, 1854-1861* (Athens, Ga., 1989), and Charles H. Brown, *Agents of Manifest Desti-ny: The Lives and Times of the Filibusters* (Chapel Hill, 1980). Walter LaFeber, *The American Age: United States Policy at Home and Abroad* (New York, 1989), 218-30; McCormick, *America's Half-Century*, 17-21; Langley, *America and the Americas*, 104-10.

2. Stewart, *Keith and Costa Rica*, 33-96; Charles Morrow Wil-son, *Empire in Green and Gold: The Story of the American Banana Trade* (New York, 1947), 20-21, 69; Newton Fuessle, "The Green Gold of the Tropics," *The Outlook* 137 (Oct. 4, 1922): 187; Charles David Kepner, Jr., and Jay H. Soothill, *The Banana Empire: A Case Study in Economic Imperialism* (New York, 1935), 34-35, 44-45; Chomsky, "Plantation Society," 22-45.

3. Wilson, *Empire*, 110, 156; David McCreery, "Wireless Em-pire: The United States and Radio Communications in Central Amer-

ica and the Caribbean, 1904-1926," *Southeast Latin Americanist* 33 (Summer 1993): 23-41.

4. House Committee on Merchant Marine and Fisheries, *Report on Steamship Agreements and Affiliations*, 63d Cong., 1st sess., 1912, 191-95; idem *Investigation of Shipping Combinations: Hearings*, 62d Cong., 2nd sess., 1913, 783-89.

5. Consul, La Ceiba, to Sec. State, Nov. 11, 1914, State Dept., Dec. File, Int. Affairs, Honduras, Record Group 59, National Archives. All State Department correspondence is from 815.00/1557, RG 59 unless otherwise noted.

6. Carleton Beals, "Baron Banana in Puerto Barrios," *The Nation*, 123 (Sept. 15, 1926): 242.

7. House Committee, *Shipping Combinations*, 728-29.

8. Charles D. Kepner, *Social Aspects of the Banana Industry* (New York, 1938), 25-57.

9. Wilson, *Empire in Green and Gold*, 94-95.

10. Raimundo Mendozas, *El Nacional* (San Pedro Sula), Feb. 13, 1931, quoted in Kepner and Soothill, *Banana Empire*, 99. See also Wilson, *Empire*, 9-11; *New York Times*, Oct. 6, 1903, 9:1.

11. Thomas Karnes, *Tropical Enterprise: The Standard Fruit and Steamship Company in Latin America* (Baton Rouge, La., 1978), 3, 11, 15-16, 48-49; *La Gaceta* (Honduras), March 19, 1907, 174; *Latin America* 3 (Aug. 1, 1914): 1.

12. Dosal, *Doing Business with the Dictator*, intro.; Stephen J. Whitfield, "Strange Fruit: The Career of Samuel Zemurray," *American Jewish History* 73 (March 1984): 309-10; Argueta, *Bananos y política*.

13. House Committee, *Shipping Combinations*, 738. See also Baker, "United Fruit II, 26-27; Kepner and Soothill, *Banana Empire*, 100-101; Wilson, *Empire*, 200; Euraque, "La 'reforma liberal' en Honduras," 32-38.

14. Richard Harding Davis, *Three Gringos in Venezuela and Central America* (New York, 1896), 5, 119, 131, 178.

15. Wilson, *Empire*, 100-101.

16. E.A. Lever, *Central America; or, The Land of the Quichés and Chontales* (New Orleans, 1885), 133-36.

17. Davis, *Three Gringos*, 28, 57-58, 79; clipping, Hermann Deutsch Papers, Tulane Univ.

18. Baker, "United Fruit II," 32-33; *New York Times*, Sept. 16, 1903, 7:2; O. Henry (William Sydney Porter), *Cabbages and Kings* (Garden City, N.Y., 1904), 8-9, 73, 98.

19. James F. Vivian, "Major E.A. Burke: The Honduran Exile, 1889-1928," *Louisiana History* 15 (Spring 1974): 175-94.

20. Guy Molony Oral History, William Ransom Hogan Jazz Archives, Tulane Univ.; Kenneth V. Finney, "Precious Metal Mining and the Modernization of Honduras: In Quest of El Dorado (1880-1900)" (Ph.D. diss., Tulane Univ., 1973), 5-6, 33; Tourist Book, Vertical File, Louisiana Coll., Tulane Univ.; *New Orleans Daily Picayune*, Feb. 11, 1890, 4:3; Feb. 14, 1890, 4:1; Oct. 1, 1890, 2:3.

21. "General Heriberto O. Jeffries," in Honduras, *Archivo Nacional* 6 (Sept. 1972): 81-84.

22. On Valentine's many activities, see Finney, "Precious Metal Mining," 14-19; Kepner and Soothill, *Banana Empire*, 102-6; Kenneth V. Finney, "Our Man in Honduras: Washington S. Valentine," *Studies in the Social Sciences* 17 (June 1978): 13-20; Kenneth V. Finney, "Rosario and the Election of 1887: The Political Economy of Mining in Honduras," *Hispanic American Historical Review* 60 (Feb. 1979), 81-107; Kenneth V. Finney, "Merchants, Miners, and Monetary Structures: The Revival of the Honduran Import Trade, 1880-1900," *SECOLAS Annales* 12 (1981): 27-38.

23. *New Orleans Daily Picayune*, Oct. 27, 1892, 3:6; Davis, *Three Gringos*, 139.

24. Acker, *Honduras*, 57-75; Woodward, *Central America*, 149-202; Euroque, "La 'reforma liberal' en Honduras," 11-34.

25. Quoted in Enrique Aquino, *La personalidad política del General José Santos Zelaya* (Managua, 1944), 57-58.

26. Davis, *Three Gringos*, 140.

27. Luis Marinas Otero, *Honduras* (Madrid, 1963), 362-69; Acker, *Honduras*, 60-64; Finney, "Precious Metal Mining," 72-73; Davis, *Three Gringos*, 148; César Lagos, *Ensayo sobre la historia contemporánea de Honduras* (San Salvador, 1908), 84.

28. Quoted in Deutsch, *Incredible Yanqui*, 8-9; see also 3-13.

29. Pablo Nuila, *Diario de operaciones de la columna expedicionaria al norte por el General Don Pablo Nuila* (Tegucigalpa, 1897), 8-9, 11.

30. Christmas to Mamie, Feb. 8, 1897, Deutsch Papers.

31. Christmas to daughter, July 4, 1897; Christmas to Mamie, Sept. 19, 1897, Deutsch Papers.

32. Christmas to daughter, Jan. 17, 1898, Deutsch Papers.

33. Christmas to Mamie, June 8, 1898, Deutsch Papers.

34. Deutsch, *Incredible Yanqui*, 29.

35. *New Orleans Daily Picayune*, Jan. 3, 1911.

36. *La Gaceta Oficial* (Tegucigalpa), Feb. 6, 1903.

37. Deutsch, *Incredible Yanqui*, 42-50; José M. Moncada, *La revolución de 1903 y el golpe de estado del 8 de febrero de 1904* (Tegucigalpa, 1904), 12-13.

38. Bonilla to Christmas, Feb. 5, 17, 1903, Deutsch Papers. In February 1905, President Bonilla presented Christmas a sword in commemoration of his contributions in the revolt of 1903.

39. Terencio Sierra to Commanding General, March 1, 1903, in *El Constitucional*, March 6, 1903; U.S. Department of State, *Foreign Relations of the United States, 1903*, 578-79. The pro-Arias *El Constitucional* (March 6, 1903) reported that in the "battle of Nacâome Lt. Col. Samuel McGill pursued fleeing enemy soldiers."

40. E.A. Lever, *New Orleans Daily Picayune*, April 28, 1903, sec. 8, pp. 2-3.

41. Ibid., 1-2.

42. Ibid., June 23, 1903. The account was rendered by Christmas to a *Daily Picayune* reporter during one of his numerous visits to New Orleans.

43. *El Constitucional*, May 14, 18, 21, 1903; *New York Times*, March 29, 1903; April 21, 1903, 4-5.

44. *New Orleans Daily Picayune*, April 21, 28, 1903; *New York Times*, April 21, 1903.

45. Moncada, *Revolución de 1903*, 48-51; Ismail Mejía Derás [pseud., Aro Sanso], *Policarpo Bonilla, algunos apuntes biográficos* (Mexico City, 1936), 343-49.

46. *New Orleans Daily Picayune*, Jan. 29, 1911.

47. Thomas L. Karnes, *Tropical Enterprise: The Standard Fruit and Steamship Company in Latin America* (Baton Rouge, La., 1978), 24. Bonilla did infuriate the Honduran Syndicate and especially Washington Valentine when he took over the Honduran railroad because of a poor repair record. Valentine argued differently, of course, and found a political spokesman in Senator Chauncey DePew of New York. As their operations increased, the banana exporters who used the railroad began to pay more attention to it.

48. Quoted in Mejía D., *Policarpo Bonilla*, 346.

49. Ibid., 356.

50. Despite his high stature in Bonilla's government, Christmas did not relinquish his U.S. citizenship. On Sept. 18, 1906, he appeared before the American consul in Puerto Cortés to register as a "citizen of the United States" (Deutsch Papers).

3. The Central American Wars

1. Thomas Schoonover, "An Isthmian Canal and the U.S. Overthrow of Nicaraguan President José Santos Zelaya," in Schoonover, *The United States in Central America*, 130-48.

2. Ibid., 130, 209 n. 2; Thomas Schoonover, "Economic Crisis,

Racism, and Relations with Central America," in Schoonover, *The United States in Central America*, 117, 122, 124.

3. The story of Estrada Cabrera's gift to TR's campaign appeared in *New York Times*, July 19, 1908, pt. 3, 3:5, and *New Orleans Daily Picayune*, July 21, 1908, 1:5. A spokesman for a Guatemalan exile group in the United States stated that the amount was $50,000. Leslie Combs, the U.S. minister in Guatemala in 1904, who allegedly transmitted the money, denied the account. In 1912 a Senate investigative committee, looking at presidential campaign contributions, probed deeply into the 1904 campaign, but the index of its thick report reveals no listing for "Estrada Cabrera," "Combs," or, for that matter, "Guatemala."

4. On Zelaya, see Stansifer, "José Santos Zelaya," 468-85; Aquino, *Personalidad política*, 57-58, 81, 103-5; *New York Herald Magazine*, Dec. 5, 1909, 2; and Schoonover, "An Isthmian Canal," 133-36.

5. Aquino, *Personalidad política*, 100. See also Healy, "A Hinterland in Search of a Metropolis," 20-43.

6. This account is based on Deutsch, *Incredible Yanqui*, 63-66. See also Victor Cáceres Lara, *Efemérides nacionales* (Tegucigalpa, 1973), 72-73, 179; Gordon Ireland, *Boundaries, Possessions, and Conflicts in Central and North America and the Caribbean* (Cambridge, Mass., 1941), 138; J. Lizardo Díaz, *Estrada Cabrera, Barillas, y Regalado: La revolución entre Guatemala, El Salvador, y Honduras en 1906* (Guatemala, 1906), 89.

7. "La Última Hora," Managua, Jan. 9, 1907; Manuel Bonilla to Zelaya, Jan. 9, 1907, State Dept., *Foreign Relations, 1907*, 612; William L. Merry to Robert Bacon, March 20, 1907, State Dept., Numerical File 3691/327; *La Gaceta Oficial*, March 30, 1907, 181; *La Bandera Liberal* (Tegucigalpa), April 25, 1907.

8. Zelaya to Theodore Roosevelt, Feb. 13, 1907, State Dept., *Foreign Relations, 1907*, 619.

9. Merry to Root, Jan. 16, 1907, State Dept., Num. File 3691/54.

10. Merry to Amer. Min., Guatemala, Jan. 30, Feb. 1, 1907, Num. File 3691/106, 107; David Bloom & Co., San Francisco, to Sec. State, March 15, 1907, Num. File 3691/167; Amer. Consul, Bluefields, to Asst. Sec. State, Feb. 23, 1907, Num. file 3691/199; *Bluefields American*, Feb. 25, 1907.

11. Merry to Root, Feb. 2, 1907, Num. File 3691/100; Pres., El Salvador, to Min. of Guatemala, Mexico, in Thompson to Sec. State, March 5, 1907, Num. File 3691/121 and 191.

12. *Bluefields American*, Feb., March 4, 1907; Amer. Consul, Bluefields, to Asst. Sec. State, Feb. 22, 1907; Merry to Root, March 1, 1907; Num. file 3691/151-3, 189.

13. Num. File 3691/158, 214-20; *Bluefields American*, April 1, 1907; W.F. Fullam to Bur. Nav., U.S. Navy, April 3, 1907, Fullam Papers, Library of Congress; Karnes, *Tropical Enterprise*, 39.

14. John Ellis, *The Social History of the Machine Gun* (New York, 1975).

15. Amer. Leg., Nicaragua, to Sec. State, March 15, 1907, Num. File 3691/245; Ellis, *Social History of the Machine Gun*, 16; Amer. Cons., Managua, May 8, 1907, Num. File 3691/670-75.

16. *Bluefields American*, April 1, 3, 1907.

17. *La Gaceta Oficial*, May 3, 1907; *New York Times*, March 26, 1907, 2:6-7; Zelaya to Gov., Bluefields, March 20, 1907, in *Bluefields American*, March 25, 1907; Merry to Bacon, April 18, 1907, Num. File 3691/544; *La Bandera Liberal*, May 6, 1907.

18. The account of this conflict and Christmas's participation in it is drawn from Deutsch, *Incredible Yanqui*, 66-68, 69-78; and *New York Times*, April 6, 1907, 4:4.

19. *New York Times*, April 11, 1907, 6:5.

20. Tracy Richardson, "A Soldier of Fortune's Story," *Liberty Magazine* 2 (Oct. 17, 1925): 39; *Bluefields American*, April 1, 1907; Amer. Cons., Tegucigalpa, to Asst. Sec. State, April 24, 1907, Num. File 3691/559.

21. Emily S. Rosenberg, *Spreading the American Dream: American Economic and Cultural Expansionism, 1890-1945* (New York, 1982), 7-62; LaFeber, *The American Age*, 218-49; Schoonover, *The United States in Central America*, 114, 118, 134, 162, 171-73.

22. Merry to Sec. State, Jan. 10, 1907, Num. File 3691/118; Fullam to Sec. Navy, May 15, 1907, Num. File 3691/613.

23. Stetson, Jennings, & Russell, Attorneys-at-Law, New York City, to Bacon, March 29, 1907, Num. File 3691/576.

24. Valentine to Bacon, April 4, 1907, Num. File 3691/576.

25. Valentine to J.W. Hein, April 30, 1907, Num. File 3691/583.

26. Root to J.W. Hein, May 28, 1907, Num. File 3691/622. See also the Valentine obituary, *Washington Star*, April 5, 1920.

27. Capt. W.J. Maxwell, U.S.S. *Marietta*, to Sec. Navy, Dec. 26, 1907, copy in Num. File 7357/43.

28. Root to Amer. Cons., Livingston, Guatemala, Dec. 27, 1907, Instructions, Honduras, RG 84, NA; Wm. P. Kent, Cons.-Gen., Guatemala, to Asst. Sec. State, Jan. 17, 1908, Num. File 7357/62.

29. W[illiam] F. Sands, Guatemala, to Sec. State, Jan. 24, 1908, Num. File 7357/81; William F. Sands, *Our Jungle Diplomacy* (Chapel Hill, N.C., 1944), 180-85.

30. Amer. Cons., Tegucigalpa, to H. Percival Dodge, Min., San Salvador [1908], Despatches, Honduras, RG 84, NA; Merry to Asst.

Sec. State, May 25, 1907, Num. File 3691/609; *La Prensa* (Tegucigalpa), Nov. 17, 21, 1908. Legation officer Thomas Riggs, a Princeton man, learned that a fellow Princetonian, Thomas Poe, languished in an Amapala jail, wearing a ball and chain, "for being a colonel on the losing side, in the revolution." Riggs obtained his release; see Riggs to Sec. State, April 10, 1908, Despatches, Honduras, RG 84, NA.

31. *New York Times,* July 8, 1908, 5:3; July 15, 1908, 4:5; July 18, 1908, 6:7; *New Orleans Daily Picayune,* July 17, 1908, 2:3; July 22, 1908, 2:5; Aug. 19, 1908, 2:3.

32. Guatemala, *Demanda entablada ante el corte de justicia centro-americana por el Gobierno de Honduras contra el Gobierno de la República de Guatemala* (Guatemala, 1908), 6, 121-22, 124.

33. Pedro Joaquín Chamorro, *Orígenes de la intervención americana en Nicaragua* (Managua, 1951), 4-5.

34. *Diario de Nicaragua* (Managua), Nov. 5, 1908; John Coolidge to Sec. State, Nov. 10, 19, 1908, Num. File 6369/36, 41; Schoonover, "An Isthmian Canal," 140.

35. Thomas Schoonover, "A U.S. Dilemma: Economic Opportunity and Anti-Americanism in El Salvador, 1901-1911," in Schoonover, *The United States in Central America,* 151-59, 165.

36. Schoonover, "A U.S. Dilemma," 153-54, 165. On the Moissant expedition, see Num. File 18432/101, 103A, 107, 115, 134, 151, 166, 190.

37. Num. File 18432/16, 17, 24; *Diario de Nicaragua,* May 6, 1909.

38. M.S. Valásquez to U.S. Min., May 14, 1909, Num. File 6369/104.

39. *New Orleans Daily Picayune,* April 5, 1910, 9:1; José Joaquín Morales, *De la historia de Nicaragua 1889-1913* (Granada, 1963), 298-301.

40. John H. Gregory, Amer. Leg., Managua, to Sec. State, Jan. 27, 1909, Num. File 6369/66.

41. Schoonover, "An Isthmian Canal," 134-37.

42. Gregory to Sec. State, March 9, 1909, Num. File 18432/43; Vice-Consul, Bluefields, to Asst. Sec. State, March 16, 1909, Num. File 18432/56; *Bluefields American,* Feb. 15, 1909; Berman, *Under the Big Stick,* 138-50.

43. Benjamin Teplitz, "The Political and Economic Foundations of Modernization in Nicaragua: The Administration of José Santos Zelaya, 1893-1909" (Ph.D. diss., Howard University, 1973), 417; Schoonover, "An Isthmian Canal," 132-33.

44. *Bluefields American,* April 19, 26; May 10, 24, 31; July 19; Aug. 23, 1909; "Aviso," June 17, 1909, Navy Dept., Area Files, 1900-

1911, RG 45, NA; Comdr., U.S.S. *Tacoma*, to Sec. Navy, July 26, 1909, Area Files, 1900-1911, microfilm (M625, reel 280).

45. Morales, *Nicaragua*, 322-23; *New York Herald*, June 1, 1910, 6:2-3.

46. Morales, *Nicaragua*, 283; Vice-Consul, Bluefields, to Asst. Sec. State, Dec. 18, 1908, Num. File 6369/59; Moffat interview with Estrada, July 4, 1909, Area Files, (M625, reel 280).

47. *New Orleans Daily Picayune*, Dec. 18, 1909, 4:5, 10:4; *New York Times*, Sept. 10, 1912, 4:5.

48. Comdr., U.S.S. *Tacoma*, to Sec. Navy, Aug. 29, 1909, Area Files, (M625, reel 281); Moffat to Asst. Sec. State, Oct. 16, 1909, Num. File 6369/227.

49. In taking the Bluff, Estrada employed John Paul Milon, an American, to operate a launch; for three months thereafter Milon piloted and repaired launches for Estrada, who promised him $1,500 for his services, payable in $100 installments. Milon complained to the American consul two years later that he was never paid. Milon to Consul, Bluefields, Aug. 8, 1911, Despatches, Bluefields, State Dept., Post Records, RG 84, NA.

50. *New Orleans Daily Picayune*, Oct. 20, 25, 1909; Moffat to Asst. Sec. State, Oct. 31, 1909, Num. File 6369/262; *El Comercio* (Managua), Oct. 30, 1909.

51. *New Orleans Daily Picayune*, Nov. 26, 1909, 1:7; Salvador Chamorro, Marcos Velázquez, Adán Dantón to Sec. State, Nov. 1909, Num. File 6369/289.

52. Moffat to Asst. Sec. State, Nov. 6, 13, 1909, Num. File 6369/275, 276; Salvador Castillo to Sec. State, Nov. 9, 1909, Num. File 6369/266; *New Orleans Daily Picayune*, Nov. 10, 1909, 3:4; *Bluefields American*, Nov. 10, 14, 1909.

53. Morales, *Nicaragua*, 312-15; *New York Herald*, Nov. 19, 1909, 2:2.

54. *New York Herald Magazine*, Dec. 5, 1909, 1-2.

55. H. Percival Dodge to Sec. State, Nov. 3, 1908; Jan. 23, 1909, Despatches, Honduras, RG 84, NA; *New York Daily Tribune*, Nov. 19, 1909.

56. *New Orleans Daily Picayune*, Nov. 19, 1909, 1:6, 7.

57. *New York Daily Tribune*, Nov. 19, 1909, 4:1.

58. Berman, *Under the Big Stick*, 143-50.

59. Morales, *Nicaragua*, 309; *New Orleans Daily Picayune*, Nov. 23, 1909, 1:6-7; *New York Times*, Nov. 23, 1909, 4:2-3; Doyle Memo, Nov. 21, 1909, Num. File 6369/343.

60. *New York Herald*, Nov. 22, 1909, 4:1; Schoonover, *The United States in Central America*, 144, 147.

61. Morales, *Nicaragua*, 323-24.
62. Zelaya, *La revolución de Nicaragua*, 125, 160; Henry Caldera to Sec. State, Nov. 20, 1909, State Dept., *Foreign Relations, 1909*, 448-49; *New Orleans Daily Picayune*, Nov. 21, 1909, 1:5.
63. *New York Herald*, Dec. 23, 1909, 2:2; *Bluefields American*, Jan. 1, 1910; Morales, *Nicaragua*, 326-27. The *New York Times* (Dec. 5, 1909, 2:4-5) reported that Zelaya ordered the bodies burned to cover his "crime." In January 1910, a month after Zelaya's abrupt resignation and departure from Nicaragua, the prosecuting attorney and the Nicaraguan officer commanding the execution of Cannon and Groce were arraigned at San Juan del Sur for having "illegally" convicted the two Americans (*New Orleans Daily Picayune*, Jan. 21, 1910, 1:5).
64. Morales, *Nicaragua*, 326-27. Groce's letter to his "Darling Momma" read: "This will be a terrible blow to you—the last words you will ever receive from your wayward son. I can't write much, as I am too nervous, and only have a few minutes to live. I joined the revolution in Bluefields and was captured and sentenced to be shot to death. I will be executed together with another young man from Virginia, LeRoy Cannon.

Now mother, dear, bear up. This is my fate—the results of war and disobedience to a loving mother.

It's hard to be shot like this, but I will die like a man. Tell all goodby."
65. Quoted in Dana G. Munro, *Intervention and Dollar Diplomacy in the Caribbean, 1900-1921* (Princeton, N.J., 1964), 176.
66. For an account of the Nicaraguan intervention of 1910-12, see Langley, *The Banana Wars*, 63-76.

4. The Campaign for Nicaragua

1. Schoonover, "An Isthmian Canal," 141-42, 146-47.
2. *New Orleans Daily Picayune*, Nov. 19, 1909, 1:6-7; *New York Times*, Nov. 21, 1909, pt. 3, 4:2.
3. *New York Times*, Nov. 28, 1909, pt. 5, 7:1; *Bluefields American*, Jan. 23, 1910. Benjamin Kidd, *The Control of the Tropics* (New York, 1898), and Alfred P. Schultz, *Race or Mongrel* (Boston, 1908), are two books that treat racism and U.S.-isthmian relations. On racism in U.S. relations with Latin America, Michael H. Hunt, *Ideology and U.S. Foreign Policy* (New Haven, Conn., 1987) 46-91; Schoonover, *The United States in Central America*, 111-29.
4. *New York Herald*, Nov. 19, 1909, 1:7. An irate New York businessman wrote to Secretary of State Knox: "What I want to know is—How long will our chicken-livered government continue to allow those damned Nicaraguan 'niggers' to insult, humiliate and injure

Americans and their interests" (T. Wesley Wright to Knox, Nov. 20, 1909, Num. File 6369/299).

5. Doyle Memo, Nov. 23 and Nov. 29, 1909, Num. File 6369/ 339, 341.

6. Quoted in *New York Herald*, Dec. 1, 1909, 9:2.

7. *New Orleans Daily Picayune*, Dec. 10, 1909, 2:5; Dec. 12, 1909, 6:6; Dec. 14, 1909, 1:5.

8. *New York Herald*, Jan. 1, 1910, 5.

9. Ibid.

10. *Bluefields American*, Jan. 9, 1910; Morales, *Nicaragua*, 381-88; *New York Times*, Jan. 2, 1910, 18:1.

11. *New York Times*, Jan. 2, 1910, 18:1.

12. *New York Herald*, Jan. 1, 1910, 5:1-2.

13. House of Representatives, 61st Cong., 2d sess.; *New York Herald*, Dec. 1, 1909, 9:2; Zelaya to Dr. Pedro González, Dec. 4, 1909, in Chamorro, *Orígenes de la intervención americana* 18-19.

14. *New Orleans Daily Picayune*, Jan. 12, 1910, 1:5.

15. *New York Herald*, Jan. 8, 1910, 4:5-6.

16. *New Orleans Daily Picayune*, Jan. 21, 1910, 1:5.

17. Ibid., Dec. 15, 1909, 1:6-7; *México Nuevo*, Dec. 30, 1909; *New York Times*, Dec. 30, 1909, 6:1; José Santos Zelaya, *La revolución de Nicaragua* (Madrid, 1910), 7-13; Kimball to Sec. Navy, Feb. 25, 1910, Num. File 6369/791; Morales, *Nicaragua*, 317-20.

18. Victor Gordon, "Revolutions Are My Business," *Bluebook Magazine* 95 (Sept. 1952): 75; *New Orleans Daily Picayune*, Jan. 1, 1911, 11.

19. Guy Molony biographical sketch, "People I Remember," Molony Papers, Tulane Univ.

20. Tracy Richardson (as told to Meigs Frost), "A Soldier of Fortune's Story," *Liberty* 2 (Oct. 10, 1925): 6.

21. Molony, "People I Remember."

22. Richardson, "A Soldier of Fortune's Story," 5-6.

23. Ibid., 6.

24. Moffat to Asst. Sec. State, Jan. 22, 1910, Num. File 6369/718; *New Orleans Daily Picayune*, Jan. 31, 1910, 1:4; Moffat to Sec. State, Feb. 9, 1910, Num. File 6369/767; Olivares to Sec. State, Jan. 31, 1910, Num. File 6369/708.

25. *New York Herald*, Feb. 10, 1910, 2:4; *Bluefields American*, Feb. 6, 1910; *New Orleans Daily Picayune*, Feb. 12, 1910, 1:5.

26. Olivares to Sec. State, Feb. 8, 10, 1910, Num. File 6369/740, 743; Caldera to Sec. State, Feb. 13, 1910, Num. File 6369/752; *New York Times*, Feb. 15, 1910, 3:5; *New Orleans Daily Picayune*, Feb. 16, 1910, 1:6.

27. *New York Times*, Feb. 21, 1910, 3:1; *New Orleans Daily Pic-*

ayune, Feb. 21, 1910, sec. 1, p. 7; *New York Herald*, Feb. 21, 1910, 5:5.

28. *New Orleans Daily Picayune*, March 4, 1910, 1:3-4; *New York Herald*, Feb. 24, 1910, 1:1; *Bluefields American*, March 13, 1910.

29. *Bluefields American*, March 20, 1910: *New Orleans Daily Picayune*, Feb. 26, 1910, 4:3-4.

30. *New Orleans Daily Picayune*, March 8, 1910, 1:2-3; Chamorro, *Origenes de la intervención americana*, 9; Samuel Lee to Elliott Northcott, Managua, March 16, 1911, Despatches, Bluefields, RG 84, NA; *Bluefields American*, Feb. 27, 1910.

31. *New York Herald*, April 8, 1910, 4:4.

32. *New Orleans Daily Picayune*, March 27, 1910, 5:2.

33. Estrada to Gen. Anastasio Ortíz, March 22, 1910, Navy Dept., Area Files, 1900-1910, RG 45, NA; Moffat to Capt. U.S.S. *Paducah*, April 1, 1910, Cons. Despatches, Bluefields, RG 84, NA; *New Orleans Daily Picayune*, April 5, 1910, 9:1-2.

34. Naval Regulations 305, 306, 307, copy in Num. File 18432/96.

35. *New Orleans Daily Picayune*, May 23, 1910, 1:1.

36. Ibid., May 19, 1910, 1:4; May 20, 1910, 1:6; May 28, 1910, 1:5; Moffat to Sec. State, May 21, 1910, Num. File 6369/958; *Bluefields American*, April 24, 1910; Rear Admiral Kimball, Report, May 25, 1910, Nicaragua Correspondence, Office of Naval Intelligence, RG 45, NA; Lowell Thomas, *Old Gimlet Eye: The Adventures of Smedley D. Butler* (New York, 1933), 126-29. The Navy Department also decreed that ships docking in Bluefields must pay duties to Estrada. Sec. Navy to Comdr. U.S.S. *Paducah*, May 31, 1910, Navy Dept. Area Files, RG 45, NA.

37. *Bluefields American*, June 19, 1910; *New Orleans Picayune*, June 3, 1910, 2:5; Schoonover, "An Isthmian Canal," 135-37, 147-48.

38. *New Orleans Daily Picayune*, June 3, 1910, 2:5; *New York Times*, June 5, 1910, 3:3; *Bluefields American*, June 5, 1910; Butler to Father, June 10, 1910, Smedley Butler Papers, Newtown Square, Pa.

39. *New Orleans Daily Picayune*, June 11, 1910, 5:3; June 18, 1910, 3:5-6. Captured federals told of officers who sold food to their soldiers at $5.00 (Nic.) for one banana, a piece of meat, or a bowl of soup (*Bluefields American*, June 19, 1910).

40. *New York Herald*, Feb. 25, 1910, 7:1; March 4, 1910, 4:6; Senate Committee on Foreign Relations, *Niicaraguan Affairs: Hearings*, 62d Cong., 2d sess., 1912, 68, *New York Times*, Feb. 25, 1910, 2:2; Moffat to J.J. Arthur, April 20, 1910, Cons. Despatches, Bluefields, RG 84, NA.

41. *New York Times*, April 24, 1910, 20:6; May 28, 1910, 1:3; *New Orleans Daily Picayune*, May 2, 1910, 2:6-7; May 16, 1910, 1:2;

Bluefields American, May 15, 22, 1910; Moffat to Capt. Gilmer, U.S.S. *Paducah,* May 27, 1910, Cons. Despatches, Bluefields, RG 84, NA. UFCO later reacquired the *Venus* and transformed it into the company's first refrigerated cargo ship.

42. On Pittman, see *New York Herald,* June 5, 1910, 5:3; *New York Times,* June 5, 1910, 3:3; June 6, 1910, 7:1; June 7, 1910, 8:1; July 17, 1910, 7:1; July 19, 1910, 3:2.

43. *New Orleans Daily Picayune,* July 22, 1910, 7:2-3; Olivares to Sec. State, June 28, 1910, Num. File 6369/1103.

44. Huntington Wilson to J.C. Needham, June 29, 1910, Num. File 6369/1020.

45. *New Orleans Daily Picayune,* July 23, 1910, 1:1; July 24, 1910, 4:3-4; Sept. 27, 1910, 5:3-4; *Bluefields American,* July 24, 1910.

46. *New York Herald,* Aug. 1, 1910, 6:6; *Bluefields American,* Aug. 21, 1910; *New Orleans Daily Picayune,* Aug. 3, 1910, 5:3-4; Aug. 22, 1910, 1:1-2, sec. 3:1-2, Aug. 28, 1910, 1:4.

47. Richardson, "A Soldier of Fortune's Story," 10.

48. Gordon, "Revolutions Are My Business," 78, 80.

49. *New Orleans Daily Picayune,* Sept. 26, 1910, 3:3-4.

50. Ibid., Oct. 24, 1910, 1:1, 3:2.

51. Nicaragua, *Report of Customs Collector, 1911-1913* (Washington, D.C., 1913), 32; *New York Times,* Aug. 23, 1912, 18:1.

52. *New York Times,* Nov. 23, 1913, pt. 6, 2:1-7; Zelaya, *La revolución de Nicaragua,* 6-7; *New Orleans Daily Picayune,* Sept. 6, 1910, 4:1-2; Ivan Musicant, *The Banana Wars: A History of United States Military Intervention in Latin America from the Spanish-American War to the Invasion of Panama* (New York, 1990), 138-44; Berman, *Under the Big Stick,* 151-65.

53. Lloyd C. Gardner, Walter LaFeber, and Thomas J. McCormick, *Creation of the American Empire: U.S. Diplomatic History* (Chicago, 1973), 273-87.

54. *El Paso Morning Times,* Nov. 27, 1913, 1:2; *New York Times,* Nov. 28, 1913, 1:3.

5. The Campaign for Honduras

1. Frank Boorman to Christmas, May 27, 1909, Deutsch Papers.

2. Honduras, Ministerio de Relaciones Exteriores, *Memoria, 1909* (Tegucigalpa, 1909), 19, 69-70; *New Orleans Daily Picayune,* July 29, 1908, 1:3-4.

3. "Honduras in 1910," *Bulletin of the Pan American Union* 33 (Aug. 1911): 313-15.

4. Gene S. Yeager, "The Honduran Foreign Debt, 1825-1953"

(Ph.D. diss., Tulane Univ., 1975), 267-71; *Diario de Nicaragua*, July 7, 1909; Percival Dodge to Sec. State, Jan. 29, 1909, and Philip Brown to Sec. State, May 6, June 12, 1909, Amer. Leg., Tegucigalpa, Despatches, RG 84, NA; *New Orleans Daily Picayune*, Jan. 29, 1911; Paul W. Drake, *The Money Doctor in the Andes: The Kemmerer Missions, 1923-1933* (Durham, N.C., 1989), 1-10, 20-24, 266; Robert N. Seidel, "American Reformers Abroad: The Kemmerer Missions in South America, 1923-1931," *Journal of Economic History* 32 (June 1972): 520-21, 541-45.

5. Munro, *Intervention and Dollar Diplomacy*, 227.

6. Invitation to Christmas, Dec. 9, 1909, Deutsch Papers; Bonilla to Christmas, Dec. 9, 1909, Deutsch Papers.

7. *New Orleans Daily Picayune*, Dec. 8, 1909, 1:3; Dec. 10, 1909, 2:5, 5:5; Feb. 3, 1910, 1:3.

8. *New Orleans Daily Picayune*, March 17, 1910; 1:1-2.

9. Ferrocarril de Guatemala to Christmas, Jan. 29, 1910, Deutsch Papers.

10. Bonilla to Christmas, April 11, 1910, Deutsch Papers.

11. Bonilla to Christmas, May 1, 1910, Deutsch Papers.

12. Bonilla to Christmas, May 18, 19, June 11, 1910, Deutsch Papers.

13. Bonilla to Christmas, June 23, 1910, Deutsch Papers.

14. Edward Reed to William F. Sands, June 23, 1910, State Dept., Dec. File, Int. Affairs, Honduras, 815.00/733; Bonilla to Christmas, June 27, 1910, Deutsch Papers.

15. Deutsch, *Incredible Yanqui*, 83-85. Bonilla added: "I see from your letter that you suppose an agreement exists between me and a high functionary of the country [Guatemala], and I do not understand the basis for your thinking this" (Bonilla to Christmas, July 23, 1910, Deutsch Papers).

16. Bonilla to Christmas, July 11, 1910, Deutsch Papers; Deutsch, *Incredible Yanqui*, 84-87.

17. Lara, *Efemérides nacionales*, 175-76; *La Gaceta Oficial*, Feb. 21, 1911, 133; Consul, Puerto Cortés, to U.S. Min., Honduras, July 25, 1910 RG 84, NA.

18. McCreery to Sec. State, July 28, 1910, Despatches, Honduras, RG 84, NA; Deutsch, *Incredible Yanqui*, 94-96.

19. *New Orleans Daily Picayune*, Aug. 8, 1910, 1:1. See also the issues of July 31, 1910, 3:1-2; Aug. 4, 1910, 1:7; Aug. 6, 1910, 1:2; Deutsch, *Incredible Yanqui*, 97-101.

20. *New York Times*, Aug. 8, 1910, 1:2; *New Orleans Daily Picayune*, Aug. 15, 1910, 1:1-2.

21. *New Orleans Daily Picayune*, Aug. 31, 1910, 5:2-3. On the

San Pedro Sula incidents, see Amer. Cons. Agent, San Pedro, to Claude Dawson, Consul, Puerto Cortés, Sept. 16, 1910, in Navy Dept., Sec. Navy, Gen. Corr., 8480, RG 80, NA.

22. *New Orleans Daily Picayune*, Aug. 9, 1910, 1:5, 2:5; Sept. 20, 1910, 4:3-4; Barahona, *La hegemonía de los Estados Unidos*, 17-19.

23. *New Orleans Daily Picayune*, Nov. 3, 1910, 1:7; Nov. 15, 1910, 3:5-6. About Dávila's notorious inability to control his generals, the diplomats accredited to his government had a saying: "In the country of Don Miguel everybody rules but him."

24. William F. Sands, Memo, Oct. 24, 1910, Dec. File, Internal Affairs, Honduras, 815.00/951.

25. R.S. Reynolds Hitt to Sec. State, Nov. 15, 1910, Dec. File 815.00/888; Hitt to Sec. State, Jan. 17, 1911, Dec. File 815.00/1022; Division of Latin American Affairs, Memo, Nov. 21, 1910, Dec. File 815.00/882; F.M. Huntington Wilson to Fenton McCreery, Nov. 25, 1910, Instructions, Honduras, State Dept. Post Records, RG 84, NA: *New York Times*, Nov. 15, 1910, 4:3; *La Prensa* (Tegucigalpa), Dec. 5, 1910.

26. "The Hornet," *New York Herald Magazine*, Jan. 29, 1911, 6; Hond. Leg. to State Dept., Dec. 8, 1910, *Foreign Relations of the United States* (hereafter FRUS) *1911*, 292-93; Edward Reed, Consul, Livingston, to Amer. Cons. Gen., Guatemala City, Dec. 14, 1910, Dec. File 815.00/946.

27. *New Orleans Daily Picayune*, Dec. 14, 1910, 1:5; Claude Dawson, Consul, Puerto Cortés, to Sec. State, Dec. 21, 1910, Despatches, Honduras, RG 84, NA; Comdr. U.S.S. *Tacoma* to Sec. Navy, Dec. 21, 1910, Office of Naval Records, Honduran Affairs, RG 45, NA.

28. "Morgan-Honduras Loan," Honduras, Treaties, Archivo Nacional, Tegucigalpa (handwritten).

29. *New York Herald Magazine*, Jan. 29, 1911, 6; *New Orleans Daily Picayune*, Dec. 21, 1910, 8:2; *New York Times*, Dec. 20, 1910, 1:2.

30. Baker, "United Fruit II," 32; Argueta, *Bananos y política*, 29-30; Barahona, *La hegemonía de los Estados Unidos*, 18-19.

31. Baker, "United Fruit II," 32.

32. Deutsch, *Incredible Yanqui*, 117-18; see also Bur. Invest. Justice Dept., New Orleans, Report of Jan. 27, 1911, in Dec. File, Int. Affairs, Honduras, 815.00/1070.

33. Amer. Min., Guatemala, to Sec. State, Dec. 21, 1910, *FRUS 1911*, 293.

34. Hitt to Sec. State, Dec. 21, 1910, Dec. File, Int. Affairs, Honduras, 815.00/929; *New Orleans Daily Picayune*, Dec. 27, 1910, 1:2.

35. *New Orleans Daily Picayune*, Dec. 29, 1910, 1:1-2, 3:3-4;

Dec. 31, 1910, 1:6, 3:4; Amer. Min., Guatemala, to Sec. State, Dec. 30, 1910, Dec. File, Int. Affairs, Honduras, 815.00/947.

36. Amer. Consul, Roatán, to Consul, Puerto Cortés, Dec. 31, 1910, Dec. File, Int. Affairs, Honduras, 815.00/947; Amer. Cons., Roatán, to Sec. State, Dec. 31, 1910, in Sec. Navy, Honduras Corr., RG 45, NA; New York Times, Dec. 30, 1910, 4:2.

37. Deutsch, Incredible Yanqui, 131.

38. Amer. Consul, Roatán, to Consul, Puerto Cortés, Jan. 7, 1911, Dec. File, Int. Affairs, Honduras, 815.00/1117.

39. New Orleans Daily Picayune, Jan. 10, 1911, 9:1; Sec. Navy to Sec. State, Jan. 14, 1911, Dec. File, Honduras 815.00/991; Thomas Dawson to Sec. State, Jan. 11, 1911, State Dept., Post Records, Honduras, RG 84, NA. Anticipating public criticism of its involvement in the invasion, the Guatemalan government denied "that the Gunboat Hornet has either been armed within Guatemalan jurisdiction or has received any armament from that source" (New York Times, Jan. 16, 1911, 5:1).

40. Deutsch, Incredible Yanqui, 134-40.

41. Bonilla to Christmas, Jan. 9, 1911, Deutsch Papers; New Orleans Daily Picayune, Jan. 4, 1911, 3:1; Jan. 7, 1911, 1:7; Jan. 8, 1911, 1:5; La Gaceta Oficial, Feb. 26, 1911, 145.

42. Dawson to Sec. State, Jan. 11, 1911, Post Records, Honduras, RG 84, NA.

43. Comdr. George Cooper, U.S.S. Marietta, to Sec. Navy, Jan. 18, 1911, Sec. Navy, Gen. Corr., no. 8480, RG 80, NA. Cooper apparently became convinced that Christmas, fearful of "assassination" by jealous Hondurans in Bonilla's command, was prepared to seek sanctuary on the Marietta. Dawson to Sec. State, Jan. 18, 1911, Post Records, Honduras, RG 84, NA.

44. Cooper to Sec. Navy, Jan. 18, 1911, Sec. Navy, Gen. Corr. 8480. Bonilla complained to Christmas about his difficulties with Cooper in a letter; Jan. 16, 1911, Deutsch Papers.

45. New York Times, Jan. 17, 1911, 8:2; see also Jan. 23, 1911, 6:4.

46. McCreery to Sec. State, Jan. 23, 1911; Consul, Ceiba, to Sec. State, Jan. 11, 1911, Post Records, Honduras, RG 84, NA; La Gaceta Oficial, Feb. 26, 1911, 146.

47. Comdr., U.S.S. Marietta, to Sec. Navy, Jan. 20, 1911, Honduras Corr., RG 45, NA; Dawson to Sec. State, Jan. 23, 1911, Post Records, Honduras, RG 84, NA.

48. Christmas to Naval Commander, Jan. 21, 1911; Comdr. Cooper, U.S.S. Marietta, and Comdr. Maurice Woollcombe, H.M.S. Brilliant, to Christmas, Jan. 24, 1911, Deutsch Papers.

49. Bonilla to Gens. Christmas and Leiva, Jan. 22, 1911, and Bonilla to Christmas, Jan. 23, 1911, Deutsch Papers; Tracy Richardson, in *New Orleans States*, Oct. 25, 1925.

50. For this account I have relied on Deutsch, *Incredible Yanqui*, 152-64; *New York Times*, Feb. 7, 1911, 4:3, which carried the story of the *Tacoma*'s eyewitness; and esp. Christmas to Bonilla, Jan. 30, 1911, Rare Book Case, Tulane Univ. Library. Commander Cooper, who had met several times with Christmas prior to the battle, wrote sarcastically that the federals could have defeated Christmas's force at the river but refused to "go out and meet the enemy" (Cooper to Sec. Navy, Jan. 26, 1911, Honduras Corr., RG 45, NA. For an account of heroics at La Ceiba, see Richardson, "A Soldier of Fortune's Story," 37-38; and Gordon, "Revolutions Are My Business," 78.

51. Christmas to Bonilla, Jan. 30, 1911, Rare Book Case, Tulane Univ. Library. Christmas cited the following Americans for valor at La Ceiba: Guy R. Molony, Joseph Reed, Jack Parker, E.J. McLaurie—colonels; Haymon Ebanks, Charles Marshall, Tony Joe, Timothy Warren, George Esche, German Woods—captains; German White—lieutenant; A. Dixon, C.L. Ebanks—second lieutenants; Luther James, Fred Bodden—soldiers. The only American killed was Louis Bier, a noncombatant who miraculously survived the explosion of a 42-mm artillery shell in his bedroom, only to be mortally struck in the abdomen by an errant bullet.

6. A Different World

1. *New Orleans Daily Picayune*, Jan. 29, 1911, 1:7. the official *Gaceta* declared: "At La Ceiba the valiant General Guerrero perished . . . and the enemy suffered many desertions" (*La Gaceta Oficial*, Feb. 27, 1911, 150). U.S. Consul Allan Gard reported: "The Americans with Christmas now say that this will be their last war for any country other than their own" (Gard to Sec. State, Jan. 29, 1911, Despatches, La Ceiba, RG 84, NA). Gordon ("Revolutions are my Business," 80) received $20,000 for his services in the rebellion.

2. Cooper, U.S.S. *Marietta*, to Sec. Navy, Jan. 26, 1911, Honduras Corr., RG 45, NA; F.C. Viguerie to Christmas, Aug. 30, 1923, Deutsch Papers.

3. Gard to Sec. State, Jan. 30, 1911, Despatches, La Ceiba, RG 84, NA; British vice-consul to Christmas, Jan. 27, 1911, Deutsch Papers.

4. McCreery to Sec. State, Jan. 28, 29, 1911, Despatches, Honduras, RG 84, NA.

5. *Washington Post*, Jan. 23, 1911.

6. Baker, "United Fruit II," 31. This article, noted Dana Gardner

Munro, was "based apparently on material obtained from Zemurray or from one of his associates" (*Intervention and Dollar Diplomacy in the Caribbean*, 227).

7. *New Orleans Daily Picayune*, Jan. 25, 1911, 2:4.

8. *New York Times*, Jan. 29, 1911, pt. 3, 4:5; McCreery to Sec. State, Feb. 2, 1911, Despatches, Honduras, RG 84, NA; Deutsch, *Incredible Yanqui*, 231-33.

9. Honduras, Congreso Nacional, *Manifiesto del Congreso Nacional al pueblo hondureño* (Tegucigalpa, 1911); Barahona, *La hegemonía de los Estados Unidos*, 180.

10. Bonilla to Christmas, Feb. 2, 1911; Capt., H.M.S. *Brilliant*, and Capt., U.S. Naval Forces in Region, to Christmas, Jan. 30, 1911, Deutsch Papers; *New Orleans Daily Picayune*, Feb. 14, 1911, 2:4.

11. *New York Times*, Feb. 5, 1911, pt. 3, 4:7; Feb. 14, 1911, 4:5.

12. Alvey Adee, "Honduran Situation," Jan. 30, 1911, Dec. File, Int. Affairs, Honduras, 815.00.

13. *New York Times*, March 3, 1911, 10:4; *Recuerdo al Gral. don Manuel Bonilla* (Comayaguela, 1918), 5; *La Gaceta Oficial*, Feb. 1, 1911, 77.

14. Amer. Consul, Puerto Cortés, to Amer. Min., Tegucigalpa [Feb. 1911], Despatches, Puerto Cortés, RG 84, NA; Lara, *Efemérides nacionales*, 65; *Actas de las sesiones de las conferencias de paz en Puerto Cortés a bordo del vapor de Guerra Americano "Tacoma" del 21 de febrero al 15 de marzo de 1911* (Tegucigalpa, 1911); Mariano Tovar, *Los hombres de América: Manuel Bonilla ante la historia* (N.p., [1911]), 6-7.

15. Comdr., U.S.S. *Chester*, to Sec. Navy, Gen. Corr. 8480, RG 80, NA.

16. McCreery to Sec. State, March 17, 1911, Dec. File, Int. Affairs, Honduras, 815.00/1195; Richardson, "A Soldier of Fortune's Story," 38; *El Nuevo Tiempo*, July 5, 1911.

17. *New Orleans Daily Picayune*, Feb. 22, 1911, 1:7.

18. Adee Memo, April 4, 1911, Dec. File, Int. Affairs, Honduras, 815.00/1316.

19. Sec. State to Atty. Gen., April 18, 1911, Int. Affairs, Honduras, 815.00/1245.

20. *New York Times*, April 7, 1911, 5:2. The *Hornet*, escorted back to New Orleans by the U.S.S. *Wheeling*, deteriorated in the humid atmosphere of the Gulf, and the captain of the *Wheeling* dispatched forty seamen with two hundred pounds of red-lead paint to coat *anything* that was rusting. The Navy sent a bill for the *Hornet's* upkeep to the Justice Department, which refused to pay; following some almost comical interdepartmental bickering, the expenses ($168.95)

were paid out of a Navy contingency fund. Federal authorities at New Orleans later sold the ship for $3,131.05.

21. *El Nuevo Tiempo,* July 25, 1911; White to Sec. State, Feb. 9, 1911; Knox to Amer. Leg., Tegucigalpa, Feb. 10, 1912; Dawson to Sec. State, March 12, 1911; J. Butler Wright to Sec. State, July 13, 1911, Despatches, Honduras, RG 84, NA; *New York Times,* Feb. 10, 1912, 3:6; "El Redacción" [A.A. Ramírez Fontecha], *El ferrocarril nacional de Honduras y el muelle y faro de Puerto Cortés* (Tegucigalpa, 1911); Finney, "Our Man in Honduras," 13-20.

22. *New York Times,* Feb. 8, 1912, 13:1; April 1, 1912, 11:1; Adee Memo, Feb. 18, 1911, Dec. File, Int. Affairs, Honduras, 815.00/1129; Honduras, Ministerio de Relaciones Exteriores *Memoria, 1912-1913* (Tegucigalpa, 1914), 49-50; Kepner and Soothill, *Banana Empire,* 100-101, 109-10; Guevera-Escudera, "Nineteenth Century Honduras," 464-65; Dosal, *Doing Business with the Dictator,* 120-22.

23. *La Gaceta Oficial,* Feb. 28, 1911, 154; Memo, Latin American Division, June 11, 1912, Meyer to Sec. State, Oct. 31, 1913, Dec. File, Int. Affairs, Honduras, 815.00/1439; Dosal, *Doing Business with the Dictator,* chap. 5; Kepner and Soothill, *Banana Empire,* 110-11. When Bonilla took power he stalled the Whitney Bank negotiations. After he died, the Wilson administration urged acceptance of a UFCO plan to rehabilitate Honduran finances, but it fell victim to consular suspicions that the "company" would not complete the interoceanic railway but instead destroy the smaller coastal banana planters. In 1926 Honduras accepted a British plan, originally proposed by Sir Lionel Carden in 1909, to pay its foreign debt; under its provisions the republic finally retired its nineteenth-century European debt in 1953 (Yeager, "The Honduran Foreign Debt," 293-309).

24. *New Orleans Daily Picayune,* Jan. 3, 1911, 1:1-2.

25. *El Nuevo Tiempo,* June 15, 1911.

26. Dawson to Sec. State, March 12, 1911, May 28, 1911; Charles White to Sec. State, Nov. 15, 1911, Despatches, Honduras, RG 84, NA.

27. Edward Welles, *Daily Mexican,* Dec. 24, 1911.

28. *El Nuevo Tiempo,* March 5, 1912; Deutsch, *Incredible Yanqui,* 170-71.

29. Charles White to Sec. State, April 24, 1912, Despatches, Honduras, RG 84, NA.

30. *El Nuevo Tiempo,* April 11, 1912; April 22, 1912; Deutsch, *Incredible Yanqui,* 170.

31. Deutsch, *Incredible Yanqui,* 172-73.

32. Bertrand to Christmas, April 21, 1913, Deutsch Papers; Consul, Puerto Cortés, to Sec. State, May 9, 1913, Dec. File, Int. Affairs,

Honduras, 815.00/1496; Dana G. Munro, *A Student in Central America* (New Orleans, 1983), 152-53. Ida Culotta Christmas bore Christmas a son, Pat; Ida died Nov. 20, 1961.

33. Hermann Deutsch Notes, Deutsch Papers.

34. Edwin Welles to Christmas, March 28, 1928, Deutsch Papers. The literary prototype of this generation of mercenaries appeared in Richard Harding Davis's *Soldiers of Fortune* (1897), in which the protagonist, Robert Clay, boasts to a Central American general interfering with his concession that if pressed he will call on a U.S. warship "and she'll blow you and your little republic back up there in the mountains." See Gerald Langford, *The Richard Harding Davis Years: A Biography of a Mother and a Son* (New York, 1961), 168-69.

35. Consul, Puerto Cortés, to Sec. State, April 28, 1914, Dec. File, Int. Affairs, Honduras, 815.00/1536.

36. John Gomin to Sec. State, Jan. 11, 1915, Dec. File, Int. Affairs, Honduras, 815.00/1565; F.J. Mejía to Christmas, Jan. 9, July 30, 1915, Deutsch Papers.

37. Amer. Min., Guatemala, to Sec. State, Feb. 15, 1915, Dec. File, Int. Affairs, Guatemala, 814.00/220.

38. Amer. Min., Guatemala, to Sec. State, June 1, 1915, and Aug. 31, 1915, 815.00/1590, 1613; Lansing to Amer. Leg., Guatemala, Aug. 20, 1915, 815.00/1607; Min. de Guerra y Marina, April 9, 1917, Deutsch Papers.

39. Amer. Min., Guatemala, to Sec. State, Oct. 7, 1915, Dec. File, Int. Affairs, Guatemala, 814.00/238; Statement of Leon Winfield Christmas, Oct. 10, 1915, Puerto Cortés, Deutsch Papers; Min. de Guerra y Marina to Christmas, Sept. 1, 1916, Deutsch Papers; *New Orleans Daily Picayune*, Oct. 14, 1915.

40. E.A. Burke to Col. Robert Ewing, April 18, 1917, Deutsch Papers.

41. Lee to Ida Christmas, May 18, 20, 25, 1917, Deutsch Papers.

42. Amer. Min., Honduras, to Christmas, June 12, 1917; copy of agreement: Christmas, F.W. Bryan, C.J. Webre, and D.B. Jones, Sept. 21, 1917; Adj. Gen. Office, Memo, Oct. 1, 1917 (copy), Deutsch Papers.

43. Consul, La Ceiba, Sept. 17, 1915; Act. Sec. State to Amer. Leg., Tegucigalpa, Sept. 22, 1915; Amer. Leg., Tegucigalpa, to Sec. State, Oct. 6, 1915; Consul, Puerto Cortés, to Sec. State, Nov. 26, Dec. 13, 1915, Jan. 29, Oct. 12, 1916, Dec. File, Int. Affairs, Honduras, 815.00/1621, 1627a, 1647, 1649, 1660, 1669.

44. Amer. Min., Guatemala to Sec. State, Jan. 5, 1918, Dec. File, Int. Affairs, Guatemala, 814.48/27, 814.00/1756.

45. Christmas to Ida and Pat, Nov. 27, 1917, Jan. 8, 1918, Mar. 16, 1918; Lansing to Christmas, May 17, 1918, Deutsch Papers.

46. Christmas to Amer. Leg., Guatemala, Dec. 24, 1918, Dec. File, Int. Affairs, Cent. Amer., 813.00/929; Amer. Leg. to Sec. State, March 9, Aug. 5, 1919, Feb. 19, 1920, Dec. File, Int. Affairs, Guatemala, 815.00/1829, 1918, 2167; State Dept. to Christmas, July 17, 1919, Deutsch Papers.

47. Amer. Consul, La Ceiba, to Sec. State, June 17, 1920; Vice-Consul, Puerto Cortés, June 14, 1920; Asst. Sec. State to *Chargé d'Affaires*, Tegucigalpa, July 9, 1920, Dec. File, Int. Affairs, Guatemala, 815.00/2195, 2194, 2204; Deutsch, *Incredible Yanqui*, 194-95; Donald A. Yerxa, *Admirals and Empire: The United States Navy and the Caribbean, 1898-1945* (Columbia, S.C., 1991) 82-83.

48. Christmas to Sumner Welles, June 1, 1921; Richmond Levering & Co. to Welles, May 2, 1921, Dec. File, Int. Affairs, Guatemala, 814.6323/17, 14. Robert Pendleton to Richmond Levering & Co., Feb. 17, 1921; Christmas to Surg. Gen., U.S. Public Health Service, July 22, 1922; Sherve, Gordon, and Crowe to Christmas, May 22, 1923; Thomas Lee, Manhattan Club, April 21, 1923; Christmas to State Dept., June 3, 1923; U.S. Patent Off., No. 1 465 808, Aug. 21, 1923, Deutsch Papers. Joseph H. Tulchin, *Aftermath of War: World War I and U.S. Policy toward Latin America* (New York, 1971).

49. J.H. Burton to Hermann Deutsch, Jan. 26, 1929, Deutsch Papers; Schoonover, "France in Central America," 192.

50. Christmas to Ida [Feb. 1920]; Invoice, UFCO Hospital, Guatemala, April 15, 1923; Ray Meaker to Guy Molony, Aug. 22, 1923, Deutsch Papers.

51. Beecher Stowe, Doubleday, Page & Co., to Christmas, June 15, 1923; Christmas to J.C. James, Nov. 23, 1923; Minor Keith to Molony, Jan. 22, 1924; *Memphis News-Scimitar* (n.d.), Deutsch Papers. Luis C. Nuila, in *El Sol* (Tegucigalpa), July 3, 1929.

52. *Los Angeles Times*, March 16, 1925, pt. 2, 1:2; March 17, 1925, pt. 2, 1-2; *El Paso World News*, Nov. 11, 1934; *El Paso Herald Post*, May 30, 1961.

53. Vivian, "Major E.A. Burke", 183-84; *New Orleans Morning Advocate*, June 30, 1939; Guy Molony Oral History, William Ransom Hogan Jazz Archives, Tulane Univ.; *New York Times*, Sept. 25, 1928, 31:5; Alfred Batson, *Vagabond's Paradise* (Boston, 1931), 87.

54. Tracy Richardson clippings, El Paso Public Library; Thomas, *Born to Raise Hell*, 260; *El Paso Morning Times*, Dec. 27, 1914.

55. Tex O'Reilly, *Roving and Fighting: Adventures under Four Flags* (New York, 1918), 250-58; Lowell Thomas, *Born to Raise Hell: The Life Story of Tex O'Reilly, Soldier of Fortune* (New York, 1936), 370; *New York Times*, Dec. 9, 1946.

56. Gordon, "Revolutions Are My Business," 81; Sec. State to Amer. Leg., Guatemala, Feb. 15, 1927; Amer. Leg., Guatemala, to Sec.

State, May 29, 1929, Dec. File, Int. Affairs, Guatemala, 814.796 Gordon, Victor D./2, 27.

57. *New Orleans Times-Picayune*, April 21, 1925, 3:7; Batson, *Vagabond's Paradise*, 85, 86.

58. *New Orleans Times-Picayune*, Jan. 18, 1929, 11:5; Nov. 15, 1932, 1:1-2; Jan. 13, 1933, 1:6, 10:1; Jan. 12, 1934, 18:5; Mil. Attaché, Managua, to Brig. Comm., April 28, 1928, War Dept., Military Intelligence Division (hereafter MID) 2610-P-25; J.B. Pate, Mil. Attaché, Nov. 18, 1938, MID 2548-150; Maj. A.R. Harris, G-2 Report, Jan. 10, 1933, MID 2657-P-439/19, RG 165, NA.

59. *New Orleans Times-Picayune*, Sept. 7, 1934; *New York Times*, Sept. 7, 1934, 19:2-6; T. Harry Williams, *Huey P. Long* (New York, 1970), 731-32.

60. Gen. Staff to Mil. Attaché, San Salvador, June 30, 1941, MID 2338-2018/1; July 10, 1941, New Orleans Office, MID, 3457-296-1; Gen. Staff, MID, to Mil. Attaché, San Salvador, July 17, 1941, MID 2271-P-171-1, RG 165, NA; Guy Molony clippings, New Orleans Public Library; *New Orleans Times-Picayune*, Feb. 15, 1922, 8:2.

61. Wilson, *Empire in Green and Gold*, 222; "El Señor Zemurray y los progresos de la Costa Norte," *Renacimiento* 4 (Jan. 15, 1921): 9-11; Decreto 139 (March 17, 1930), Archivo del Congreso Nacional, Honduras.

62. Amer. Leg., Tegucigalpa, to Sec. State, Aug. 18, 1919, Dec. File, Int. Affairs, Honduras, 815.00/2093.

63. Alfredo Trejo Castillo, *El Señor don Samuel Zemurray y la soberanía de Honduras* (Tegucigalpa, 1926).

64. Kepner and Soothill, *Banana Empire*, 118-21; Manuel Galich, *Del Pánico al ataque* (Guatemala, 1977), 27-31; Mil. Attaché, San José, March 10, 1931, MID 265-P-83/24, RG 165, NA.

65. MID 265-P-83/20-23, RG 165, NA; Karnes, *Tropical Enterprise*, 178; Dosal, *Doing Business with the Dictator*, chap. 5.

66. *New York Times*, Dec. 2, 1961, 23:3; Baker, "United Fruit II," 29. See also Thomas McCann, *An American Company: The Tragedy of United Fruit* (New York, 1976), 21-22; and Whitfield, "Strange Fruit," 312-13, 319-31.

67. Dosal, *Doing Business with the Dictator*, chap. 10.

68. Quoted in Baker, "United Fruit II," p. 26.

Epilogue

1. See Dosal, *Doing Business with the Dictator*, chaps. 5 and 10, for background on the Cutter-Zemurray relationship.

2. For this account we have relied extensively on Wilson, *Em-*

pire in Green and Gold, 258-66; and the undeniably biased summary in McCann, *An American Company* (esp. 18-24), which has been revised and reissued as *On the Inside: A Story of Intrigue and Adventure on Wall Street, in Washington, and in the Jungles of Central America* (Boston, 1987).

3. Quoted in Wilson, *Empire in Green and Gold,* p. 264.

4. Juan del Camino, "El monstruo de la United Fruit sigue tragándose las tierras del sur," *Repertorio Americano* 31 (April 23, 1936): 285-86. On the "ethnic question" in the banana industry, see the important study by Bourgeois, *Ethnicity at Work.*

5. Aviva Chomsky, "Plantation Society"; Kepner, *Social Aspects of the Banana Industry,* 27-44, 157-218; Whitfield, "Strange Fruit," 316-17.

6. Zemurray quoted in Steve Volk, "Honduras: On the Border of War," *NACLA: Report on the Americas* 15.6 (1981): 5; Whitfield, "Strange Fruit," 322-23.

7. Sam Stone, *The Heritage of the Conquistadores: Ruling Classes in Central America from the Conquest to the Sandinistas* (Lincoln, Neb., 1990).

Bibliographical Note

Soldiers of fortune in early twentieth century Central America were not the literary type, and the researcher must piece accounts of their careers together from a variety of sources. The Hermann Deutsch Papers, Tulane University Library, New Orleans, contain three boxes of Lee Christmas's letters and one box of photographs. Deutsch supplemented this frankly sparse collection with extensive interviews with Christmas's contemporaries (especially Guy Molony), both in New Orleans and in Honduras. Regrettably, the Molony Papers at Tulane contain only a few items. The oral history in Tulane's William Ransom Hogan Jazz Archives, conducted in the 1960s, offers some personal reminiscences about the isthmian adventurers, mostly Major Edward Burke, and there are small collections of Burke Papers in the archives of Louisiana State University and the Bancroft Library of the University of California, Berkeley. The John D. Imboden Papers in the Alderman Library, University of Virginia, contain correspondence from and to Frank Imboden. Far more useful for this study were the two dozen or so Manuel Bonilla letters in the Deutsch Papers.

U.S. officials dutifully reported on the activities of American adventurers and entrepreneurs in Central America between 1896 and 1929. The State Department's consular reports (filed separately until 1906 and available on microfilm) chronicle isthmian revolutions and occasionally note American participants. The diplomatic correspondence is available on microfilm in three series. The first covers the years from 1821 to 1906. The second, called the Numerical File (1906 to 1910), contains numerous reports on American filibustering in this era, but identifying participants requires imaginative use of the index. The third series, the Decimal File (1910 to 1929), contains various subseries, among which the Records of the Department of State Relating to the Internal Affairs of Central America, with separate files for Honduras, Nicaragua, and Guatemala, proved useful in tracking the soldiers of fortune. The Post Records of the Department of State (Record Group 84), particularly for Honduras, were invaluable for detailing the Honduran rebellion of 1910-11. By careful perusal of the "contents" listing at the beginning of each collection, the researcher can readily locate references to filibustering.

The activities of Christmas's generation also figured in U.S. military accounts, since naval officers patrolling tropical ports or policing banana towns often had direct contact with filibusters. For this study the most useful were Department of the Navy, Naval Records Collection of the Office of Naval Records and Library, Office of Naval Intelligence, "Honduras Correspondence, 1910-1911," and "Nicaragua Correspondence, 1909-1910"; and Department of War, Military Intelligence Division, 1917-41, which contains a name index. For U.S. agencies the most useful guide to materials in the National Archives is George S. Ulibarri and John P. Harrison, *Guide to Materials on Latin America in the National Archives of the United States* (Washington, D.C., 1974). Other essential guides to research on Central American-U.S. relations are Kenneth J. Grieb, ed., *Research Guide to Research on Central America and the Caribbean* (Madison, WI, 1985); Richard Dean Burns, ed., *Guide to American Foreign Relations Since 1700* (Santa Barbara, Calif., 1983); and U.S. National Archives and Records Administration, *Diplomatic Records* (Washington, D.C., 1986).

References to filibustering also appear in the following Central American documentary publications: Guatemala, *Demanda entablada ante el corte de justicia centro-americana por el gobierno de Honduras contra el gobierno de la República de Guatemala* (Guatemala, 1908); Honduras, Congreso Nacional,

Manifiesto del Congreso Nacional al pueblo hondureño (Tegucigalpa, 1911); Miguel Dávila, *Manifiesto que el señor presidente dirige a los hondureños* . . . (Tegucigalpa, 1908); Honduras, Secretaría de Relaciones Exteriores, *Actas de las sesiones de las conferencias de Paz en Puerto Cortés* . . . (Tegucigalpa, 1911); Nicaragua, "Documentos de la revolución de la costa atlántica de Nicaragua, 1909-1910," *Revista de la Academia de Geografía e Historia de Nicaragua* 22-23 (Jan.-Dec. 1961): 71-97; and Nicaragua, Ministerio de Relaciones Exteriores, *Documentos oficiales referentes a la guerra entre Nicaragua y Honduras de 1907, y a la participación de El Salvador* (Managua, 1907).

Newspapers of Christmas's era chronicled the careers of American soldiers of fortune in the tropics in the heyday of militant American empire building—not surprisingly, often exaggerating their exploits—and supplying a generally reliable chronology of their activities. *La Gaceta Oficial* (Honduras, 1900-1912) provides occasional references to Christmas's contributions to Honduran order and disorder. The *Bluefields American* reflects, often in spirited fashion, the views of coastal residents toward Zelaya. Since New Orleans was the "capital" for isthmian Caribbean coastal residents of these years, the New Orleans papers, especially the *Daily Picayune*, are essential reading. Many city libraries maintain name indexes compiled from local newspapers (the New Orleans public library has such a file) and can often provide clippings on "hometown boys" in Central America between 1900 and 1920.

Memoirs and biographies of Christmas's revolutionary confreres range from Sunday-supplement tales, often sensational and predictably shallow, to more substantial accounts. For "Tex" O'Reilly, the Texas journalist, soldier of fortune, and sheriff, see his own *Roving and Fighting: Adventures under Four Flags* (New York, 1918); and the biography by Lowell Thomas, *Born to Raise Hell: The Life Story of Tex O'Reilly, Soldier of Fortune* (New York, 1936), both of which may be characterized as "Sunday-supplement" material. Tracy Richardson told his story in five articles in *Liberty* (Oct.-Dec. 1925). They are considerably more helpful in reconstructing the battles of Central America than Victor Gordon, "Revolutions Are My Business,"

Bluebook Magazine 95 (Sept. 1952): 72-81, which is laughably inaccurate. For Edward Burke, see James Vivian, "Major E.A. Burke: The Honduran Exile, 1889-1928," *Louisiana History* 15 (Spring 1974): 175-94.

Despite its title, Ivan Musicant, *The Banana Wars: A History of United States Military Intervention in Latin America from the Spanish-American War to the Invasion of Panama* (New York: Macmillan, 1990), treats the U.S. military intervention in Nicaragua but not the smaller incursions into Honduras or the wars involving the banana barons and their mercenaries. José Santos Zelaya, *La revolución de Nicaragua* (Madrid, 1910), offers essentially a defense of the dictator's anti-American policies but does contain some useful documents, among them the last letters of Lee Roy Cannon and Leonard Groce. Enrique Aquino, *La personalidad política del General José Santos Zelaya* (Managua, 1944), is more balanced. The best study of Zelaya in English is Charles Stansifer, "José Santos Zelaya: A New Look at Nicaragua's 'Liberal' Dictator," *Revista/Review Interamericana* 7 (Fall 1977): 468-85; but see also the assessment of John Findling, "The United States and Zelaya" (Ph.D. diss., Univ. of Texas, 1971), written under the direction of the distinguished U.S. diplomatic historian Robert Divine.

Manuel Bonilla—Zelaya's enemy and Zemurray's and Christmas's benefactor—was a warrior, not a philosopher, and left only a few pamphlets to explain his political purpose. Rafael Bardales Bueso has supplied a biography, *Imagen de un líder: Manuel Bonilla* (Tegucigalpa, 1985), which reprints many documents about domestic politics but largely ignores the international aspects of Bonilla's career. His adversary, Policarpo Bonilla, a Honduran thinker and statesman, is a more attractive subject, as Ismael Mejía Deras (pseud. Aro Sanso) revealed in his ample biography, *Policarpo Bonilla, algunos aspectos biográficos* (Mexico City, 1936).

Zemurray's biography awaits the revelations and release of papers (if any exist) by his daughter, Doris Zemurray Stone, and grandson, Sam Stone. Until then one must rely on the diverse accounts of the Banana Man's activities in Charles Kepner and Jay Soothill, *The Banana Empire: A Case Study in Economic*

Imperialism (New York, 1935), a socialist-flavored critique; Alfredo Trejo Castilla, *El Señor don Samuel Zemurray y la soberanía de Honduras* (Tegucigalpa, 1926), which warned of Zemurray's expanding influence in the country; Marvin Barahona, *La hegemonía de los Estados Unidos en Honduras (1907-1932)* (Tegucigalpa, 1989); Ernest Baker, "United Fruit II: The Conquest of Honduras," *Fortune* 7 (March 1933): 25-33, which covers the revolution of 1911 and Zemurray's takeover of UFCO; Charles Morrow Wilson, *Empire in Green and Gold* (New York, 1947); Thomas McCann, *An American Company: The tragedy of United Fruit* (New York, 1976), which has been updated by McCann as *On the Inside: A Story of Intrigue and Adventure on Wall Street, in Washington, and in the Jungles of Central America* (Boston, 1987); Stephen J. Whitfield, "Strange Fruit: The Career of Samuel Zemurray," *American Jewish History* 82 (March 1984): 307-23; Darío A. Euraque, "La 'reforma liberal' en Honduras y la hipótesis de la 'oligarquía ausente,' 1870-1930," *Revista de historia* 23 (Jan.-June 1991): 7-56; Mario R. Argueta, *Bananas y política: Samuel Zemurray y la Cuyamel Fruit Company* (Tegucigalpa, 1989); and Paul Dosal, *Doing Business with the Dictator: A Political History of United Fruit in Guatemala, 1899-1944* (Wilmington, Del., 1993).

Christmas's adventures spawned a hundred journalistic pieces that appeared in American newspapers from 1900 until long after his death. His biographer, Hermann Deutsch, a journalist by trade, somehow managed to penetrate the adulatory mists surrounding his life and to produce, in *The Incredible Yanqui: The Career of Lee Christmas* (London, 1931), a work that artfully combines detail and drama in a readable and sympathetic but not glorifying manner.

Index

Accessory Transit Company, 13
Aceituno, 53
Acoyapa, 101
Adams, Brooks, 9
Adee, Alvey A., 72, 143, 145
adventurers, 86, 91. *See* mercenaries and soldiers of fortune
Alfaro, Prudencio, 76-77
Alfonso XIII, King of Spain, 62
Alguín, "Little Phil," 159
Allgemeine Elektrizitäts-Gesellschaft (AEG), 29
Altschuhl, Francisco, 104
Amapala, 53, 67
American, 81; as used in this book, 5; customs collectors, 113; entrepreneurs, 33, 47
American Mediterranean, 13, 24, 116
Anglo-American paternalism, 142
anti-Americanism, 2, 65, 125, 144
anti-Manuelistas, 73
anti-Nicaraguan propagandists, 77
anti-Zelaya activity, 76, 86, 98
Arauz, Eugenio, 75-76
Arbenz, Jacobo, 171
Argueta, Mario, 16
Arias, Juan Ángel, 52-55
Atlantic Fruit and Steamship Company, 35-36

Atlantic Navigation Company, 104
Austria, 16

Baker, Ernest, 4, 143
Baker, Lorenzo, 34, 38, 168
banana companies, 39-40, 117, 149, 155, 172
"Banana diplomacy," 174
banana empire, 38
"Banana gate," 171
banana men, 7, 11, 23, 28, 31, 57, 74, 79, 167, 174; barons, 3-4, 173, 175
banana wars, 174
bananas, 14, 34-35; sigatoka or Panama disease, 170; trade in, 37, 39, 46
Banco Atlántico, 38
Banking Acts of 1862 and 1864, U.S., 18
Baptist Memorial Hospital (Memphis), 158
Barahona, Sotero, 67
Barrios, Justo Rufino, 14, 45
Batson, Alfred, 161-62
Bay Islands, 122, 130
Beals, Carleton, 36
Beers, Joseph, 78, 83, 147
Belgium, 9
Belize, 5, 11, 40, 67, 87, 121. *See* British Honduras

Bertrand, Francisco, 146, 148, 152-53; stripped Christmas of subcommandants at Omoa and Cuyamel, 152
Big Stick militarism, 174
Bills, Waldemar Harold, 65-66
Black, Eli, 171
Bluefields, 2, 35, 41, 63-66, 80, 85, 87, 93, 96, 98, 103-9; harbor, 83; blockade of, 110; revolt, 113; settlers from the West Indies, 80
Bluefields American, 63, 79-80, 103, 110
Bluefields Banana Company, 37
Bluefields Steamship Company, 80-84, 104, 110
Bluefields Tanning Company, 104
Bluff, The, 83, 100, 106, 111, 189 n 49
Boaca, battle of, 101
Boca San Carlos, 84
Bocas del Toro, Panama, 35
Boer War, 99, 109
Bográn, Luis, 42-43, 45
Bonilla, Manuel, 4, 27, 47, 51-57, 60-62, 64, 66, 70-71, 73, 110, 115, 117-18, 120, 123-26, 129, 133, 141, 147, 150, 172; animated by Zelaya's difficulties, 119; borrowed from Theodore Rössner, 120; death of, 152; denies agreement with Estrada Cabrera, 194 n 15; difficulties with George Cooper, 196 n 44; gravely ill from Gresham's disease, 152; Manuelistas, 123-24, 146, 151; presents sword to Christmas, 185 n 38; rendezvous for 1909 invasion forces, 121; revolt of 1903, 52-55; revolt of 1910, 119-24; revolt of 1911, 130-45; stalls Whitney Bank loan, 199 n 23; supporters, 72; takes over Honduran Railroad, 185 n 47
Bonilla, Policarpo, 46-47, 51-52,

55-56, 59, 60-61, 68, 70, 124-25; government of, 48
Born to Raise Hell, 161. See Edward O'Reilly
Boston, 33-34, 36; banana barons, 164
Boston Fruit Company, 34
Bourbon era, 13
Boxer Rebellion, 107
Bransfield, James, 96
British, 24, 28; economic presence, 116; in El Salvador, 25; merchants, 41
British Free Trade, 28
British Honduras, 33, 40, 73, 115, 119-22, 126. See Belize
British navy, 130, 135-37, 142, 145; marines on the Mosquito coast in 1894, 31
Brittanic, 121
Brown, "Cashier," 41
Bryan, William Jennings, 113
Budde, Fred, 43
Bulger, James, 66
Burke, Edward A., 42-43, 154, 159-60; death of, 160
Burke, Lindsay, 160
Busby, G.T., 103
Bush, George, 174
Butler, Smedley, 106-9

Cabbages and Kings, 41
cacique, 15
California, 13
Canal Zone, 99, 107
Cangrejal ford, 139
Cangrejal River, 137
Cannon, George, 108
Cannon, Lee Roy, 74-75, 85-89, 92; charges against prosecuters, 190 n 63; culpability, 91; no right to U.S. protection, 89; trial and execution, 85, 89
Carden, Lionel, 117, 199 n 23
Carías Andino, Tiburcio, 162, 168
Caribbean, 3, 9-11, 13, 17, 22, 59, 90

Caribbean coast of Central America, 14, 31, 83, 113
Carrera, Rafael, 15
Carter, Jimmy, 3, 173
Caruso, Adelaide, 50, 55. See Christmas, Adelaide
cash tax obligations, 15
Castrillo, Salvador, 85, 88, 111
caudillo, 15
Centinella, 121-22, 127, 129, 131
Central America, as used in this book, 5; development, 4; disorder, 2; geography, ll-12; Liberal policies, 14; nationalists, 172; politics, 13-14; population, 12; transit, 29
Central American Court of Justice, 30, 75
Central American Treaty of 1907, 72, 75, 77
Chamelecón River, 44
Chamorro, Emiliano, 78, 81, 85, 90, 101-3, 114; aided Zelaya to suppress a revolt in 1896, 78
Chamorro, Pedro Joaquín, 81
Chamorro, Violeta, 174
Chile, 34
Chinandega, 77
Chinese, 41; merchants, 107
Chino, 102
Choloma, 50-51
Choluteca, 73, 87
Chontales, 101
Christmas, Adelaide, 67, 69, 152. See Caruso, Adelaide
Christmas, Ida, 156-58; death of, 200 n 32. See Culotta, Ida
Christmas, Lee, 4, 7, 31, 41, 47-49, 52-57, 64, 67-69, 72-75, 87, 92, 98, 115, 118, 122-26, 131-33, 135, 137, 139, 141, 144, 146-47, 150, 167, 218; assassination attempts, 51, 196 n 43; assistant inspector of the Republic, 153; called the "incredible yanqui," 141; "Chief of Sanitary Police," 156; colonel and the police chief of Tegucigalpa, 51; commandant at Amapala, 52; commandant at Puerto Cortés, 151, 153; director general of police, 150; divorced from Mamie, 50; Doubleday, Page, interested in a biography of, 158; fatal illness: tropical sprue, 158; Guatemala's secret police, 69, 72, 115, 156; house prisoner of Estrada Cabrera, 153; inspector of the Guatemalan Army, 153; invents a locomotive throttle-adjusting device, 157; joins American lumber concern, J.H. Burton and Company, 156; legends of, 48, 68-69, 115; locomotive engineer on the Guatemalan national railroad, 119; met with one of Pancho Villa's emissaries, 153; military inspector of the Departments of Cortés, Atlántida, Colón, and the Bay Islands, 154; obtained U.S. Patent No. 1465808, 157; offered another sinecure, 154; preserved U.S. citizenship, 185 n 50; received his long-sought appointment as "Special Agent" of the State Department, 156; received sword from Bonilla, 185 n 38; returned to New Orleans with family, 157; subcommandant of several northern posts, 151; volunteered to serve with U.S. Army in Mexico, 153
Christmas, Lee, Jr., 67
Christmas, Magdalena, 50-51
Christmas, Mamie, 49-50
Christmas, Pat, 200 n 32
circum-Caribbean, 24, 27, 107, 172
Ciudad Juárez, 159
Clarence, Robert Henry, 46
class, 3, 24
Cleveland, Grover, 9

Code of Naval Regulations, 105
coffee, 14
Colombia, 5, 35; Liberal revolt of
  1885, U.S. military suppression
  of, 33
Colorado Junction, 85
Comayagua, 40, 44
Combs, Leslie, 176 n 3
communal lands, 15
compradores, 16, 22, 79; alliance
  of, 172; elite, 15, 22, 26, 28
Conrad, Gabe, 95-96, 101-04
conscript labor, 15
Conservatives, 13-14, 81, 85, 103,
  175; associates, 83; enemies,
  84; exiles, 112
contra war in Nicaragua, 31, 174
Cooper, George, 134-36, 196 n 44,
  197 n 50
core, 7. See metropole
Corinto, 2, 63, 93, 112
corporation, 149
corporatist, 13
Costa Rica, 3, 5, 12, 14, 21,
  26-27, 33-35, 75, 85; Caribbean
  coast railroads, 34; nationalism
  and United Fruit, 170
Craven, Phil, 95-96, 112
Cuba, 17, 33, 35; Cuban independence, 9; U.S. protectorate, 9
Culotta, Ida, 152. See Christmas,
  Ida
Cutter, Victor, 31, 168
Cuyamel Fruit Company, 7, 16,
  27, 36-37, 39, 142, 148-49, 152,
  163-64, 170; South Dakota
  company, 142
Cuyamel River, 149

D'Antoni, Salvator, 37-38
Dávadi, Florian, 128, 132, 147
Dávadi brothers, 118
Dávila, Miguel, 46, 73-74, 87,
  115-16, 118-19, 124-30, 133,
  135, 141-47; plot against, 119;
  weak control of military, 195 n
  23

Davilistas, 122, 146
Davis, Richard Harding, 39-41,
  45, 200 n 34. See Three Gringos
  in Venezuela and Central
  America
Dawson, Thomas, 133, 146
dependency theory, 10-11
DePew, Chauncey, 185 n 47
depression, 20, 165, 169; of
  1873-78, 19-20, 44; of 1883-85,
  19-20; of 1893-95, 19-20; the
  Great Depression (1929-41), 168
Deutsch, Hermann, 4, 50
development, 12, 27, 175
Díaz, Adolfo, 81, 94, 112, 114,
  123, 172
Díaz, Fornos, 97
Díaz, Pedro, 122, 142
Díaz, Porfirio, 152
DiGiorgio, Joseph, 36
Dinamante, 85
Dodd, Harvey, 112
Dodge, Percival, 87
Dolan, Pat, 95-96
dollar diplomacy, 20, 36
Dominican Republic, 35
Dreben, Samuel "Jew Sam," 31,
  99-100, 102, 111, 121, 146, 159;
  death of, 159
Drexel Institute, 86
Drummond, William, 49
Durón, José Manuel, 47-49

earthquakes, 12
East Asia, 8
edad de oro (the Golden Age), 42,
  46
Edwards, James, 96
ejido, 15
El Amigo, 4, 118-20, 123, 129. See
  Samuel Zemurray
El Castillo, 89
El Porvenir, 37-38, 74
El Rey, 94
El Salvador, 1, 5, 12, 22, 27, 30,
  43, 55, 59, 61-62, 64, 74-78;
  counterguerrilla campaign in El

Salvador, 174; government, 63;
invades Guatemala, 61
Elliott, LeMann, 122
Emery, George D., 78
Emma, 121-22, 129
enclaves, 14-15, 22, 30, 79, 88
entrepreneurs, 3, 167, 174; profit
from periphery labor, 24
era of liberal dictators, 167
Escondido River, 83-84, 93, 105,
110
Estrada Cabrera, Manuel, 27,
58-59, 61, 64, 73, 75, 77-78, 81,
87, 90, 98, 113, 125-26, 130,
155-56, 172; alleged contribution to Roosevelt, 59, 186 n 3;
expels Bonilla and Christmas,
127; hired lobbyist in Washington, 59; secret service, 69, 72,
115, 156; used Bonilla and
Christmas in campaign against
Zelaya, 125
Estrada, Juan J., 66, 74-75, 79,
81-85, 88, 90-92, 96, 99, 101,
105, 108, 110-12, 114, 156; rebellion against Zelaya in 1909,
81-90, 115
ethnicity, 3, 203 n 4
Euraque, Darío, 16
European consuls, 133
European creditors, 113
evacuation of Puerto Cortés, 145
Evans, May, 128
expansionism of the industrial
states, 23

Falcón, 94
Figueroa, Fernando, 76, 78; Doña
Lastenía, lover of, 78
filibusters, 6, 30-31; Americans,
12, 17, 106; three eras of, 6-7,
12, 31-32
Filipino rebels in 1899-1902, 33,
66
financial imperialism, 20
Fletcher, Gilmore, 88
Fletcher, Henry, 88

Fletcher family, 87
foreign entrepreneurs, 15-16, 79,
88
Fowler, Godfrey, 95-96, 103-4, 109
France, 9, 16, 29, 172
free market capitalism, 10, 17-18,
22-23, 27, 29; imperialism, 24.
See also laissez-faire and
liberalism
Fremont, Emile, 122
French, 28; in El Salvador, 25
fruit companies circumvent the
1899 Honduran land law, 47
Fullam, William F., 65, 70

Galveston, 37, 87
Gard, Allen, 135, 197 n 1
Gatling gun, 54, 65, 100, 141
Germans in Central America,
24-25, 28; businessmen, 28-29,
41
Germany, 8-9, 28, 109, 172; ma-
rines at Corinto in 1878, 31;
vessel used for surrender of
Honduran arms, 125
Gilsley House (New York City),
81
Glover's Reef, 121
González, Roberto, 94
Gordon, Victor, 31, 98-99, 101-2,
104, 108, 111-12, 146, 161
Gracias, 73
Granada, 40, 76
Great Britain, 8, 9, 18, 172
Greely, A.G. 144
Greytown, 41
Grimer, Louis, 100
Groce, Leonard, 66, 75, 85-89, 92;
charges against prosecutors, 190
n 63; culpability, 91; letter to
mother, 190 n 64; no right to
U.S. protection, 89; trial and ex-
ecution, 85, 89
Guardia, Tomás, 14
Guatemala, 4-5, 11-12, 15, 21-22,
27, 30, 45, 47, 49, 58, 61, 69,
75; denies aiding *Hornet*, 196 n

39; oil exploration, 157-58; police state, 58; secret police, 69, 72, 115, 156
Guatemala City, 11, 59, 74, 77
Guerrero, Francisco "Chico," 135-39, 142; death of, 197 n 1
Gulf of Fonseca, 6, 25, 76, 98
Gulf of Mexico, 40
Gutiérrez, Rafael, 59

HMS Brilliant, 122, 136, 144
HMS Scylla, 123
Haiti, 17
Hanson, Olaf, 122
Hapsburg, 13
Hardy, John, 66
Hardgrave, O.L., 130-31
Harrison, Benjamin, 9
Hawaii, 8-9
Hearst, William Randolph, 89
Henry, O., 41
Herno Mountain, 151
Hill, F.K., 81
Holland, 9
Holland, G. Spencer, 88
home country, 21, 26
Homestead Act of 1862, 18
Honduran National Railway, 44, 116
Honduran-Salvadoran Treaty of 1878, 64
Honduras, 2, 5-7, 12, 14, 16, 21, 27, 30, 35-36, 41-44, 56, 61-64, 71, 73, 77, 110; banana tax of 1892, revoked in 1912, 47; civil war of 1894, 46; development as a partnership with foreign capital, 56; invasion by exiles from El Salvador, 130; historians of, 15; legation in Washington, 127; military campaign of 1907, 81; neutrality, 77; north coast 4, 11, 16-17, 37, 40, 48, 69, 116, 133, 135, 138, 142, 145; officials, 16; public debt, 116; revolt of 1897, 47-48, 51; revolt of 1903, 52-55;

revolt of 1911, 4; society turmoil, 57
Honduras Syndicate, 185 n 47
Hornet, 110, 127-34, 146, 196 n 39, 198 n 20
host country, 21-22, 26
Hotchkiss guns, 65, 94, 102, 137-38
Hotel Dewey, 154
Hotel Lafebre, 145
Hotel Monteleone, 84
Hotel Tropical, 98, 100, 104
Hotel Varnum, 84
House Committee on Merchant Marine and Fisheries, 35
Hubbard, Ashbel, 39
Hubbard, Zemurray Steamship Company, 39

Imboden, Frank, 43
Imperial America, 20, 26
in kind services, 15
individualism, 22
industrialization, 7-8, 16
International Railroads of Central America, 22
interoceanic cable connection, 18
isthmian interoceanic communications, 8, 32
isthmian political culture: described in the Heritage of the Conquistadores, 173. See Samuel Stone
isthmian union, 45
Italy, 9, 16

Jalteva, 94-95
Jamaica, 34-35, 41
Japan, 8, 172
Jeffries, Herbert "General Heriberto," 43
Jeffs, Charles, 41, 146
Jersey City, 34
Johnson, Charley, 128, 147

Karnes, Thomas, 56
Katz, Adolph "Dolly," 39

Keith, Henry Meiggs, 34
Keith, Minor Cooper, 3, 31, 34, 38, 158, 168, 172
Kimball, W.W., 82, 98, 102, 109
King of Spain: 1906 Nicaraguan-Honduran boundary award, 62, 164
Kinney, Henry L., 31
Knox, Philander C., 36, 87, 89, 105, 109, 143; receives complaint of weak U.S. policy, 190 n 4
Knox-Parades convention, 143-44, 148
Krupp guns, 54, 64-65, 84, 132, 137-38, 141

La Ceiba, 36-38, 41, 64-65, 74, 83, 116, 123, 129-30, 135-39, 142; consular corps in La Ceiba, 115; surrender of, 141, 143
La Luz and Los Angeles Mining Company, 81, 87, 104-7, 112
labor relations abroad, 24
La Garita, 102
Laguna Trestle, 48-51
laissez-faire, 28-29. See free market and liberalism
Lake Managua, 103
Lake Nicaragua, 12, 85, 103
Lala-Ferreras-Cangelosi Steamship Company, 80
Lamini, battle at, 54
land privatization, 15
Lansing, Robert, 155
LeBlanc, Alcée, 41
Lees, Ralph, 96
Leiva, Andrés, 137-38
León, 40
Lesseps, Ferdinand de, 29
Lever, E.A., 53, 74
Liberal regimes, 21
Liberals, 13-14, 18-19, 81, 175; and foreign capitalists, 14
liberalism, 11, 15. See free market and laissez-faire
Linard, Drew, 147

Lincoln, Abraham, 19
Lindbergh, Charles "Lucky Lindy," 160
Long, Huey, 162-63
López Gutiérrez, Rafael, 157; heads revolt, 163
Louisiana bond frauds, 160
Louisiana State Lottery, 41, 152

machine guns, 151
Madriz, José, 79, 93-94, 97-98, 102-3, 105-7, 111
Malthus, Thomas Robert, 9
Manabique Point, 129-30
Managua, 12, 40, 78, 84-85, 97, 111
Manhattan Club, 158
Maraita plain, 67, 69, 139
Marblehead, 61
Marín, Ramón Octavio, 121, 123
market economy, 18, 23, 27
Matagalpa, 101-3
material progress, 17-18
Mausers, 95
Maxim, Hiram, 65
Maxim guns, 66, 95, 127
Mazatlán, 25
McCreery, Fenton, 146
McGill, Samuel, 185 n 47
McLaurie, Ed, 132, 151
Meiggs, Henry, 34
Membreño, Alberto, 143
Mena, Luis, 93-94, 101-2, 111-12
Méndez, J.J., 159
mercenaries, 2, 4, 7, 30-31, 79, 85, 167. See soldiers of fortune
Merry, William, 70
mesa central (central plateau), 34
metropole, 9-11, 17, 21, 26-30; and multinational leaders, 173; businesses, 21-22, 26, 28; control over peripheral labor, 15, 24; rivalry, 27
metropole-comprador relationship, 172
Mexico, 16, 22, 71, 98, 159
Mico River, 93-94

militarization of tropical America, 174
Mills, Fred, 68
Milner, Joseph, 43
Milon, John Paul, 189 n 49
minerals, 14
Miskito indians, 101. See Mosquitia
modernization, 1, 11, 14
Moe, Alfred K., 55
Moffat, Thomas, 82, 85, 101, 104, 108-9
Moissant, John, 76-77
Molony, Guy "Machine-gun," 31, 99-100, 121-24, 128, 131, 138, 152, 158, 160-62; superintendent of New Orleans' city police, 161; general of the army and bodyguard to Honduran President Miguel Paz Barahona, 162; death of, 163
Moncada, José María, 110
Monkey Point, 85; railroad construction project at, 63
Monroe Doctrine, 8, 17, 27, 29
Morgan, J.P., and Company, 105, 107, 116-17; Morgan loan to Honduras, 133, 143-44, 147-48
Morrill Land Grant Act of 1862, 18
Morris, John, 41
Mosquitia (or Mosquito Coast), 11, 46, 78, 80, 83, 93. See Miskito indians
Motagua River, 73, 149
multinational corporations, 21-22, 30, 175
Munro, Dana Gardner, 152

Nacaome, 53, 116
Namasigüe, 67, 94, 138
national development, 16, 88
national security, 9, 17
New Orleans, 4, 7, 37, 40-42, 45, 47, 49, 69, 74, 91, 99, 103, 106-7, 143; World's Industrial and Cotton Centennial Exposition of 1884, 21; French Quarter, 84
New Orleans Daily Picayune, 84, 101, 112, 118, 125, 130, 140, 190 n 63
New York and Honduras Rosario Mining Company, 44, 71
New York banking houses, 113
New York Herald, 92, 94-95, 97, 104, 127
New York Times, 96, 190 n 63
Nicaragua, 1-5, 11-14, 21, 25, 27, 30, 35-37, 45, 58, 62-63, 66, 106-7, 112; alternative transit route with European or Japanese assistance, 79; American property in, 88; boundary dispute with Costa Rica, 25; boundary dispute with Honduras, 62, 164; Conservatives, 60, 77, 99; development, 60, 83; gunboats, 49, 94; Liberal revolt of 1893, 46; Liberals, 6; nationalists, 83; north coast, 59, 75, 79, 113; revolt in, 113; sovereignty, 108; transit route, 6, 25
Nicaraguan Canal: foreign investment considered, 25
Nicaraguan Fruit Company, 83
no transfer principle, 17
Noriega, Manuel, 174
Norway, 109

Odendahl, Alex, 41
Oleson, Ole, 122
Olivares, José de, 77
Olsen, Hans, 122
open door policy, 28
O'Reilly, Edward "Tex," 161; death of, 161
Ortega, Daniel, 174
overproduction, 19

Pacific basin, 10, 13, 28
Pacific coast of Central America, 11, 170
Pacific Ocean, 8, 12

Palm Hotel, 152
Pan-Americanism, 8, 23, 27, 29
Panama, 2, 5, 12; independence,
    9; invasion of Dec. 1989 (Oper-
    ation Just Cause), 174; railroad,
    13; U.S. protectorate of, 9
Panama Canal, 25; Zone, 91,
    103
Panama City, 99
Paredes, Juan, 128, 133
Patuca River, 61
Pax Americana, 116
Paz Barahona, Miguel, 162
peasant societies, 15
Peking, 107
Pentada, Pedro, 123
periphery, 7-10, 168; economy, 11
Pershing, John J., 159
Peru, 34
Philippines, 9, 99; struggle against
    U.S., 33, 66
Pioneer, 94
Pittman, William, 109
plantation cash-crop system, 16
Poe, Thomas, 188 n 30
Porter, William S. (O. Henry), 41
Preston, Andrew, 34-36, 38, 80,
    168-69
Preza, José Dolores, 66
pro-Americanism, 2, 151
productionism, 8-10; use of tech-
    nology, science, and educational
    system, 8
professionalized military, 15
pronunciamiento, 83
protective tariff laws, 18
Prussia, 16
Puerto Barrios, 4, 36, 67, 72
Puerto Cortés, 2, 37, 40-41, 44,
    47, 49, 51, 54, 57, 65, 69, 72,
    74, 87, 116, 121, 129, 132, 135,
    160, 163; wharf, 117, 147
Puerto Limón, 3, 35, 83
Puerto Rico, 9

racism, 3, 9, 24, 190 n 3, 203 n 4
radio stations, 35

Rama, 84, 93, 96, 101, 103, 106,
    108-9
raw materials, 8-9, 11, 20, 23,
Reagan, Ronald, 3, 173-74
Realejo, 12
Recreo, 93, 95, 97
Reed, Joe, 137-38
Regalado, Tomás, 53, 61
Remingtons, 95
Republicans, 18
Richardson, Tracy, 31, 69, 99-100,
    111, 146, 158, 160; death of,
    161
Richmond Levering Company
    (New York City), 157-58
Riggs, Thomas, 188 n 30
Riis, Jacob, 9
Rolston, H.V., 149
Roosevelt, Theodore, 3, 62-63, 66,
    76, 105, 141, 172, 174; adminis-
    tration, 70
Root, Elihu, 70
Rössner, Theodore, German firm,
    120
Rothschilds, 42-43
Roving and Fighting, 161. See Ed-
    ward O'Reilly
ruling elites, 173
rural police, 15

Samoa, 8
Samuel Weil Company, 83
San Antonio del Norte, 54
San Juan del Norte, ll, 85, 97
San Juan del Sur, 12
San Juan River, 12, 84-85, 88
San Pedro Sula, 41, 44, 48-49, 54,
    69, 146
San Salvador, 43, 61, 77
Sandinistas, 173-74
Sandino, Augusto César, 12, 162;
    civil war, 30
Sands, Christian, 108
Sands, William, 73
Santa Clara, 102
School of Pan American Agricul-
    ture, 170

Secrest, H. Nathan, 112
Segovia River, 61
semiperipheral society, 10
Siemens, 29
Sierra, Terencio, 48, 50-54, 67
slavery, expansion, 7; colonizing
    freed slaves, 17
social imperialism, 4, 8, 10-11,
    21, 23-24; and foreign competi-
    tion, 8; exporting social prob-
    lems, 10; exporting unemploy-
    ment, 10
soldiers of fortune, 3-4, 7, 41,
    43-44, 47, 64, 86, 88, 91, 101,
    104, 155, 174. See mercenaries
Somoza García, Anastasio, 79,
    168, 172
Soto, Enrique, 47
Soto, Marco Aurelio, 42, 46
sovereignty, 16, 22, 28, 107; and
    development of the periphery,
    10; loss of, 22; of a peripheral
    state, 27
Spanish-American War, 3, 9, 19
Spengler, Otto, 9
St. Charles Hotel, 84, 162
Stann's Creek, British Honduras,
    115, 118
Standard Tropical Trading and
    Transport Company, 36-37
Stone, Doris Zemurray, 117
Stone, Samuel, 173. See isthmian
    political culture
Storyville, 128, 161
Streich, William, 37, 148
struggle for isthmian domination,
    58
Suez, 17
Sussman, Richard, 85, 110, 112
Syrians, 41

Taft, William Howard, 76-77, 119,
    145; administration, 88; dollar
    diplomats, 125-26
Tatumbla (place), 94-95
Tatumbla (ship), 64, 121, 129-30
technology, 8

Tegucigalpa, 33, 40, 46-47, 54-55,
    145-46
Tejeda Reyes, 68
Tela, 37-38, 116, 136, 149
Tela Railroad Company, 149
telegraph, 34
Teplitz, Benjamin, 81
Thomas, Lowell, 161
Three Gringos in Venezuela and
    Central America, 40. See Davis,
    Richard Harding
Tipitapa River, 103, 111
Tisma, 103, 109
Toncontin, 55
transcontinental railroad, 18
transisthmian routes, 13, 23
Trautwine, John, 44
Trujillo, 6, 65, 135, 139; taking of,
    132-33
Turks, 41

U.S. arrogance, 2
U.S. Canal Commission in Nica-
    ragua, 86
U.S. Civil War, 17-19
U.S. Department of State, 23, 25,
    127, 147-48, 153-56; consular
    officials, 73, 129, 132-33, 135,
    147, 156; diplomats, 151
U.S. economy, 19
U.S. entrepreneurs, 1, 6, 24, 57,
    79, 100, 104, 113; fruit compan-
    ies, 16
U.S. government, 23, 72, 82, 116,
    155; fear of German activity in
    Central America, 156; objective
    to dominate the isthmus, 45;
    security in the region, 25
U.S. hegemony, 167
U.S. imperialism, 2, 23, 92; mate-
    rial objectives over values and
    ideology, 26
U.S. intervention, 2-3, 79, 130;
    bombardment of San Juan del
    Norte in 1854, 31; in Central
    America, 1980s, 1-3, 6-7, 31,
    173-75; in Guatemala's domes-

tic order, 59; in Honduras in
1906, 31; in Nicaragua in
1911-12 and 1926-32, 31, 167;
marines, 108-9, 113, 148; three
eras of, 6-7, 12, 31-32
U.S. liberals, 17
U.S. Navy, 82, 90, 93, 107, 118,
125, 128, 130, 133-37, 142-46,
157; decree for ships in Bluefields to pay duties to Estrada,
192 n 36
U.S. Special Service Squadron, un-
officially designated the "Central American Banana fleet,"
157
U.S. Treasury agents, 128
USS *California*, 113
USS *Chicago*, 67
USS *Des Moines*, 96
USS *Dubuque*, 79
USS *Marietta*, 65, 131, 133, 136,
138, 142, 144
USS *Paducah*, 108
USS *Petrel*, 148
USS *Tacoma*, 128, 131-36, 138,
145, 147; negotiations aboard,
150
Ubico, Jorge, 168
Ulua River, 168
United Fruit Company (UFCO), 3,
7, 16, 27, 33, 35-36, 74, 149,
164, 166, 169-71; called "the
Octopus" or "el pulpo," 170-71;
changed name to United
Brands, 171; stockholders, 35,
166, 168-69; Zemurray in
charge, 166-71
United Provinces of Central
America, 12
Universal Canal Company, 29
Utila, 130

Vaccaro, Felix, 37
Vaccaro, Joseph, 37
Vaccaro, Luca, 37
Vaccaro brothers, 4, 31, 37-38, 65,
74, 149

Vaccaro Brothers Company: headquarters, 37-38; company town
of La Ceiba, 164
Valentine, Julius, 44
Valentine, Washington S., 4, 44,
71, 114, 116-17, 143-44, 147-48;
the "king of Honduras," 71, 143
Valladares, José María, 61-62,
67-68, 119, 125, 150-51
Vanderbilt, Cornelius, 6, 13, 31
Vásquez, Domingo, 43, 46-47, 159
Venus, 99, 193 n 41
Villa, Francisco "Pancho," 153,
159
volcanoes, 12

wage-labor system, 15
Walker, J.A., 103
Walker, William, 6, 12-14, 31;
death of, 6
Wall Street, 125
Waller, Dr., 69
Weil, Samuel, 78; business, 83
Weinberger, Jacob "Jake," 31, 37,
39, 80, 110; the "Parrot King,"
37, 80
Welles, Sumner, 157
Western Hemisphere, 17
Whitney Bank in New Orleans,
148, 199 n 23; loan to Hon-
duras not made, 149
Wilkins, William, 102
Williams, William A., 26; work
challenged, 180 n 38
Wilson, Francis Mairs Hunt-
ington, 110
Wilson, Woodrow, 113, 141, 154;
fourteen points, 28; urges stabi-
lization of Honduran finances,
199 n 23
world transit systems, 17
World's Industrial and Cotton
Centennial Exposition in New
Orleans, 42

Yerex, Lowell, 162; president of
TACA (Honduran national
airline),162

DATE DUE